Psychoanalysis and Social Involve

Studies in the Psychosocial

Edited by Peter Redman, The Open University, UK Stephen Frosh, Centre for Psychosocial Studies, Birkbeck College, University of London, UK and Wendy Hollway, The Open University, UK

Titles include:

Stephen Frosh
HAUNTINGS: PSYCHOANALYSIS AND GHOSTLY TRANSMISSIONS

Uri Hadar
PSYCHOANALYSIS AND SOCIAL INVOLVEMENT
Interpretation and Action

Margarita Palacios
RADICAL SOCIALITY
Studies on Violence, Disobedience and the Vicissitudes of Belonging

Studies in the Psychosocial Series
Series Standing Order ISBN 978–0–230–30858–9 (hardback)
                                    978–0–230–30859–6 (paperback)
(outside North America only)

You can receive future titles in this series as they are published by placing a standing order. Please contact your bookseller or, in case of difficulty, write to us at the address below with your name and address, the title of the series and one of the ISBNs quoted above.

Customer Services Department, Macmillan Distribution Ltd, Houndmills, Basingstoke, Hampshire RG21 6XS, England

Psychoanalysis and Social Involvement

Interpretation and Action

Uri Hadar
Professor of Psychology, Tel Aviv University

Translated from Hebrew by Mirjam Meerschwam-Hadar

First published 2013 by
PALGRAVE MACMILLAN

Palgrave Macmillan in the UK is an imprint of Macmillan Publishers Limited,
registered in England, company number 785998, of Houndmills, Basingstoke,
Hampshire RG21 6XS.

Palgrave Macmillan in the US is a division of St Martin's Press LLC,
175 Fifth Avenue, New York, NY 10010.

Palgrave Macmillan is the global academic imprint of the above companies
and has companies and representatives throughout the world.

Palgrave® and Macmillan® are registered trademarks in the United States,
the United Kingdom, Europe and other countries

ISBN: 978–1–137–30107–9 (hardback)
ISBN: 978–1–137–30108–6 (paperback)

This book is printed on paper suitable for recycling and made from fully
managed and sustained forest sources. Logging, pulping and manufacturing
processes are expected to conform to the environmental regulations of the
country of origin.

A catalogue record for this book is available from the British Library.

A catalog record for this book is available from the Library of Congress.

Contents

Preface

Like many others, my book carries one title and a single author, but these singularities are critically misleading. To begin with, take the title. For a long time, throughout the process of first-draft writing, the book had a title totally different from the present one. It read *How Healthy to Be Good.* I liked it because of its mysterious suggestions, as well as because of its stitching together of mind (*good*) and body (*healthy*) and its indeterminate nature as a written act, between question and exclamation. Yet, it was too uninformative as a title. Even with its subtitle, *Psychoanalysis as an Ethical Process*, it still missed one of its main themes – social involvement and activism – as well as one of its main methods, the movement to and fro between interpretation and action. Therefore, that title gave way to the present one, but not without leaving its traces in the text. The detective-minded reader is welcome to mark these traces.

With regard to authorship, the situation is endlessly more complicated than it is with the title and I do not really have a good idea about the relationships between Uri Hadar and the contents of the book. Sure, I was critically instrumental in the process of writing the book, but then, so were many others: Hebrew, English, Mirjam, Lynne, Stephen and Jessica. I write these names here without a surname, to indicate their intimate contribution, as if they were a kind of pronoun, an almost first person, but I will name them fully soon, to indicate something about their contribution. Still, I must defend my good name. This book is, in many ways, more personal than other books I have written. It tells of many of my experiences; many of the stories it tells are my experiences. At times, this has far-reaching implications. For example, in presenting clinical vignettes, which I do quite a lot in the book. Each case is, in crucial ways, *my* experience of a case, the lessons it has taught me, the scars it left in me. In fact, in this respect, no case in the book can be treated as naturalistic documentation. Rather, it combines experiences that I had in therapy, as a therapist, so as to illustrate a particular theoretical theme. This strategy has two major advantages: It clarifies well, I think, the theoretical theme with which it is associated and it effectively removes the personal identity of the patient from the vignette. This allows me to keep my patients' privacy. They cannot be identified simply because the protagonist of the vignette, the one who holds the patient position, does not have a singular identity. For that matter, and to link up to the issue of authorship, the analyst also does not always hold a singular identity, even if he does enough of it to be considered the author. My patients may well find themselves in a strange situation while reading the book. They will encounter familiar moments in the vignettes, but also much strangeness. Perhaps, in that sense, the book may act as an addendum to the analytic sessions, for better or for worse. Either way, I am endlessly grateful to my patients for giving me their lessons and for being patient with the discomfort that may accompany their refractions and reflections in my text.

I hope that it is clear by now that this preface is not only a confession, but also an acknowledgement of the diverse subjectivities that went into writing the book. Two of them, who appear as the odd ones out in list of first names that I have previously given, are Hebrew and English. These both enact and interpret my thoughts. The book was written in Hebrew first, but substantially re-written in English, so that both languages inform the text, each with its characteristic capacities, each doing something that the other does not. There are many examples of this, but I illustrate only a couple of instances.

Hebrew is a heavily gendered language, as each noun is gendered and verb phrases must agree with nouns for gender. This burdens the text with gendering far more than the English does. For example, in English I can stick with the neutral inflection of 'being a subject', but in Hebrew 'subject' must be either a he-subject or a she-subject, subjectess, as it were. As a result, I shifted arbitrarily between the male and the female in neuter sentences which, initially, makes the female sentences very marked. Paradoxically, if one sticks with gendered language in English, the effect gets more marked, because English does not have to lend itself to global gendering. Yet, I did not want to let the gender beauty sleep, so I kept shifting between the gender of the neuter (human) nouns one part in male inflections, one in female, then in male again, and so on. This creates a slightly chaotic effect but, with it, the need for the reader to clarify to herself the generality or specificity of the gendered form. It may be inconvenient in some cases, but I feel that this serves an important task of drawing attention to gender in language and thought. I hope this does not too much interfere with the flow of reading.

In a similar fashion, I used different terms to refer to the therapeutic process in the various psychoanalytic practices. Unless otherwise stated, I refer to this process with terms such as therapy, psychotherapy, psychoanalysis, analytic psychotherapy and psychoanalytic psycho-therapy, all in a similar vein. This is a somewhat unusual choice in the professional literature, where attention is often given to designate different terms to different schools of practice. Yet, the universe of discourse that the book enacts derives entirely from language based thinking and language based communication. Within this universe, I emphasize the amelioration of suffering by using 'therapy', whereas I emphasize interpretative elaborations by using 'psychoanalysis'. Yet, I use these quite loosely. Various combinations of the amelioration of suffering and the articulation of thoughts are represented by the various combinations of 'therapy' and 'analysis'. I assume the related mental processes to be largely similar across psychoanalytic schools and practices.

The word 'occupation' (as in 'the occupied Palestinian territories') translates as 'kibush' in Hebrew, which means something nearer to 'conquest' than to 'occupation'. It served me well in the Hebrew to use this term in order to generally indicate social oppression because, for the Hebrew reader, it ties up oppression with the particular political and social reality of Palestinian (but not only Palestinian) lives in Israel and Palestine. By fortunate coincidence, 'colonization' also often translates to Hebrew as 'kibush'. 'Occupation' is more confusing in this regard, because of its prime association with having a vocation or even with being busy. Nevertheless, I often preferred to keep 'occupation' in the sense of social oppression. This also may keep the reader busy with the linguistic rendering of ideas, which probably is sometimes a from of oppression in its own right, but may be in the service of clarifying ideas. 'Clarifying ideas can be dangerous', to take a loan on Chomsky's most celebrated illustration of syntactic ambiguity. The danger can come either from the ideas themselves or from the process of clarifying them.

Generally speaking, the text has many comments about transitions between Hebrew and English. It creates a certain echo, if one tries to keep it in mind, not an unpleasant echo, in my experience, but I hope the echo does not become a noise. The comments are clearly those of Uri Hadar, unlike the text itself, in which Mirjam has an immeasur-able share. My translator and lifelong partner, Mirjam, has often shared with me in the manner in which clarifying ideas can be dangerous. For example, on the early morning in which two policemen in civilian clothes knocked on our door and took our laptops for examination in the police station. This was because Mirjam served, at the time, as official chair of New Profile, a feminist NGO whose aim is to raise consciousness of, and reduce, the weight of the military in Israeli daily life – in schools, books, politics and defence. Someone in government did not like this activity. Mirjam has been my prime partner for numerous discussions about all aspects of living and non-living. Her influence on the text and its ideas is probably my best example of how the notion of authorship can be subverted. So can the notion of gratitude.

In January 2004, the Faculty for Israeli Palestinian Peace organized an international conference in Jerusalem on ending the Occupation. In many ways, this was a remarkable political and intellectual event, but it enters this preface because it created the occasion for my meeting with two of its participants, Lynne Segal, a pioneering feminist, activist and thinker of living in the social domain and Jessica Benjamin, a Relational psychoanalyst and a leader of contemporary psychoanalytic theory, not least in its application for conflict resolution. Over the years, I have had numerous conversations with both Jessica and Lynne about issues that preoccupy this book and, in many places, their contribution is described in some detail. Their friendship and conversation encouraged me in writing the book and influenced me in ways that are not always accountable, as is my gratitude.

Lynne is the one who made the initial connection with the publishers, a move that effectively brought the book to publication. Also, it was Lynne who introduced me to Stephen Frosh a few years ago, an acquaintance which led to many fertile and engaging discussions of psychosocial studies generally, and the Israeli-Palestinian conflict in particular. Back in 2009, Lynne organized and chaired an evening in which Stephen and I discussed – indeed, argued over – Israeli violence towards Palestinians in terms of its cultural and historical context. This was eventually published in both *OpenDemocracy* and *The Jewish Quarterly*, and has been a landmark in my thinking of the current situation in terms of victimhood and victimization. Stephen is also the academic editor of the current Palgrave Macmillan series. Lynne, Stephen, many thanks.

My colleagues and friends in Psychoactive read the chapter on Psychoactive and made specific good suggestions. Some in Psychoactive also read and commented on some of the other chapters, but beyond this, Psychoactive is a major inspiration for the book and I am indebted to the thought, goodness and energies that characterize its activities and nourished my involvement with them. I would have liked to name everybody, all 300 members, but I realize that this is not done.

In addition, some of my ex-students read and commented on parts of the book. I am grateful for comments to Jonathan Handelzalts, Irit Aviram and Efrat Even-Tsur. Finally, my very good and learned friends, Moshe Talmon, Yosef Triest, Levana Marshal and Yosef Grodzinsky encouraged me throughout, commented about various points and tried to help me with the Hebrew publication of the book. I am endlessly grateful to them.

Introduction: Structure and Overview of the Book's Main Themes

What are the human values, the life values, which may offer psycho-analytic psychotherapy some general guidelines about its goals and the reasons that make it worthwhile for a person to take up such an expansive and expensive process? The classic answer to this question is based on the medical model and it is formulated in the 'technical' terms of mental health. Our aim is to cure the mind of its diseases or, in a milder formulation, to enable the individual to function better in such contexts as work, family and social intercourse. The stronger, medical formulation is problematic because the psyche is not a machine, not even a biological one, and hence it is hard to define what constitutes a disease, a cure or a mental health. Similar considerations apply to social functioning, where mostly we feel our way around in the absence of well-defined standards. If half a century of cultural criticism and the critique of modernism have taught us anything, it is that in the sphere of culture, meaning and the psyche there are no external criteria of functionality and our choices are ethical rather than technical. To the extent that psychoanalytic psychotherapy has a technical dimension – and I believe that it does – the technical subserves the ethical and it is the latter that dominates our decisions on the macro level, whether we are therapists or patients.

The range of questions that I consider as ethical rather than tech-nical is wide: Who should go to therapy? When should she go? To what extent can we know that somebody needs psychotherapy? What kind of therapy would be best for a person? When should a person in therapy consider it as complete or exhausted? And so on and so forth. The answers to all of these questions are to be found in a dynamics of agreement and disagreement between approaches that differ markedly among them, in a way that is reminiscent of approaches regarding the governing of a state, for instance. In the domain of government – and I emphasize this comparison for reasons that are at the heart of the present book (Chapters 6 through 8) – we accept as a matter of self evidence that the various answers to questions like the preceding are ethical rather than technical. This comparison between psychoanalytic psychotherapy and government has not been invented by me: Freud (1937) drew it in one of his best known papers, 'Analysis Terminable and Interminable', where he discussed the place of psychoanalytic psychotherapy in the wider context of life as such. These matters, ever since, have been widely debated in various contexts and from different vantage points. Though very close to its heart, they are not, however, the main issue of the present book.

The notion of the ethical that the present book promotes is more radical than the preceding in the sense of informing analysis on a more technical level. Here the idea is that the ethical does not merely set the goals of therapy in order, then, to relegate the work to a process that is essentially technical, but rather that the ethical is so deeply implicated in the technical that they cannot be considered separately. By way of a first, introductory statement, I may say that it is healthy to be ethical. Therapy aims for the ethical because this improves the individual's mental life. Or, formulated by way of Lacan's (1963/2006, p. 646) rendering of Kant's notion of good will: It is healthy to be good. Of course, if psychological well-being can be exhausted by reference to the ethical – which is how the three monotheisms that are based in the Bible would see this – then what have we achieved with two centuries of modernity (and over a century of psychoanalysis)? This is why I believe it is important to stress from the outset that the approach I develop here does not come to equate the psychologically healthy with the ethical, does not reduce the one to the other, but argues that, in psychoanalytic psychotherapy, therapeutic considerations are *saturated* with ethical considerations. Or, to speak in the language of mental health – something about which I have reservations but which I do here nevertheless for the sake of simplicity, as well as by way of tapping into a particular terminological history – then what is psychologically healthy will usually also involve something ethical. The psychologically healthy is not wholly ethical, but it always includes something of that kind. Not everything, but never none at all. Especially, in the set of practices in which we as psychotherapists engage, particularly when we offer psychoanalysis we never deal with purely technical considerations. Here I would like to offer an illustration.

My illustration is based on a discussion which occurred a few years ago in the department of psychology at Tel Aviv University, at which I work. A departmental seminar discussed which type of therapy was better: psychoanalysis or cognitive-behavioural therapy (CBT)? Those who spoke in favour of psychoanalytic approaches argued that these approaches touch the psyche of the patient more deeply and hence do a more thorough job. Those who supported CBT said that it was more scientific because its foundations, as well as its outcome, were evidence based – something psychoanalysis cannot claim. In my contribution to this debate, I said that both arguments, either way, seemed mistaken. The first, because we have no clear idea of what 'more deeply' might constitute (other than the manner in which psychoanalysis itself would have it according to its own, inner logic, but this would yield a circular argument). I myself would not describe a successful psychoanalytic move in terms of depth, but rather in terms of imaginary and metaphorical wealth, as indeed I have done in the past (Hadar, 2001). The argument regarding the evidence in support of CBT, I felt, was erroneous for a number of reasons. First, the evidence that CBT refers to assumes that we can or should be able to have a strong definition of what it is we are treating. Evidence is then based on isolating and quantifying the target variable (the symptom). If the patient came to therapy with a specific problem, then effectiveness could, perhaps, be evaluated by the extent to which the patient was relieved of his or her symptoms. But if the patient has sought therapy without a specific reason, or if the specific complaint proves to mask another, more pertinent problem, then the existing forms of assessment are irrelevant. Second, I claimed, there was ample evidence in support of psychoanalytic psychotherapy. Thousands of case descriptions analyse the logic of the processes a particular individual goes through in the course of her or his therapy. All this, for some reasons, does not count as evidence by proponents of the so called Evidence Based Psychotherapies. Finally, I argued, there is an ethical dimension that eludes statistical arguments on the effectiveness of psychotherapy despite its centrality to the therapeutic enterprise, namely, the patient's ability to make his stand and insist on what is important to him or her in circumstances when this is not easy, for instance, under the conditions of Milgram's (1965) famous experiment, where subjects were pressured to perform acts with which they felt ill at ease. In conditions like Milgram's experiment, the ability to resist the pressure, I argued, is more pertinent to mental well-being than various other aspects of social functioning. I suggested that, all other factors being equal, patients who had been in psychoanalysis would probably be better able to resist social pressures than those who had been in behavioural-cognitive therapy. For me, this is more meaningful evidence of the value of therapy than, for instance, the patient's ability to cope with certain work conditions or with the hardships of, say, military service. Types of therapy that are aimed to further adjustment to particular work conditions will obviously score higher on adjustment, but what about a person's ability to assert him or herself, to feel compassion or to be conscientious? It seems to me that these are no less important – and in the long run even more important – than functioning in difficult physical or social conditions. In this book, it is my intention to argue that such factors as self assertion and compassion are not only moral issues, but also a matter of mental well-being.

The previous argument, I think, bears out that the ethics which I have in mind as formative of psychoanalytic psychotherapy is of a particular kind. It is an ethics which, unlike religion, has no claims on specific behaviour as such. While the ethical in psychotherapy includes rules that guide behaviour, that guide life, these rules are not formulated in terms of dos and don'ts. Rather, they occur on a meta-level whose guiding principle, in an imperative form, is: *Be sensitive to yourself and insist on what you perceive as pertinent to yourself*. Hence, taking up the previous illustration, I do not suggest we check whether someone managed to take a certain position (e.g., to discontinue the experiment), but rather, in the case he reached such a decision, to consider whether he can put himself behind that decision and insist on it. Here however, we face a critical question which we traditionally perceive as the fundamental moral question. In terms of the ethics of therapy, what is the status of a person who, in Milgram's experiment, actually benefits somehow from inflicting pain or continues to inflict electric shocks because he has faith in the experiment's objective? What if a person asserts himself by hurting another: is therapy also bound to assist him in this? My formulations, so far, do not contradict this notion and perhaps even support it. This may be construed as the difference between morality as such and psychoanalytic ethics, but we also need to consider the mental effects of taking into account how the individual's actions affect his fellow humans. Morally speaking, the place of the other is rather clear: the prohibition to harm him if he does not constitute a threat is categorical. But does this clash with the psychoanalytic ethics of being yourself? This is the topic of Lacan's paper 'Kant with Sade' (1963/2006), which I have already mentioned and in which he discusses the good as opposed to the healthy or the pleasurable.

In Kant's *categorical imperative* – a principle of ethics that is shared by the monotheisms originating in the Bible – an act or a principle of action is moral to the extent that it can be generalized to all people, that is, to the extent that it can be universalized without risking contradiction; accordingly, if it applies to one person, this does not contradict the possibility of applying to another person (Kant, 1788/2004). Rules of conduct like 'Everything belongs to me' or 'A person is entitled to harm another if the person enjoys it' create a contradiction and hence are immoral. The first rule introduces contradiction for any two people, whereas the second leads to contradiction wherever there are two people who derive pleasure from hurting their fellow person. Nevertheless, it is something like the latter rule that Sade promotes as ethical and which forms the basis of sadism. Sadistic morality is characterized by the assumption that it is every person's right to pursue what pleases them regardless of how this affects the other. Kant's and Sade's seem to be fundamentally clashing principles – but are they really?

Lacan says that the contradiction arises due to the assumption of categorical separateness between self and other, or, in Lacan's terms, between the subject and the other. Here Lacan develops ideas that originated in Hegel, according to which a person cannot know himself from within himself, cannot be a subject, without becoming conscious of the other. The subject can only evolve in interaction with the other. The consciousness of the other constitutes the subject in such a way that the latter cannot exist without the former. Psychoanalysis, moreover, presupposes that the subject starts developing only as a result of internalizing a subjectivity which already exists in someone else. In psychoanalytic theory, this subjectivity is usually that of the mother. The infant becomes aware that he is in pain to the extent that his mother says: 'You are in pain', or hungry to the extent that his mother says: 'You are hungry'. Self-consciousness does not exist without the reflection of the other. 'Be yourself', therefore, can only be a meaningful statement where there is an other who recognizes this selfhood. 'Be yourself' is effectively a principle of searching for the other's recognition, because one cannot be himself in the absence of another who recognizes him as such. If we want to learn about the individual's ability to be 'himself', we must learn how he represents his fellow individual, along with the way in which this representation is closely and mutually interrelated with his self-representation. Indeed, in Sade's texts, the subject who exercises pleasure at the expense of another's suffering is continuously talking to this other person, explaining himself. He is never simply sadistic, but always philosophically so.

Chapter 1 begins this book with a construction of the basic principle of analytic psychotherapy, according to which psychological health is guided by the injunction 'Be yourself' or, to be precise: 'Be a subject'. This is a fundamentally ethical imperative. Chapter 1 discusses the diverse ways in which the individual becomes herself or takes her place as a subject, and how psychotherapy addresses itself to this, and may be helpful. In the approach I develop here, there is a crucial difference between subject and self, because the self is thought of as intrinsic to and independent of the individual's actions, as a type of internal essence, whereas the subject is constituted by the individual's actions and changes according to these actions. The subject, we may say, is an entity that is more external than the self, and is more accessible, conceptually and otherwise, to the observer. The notion of 'observer' is not trivial here: it applies to any social context and effectively holds for whoever perceives the individual as a subject, whoever acts as a witness. Indeed, the observer may be seen as a witness in precisely the sense of *observing the individual in a way that recognizes him as a subject*. Now, the question arises as to whether all of the individual's actions constitute him as a subject, whether the subject is the sum of his actions. My answer to this question is negative. The individual's actions constitute him as a subject in a variety of dimensions, such as self-consciousness and responsibility, but they are 'subject acts', acts that constitute the agent as subject, only to the extent that they address the other and respond to his or her presence. In this sense of addressing the other, the subject is also an external entity. Therefore, the ethics of subjecthood does not negate the other, but on the contrary, it seeks her. Put in psychoanalytic terms, the proposed ethics implies a notion of development in which becoming a subject is simultaneously tied up with an intentional relatedness to the other and to the place the other occupies in the individual's life. Taking one's subject position is a matter of neither egotism nor altruism and seeks to exclude neither self nor other; it constitutes the individual as a social entity (Butler, 2005). There is no other psychoanalytic way to be a subject. Chapter 2 develops this idea, along with the question of how this is enacted in psychoanalysis (Chapter 3).

If subjecthood means being social and if psychotherapy purports to advance subjecthood, then it is hard to avoid the conclusion that psychotherapy is in close dialogue with social processes. Yet, this idea, which I just formulated in the space of one economical sentence, is not a player in the field of analytic psychotherapy. Or not, in any case, a direct player. Patients do not usually talk about socio-political issues in their psychotherapy and few theorists so far have addressed the discussion of such issues within the frame of psychoanalytic psychotherapy. Yet, a few theorists have done so (e.g., Samuels, 1993; Frosh, 2010) and I discuss their ideas in Chapter 8, 'Activism', where I investigate the possible contributions of the theory of analytic psychotherapy to social and political activism, especially as it unfolds in the context of the Israeli military occupation in the West Bank and the Gaza Strip. I propose that activism can gain from therapeutic considerations, but can analytic therapy gain from social and post-colonial considerations? I discuss this issue in Chapter 7.

What can we gain from a social perspective in therapy, from including socio-political issues in therapeutic theory and practice? It seems to me that often theoretical blind spots come into being only because the perspective from which we examine our issues becomes fixed or rigidified. Even such a wide perspective as individual psychotherapy may suffer from this, as I illustrate in the following discussion. Being able to approach old issues from a different angle can help us shed a new light on persistent blind spots. In my opinion, this is the service Frantz Fanon (1952) rendered psychoanalysis when he used its terms in order to understand colonialism. In doing so, he more or less established what has come to be known as post-colonial theory. 'Post' because until the world assimilated Fanon's original ideas, the crude and most offensive forms of colonialism were becoming history, leaving intact more sophisticated forms of large scale domination, which are now being discussed under the heading of 'post-colonial studies'. In Chapter 8, which is dedicated to 'activism', I also look into a deeper significance of the various theories that reflect a worldview and are marked by the prefix *post-*. I believe that this *post-ism* represents approaches that remember the ideological positivity of modernism (e.g., communism, capitalism, Zionism), while insisting to remember also the terrible malformations, the destruction and the suffering that this ideological positivity brought upon the twentieth century, in the Middle East no less than elsewhere in the world. It is in recognition of this that what we could call the *post-ist* approaches represent the loss of ideological innocence and the quest for views that preserve humanity without promoting absolute ideals.

By introducing psychoanalytic terms into the discussion, Fanon mainly meant to contribute to the understanding of colonialism and this, indeed, was the case for many years. Recently, however, we witnessed some development in the opposite direction, that is to say, we began having psychoanalytic insights into the therapeutic situation which originate in social studies (Frosh, 2010). Take, for example, the dynamics related to the notion of *injury* (e.g., Benjamin, 2009a). Psychoanalysis set out from this notion by viewing psychological problems of the individual as originating in a traumatic interpersonal event (Freud & Breuer, 1895/1955). In those early days, Freud even believed that this traumatic event always involved sexual exploitation or abuse, that is to say, an event with a perpetrator and a victim. The perpetrator could be a parent but also someone else in a position of power vis-à-vis the victim. In psychoanalytic therapy, the *patient* – as the epithet indicates – was first of all there in his role as a victim. Victimhood was his initial position within the therapeutic process. Indeed, the aim of therapy was to allow the patient to move away from his victim position. Over time, due to various – in part good – reasons, the initially lucid presence of injury grew weaker, theoretically speaking. There is personality, there are the circumstances of life, there are fantasies and a choice of deprivations – no need for injury. I obviously agree: no intended, traumatic injury is required for psychological problems to arise. Life as such is sufficiently complex. But it seems to me that the concept of injury allows some insights regarding the therapeutic process that none of these other notions affords. Because I consider this insight the central axis of this book, Chapter 5 is devoted to it. This part of the book discusses a number of issues which can be made meaningful through the prism of injury. First, the notion of injury adds a dimension to our understanding of the key role of the ethical in the praxis of analytic psychotherapy. Here the ethical refers simply to the recognition of injury, the injustice in which it inheres. Such recognition, I think, is crucial to psychoanalysis if it wants to steer clear of entering – and getting caught in – a discussion that is enclosed within itself, without seriously examining the external implications of the themes that arise from it. Many times, these implications may be sacrificed by both patient and therapist on the altar of analytic interpretability. The perspective of injury, however, also gives access to insights that are not fundamentally ethical, such as the understanding that transference has a negative core – the understanding that no transference in analytic psychotherapy can be wholly positive. This is not the place to go into the related arguments, but I deal with it extensively in Chapter 5, because it has important clinical implications.

On a more theoretical level, as I previously mentioned, the perspective of injury offers psychoanalysis the benefit of insights derived from the understanding of the (post-)colonial condition. For example, take the basic definition of the place of the patient in therapy. Of course, one has to accept, as all theoreticians do, that this place is defined by negativity – dissatisfaction or suffering in one of their forms – but the medical perspective conceptualizes this in terms of pathology. This has been seriously and extensively criticized on grounds of ignoring the extent to which culture influences our notions of mental and functional norms. The notion of injury, as it is thought of in (post-) colonial theory, seems to offer therapy an alternative to the notion of pathology in defining the place of the patient. In this perspective, the patient is someone who has been injured by acts of domination that damaged their ability to take subject positions, to make decisions and take responsibilities. Chapter 7 elaborates on these matters, as well as on other ways in which therapy and (post-)colonial theory may enrich each other.

Because the social-therapeutic context is prominent among the insights that this book offers, I would like to briefly present here in the Introduction one topic that stands to gain from being considered through the prism of the comparison between therapy and the colonial situation. Consider, for that purpose, the concept of *resistance,* which is central in both post-colonial and psychoanalytic theory. In psycho-analysis, resistance is conceived of as an obstacle to the therapeutic process and it is supposed to be reflected in a variety of forms of failure to communicate fluently, be it in the context of remembering or in the context of (free) associating. This failure often reflects in diverse types of *enactment* such as frame violations, silences, empty speech, infatuation, and so on. This notion of resistance is often summarized by the formula whereby 'Whatever is not articulated in speech finds expression in action'. The notion of resistance here opposes action to psychoanalytic work. In post-colonial theory, by contrast, it is mainly through resist-ance that the oppressed (and there are various ways in which people can be colonially oppressed) can take their place as subjects (Jefferess, 2008). Clearly, then, while resistance is classically thought of as an obstacle to personal freedom in psychoanalysis, it is thought of as the prime instru-ment of liberation in post-colonial theory. This contrast in viewing resistance between psychoanalytic and post-colonial theory causes us to feel that they belong to absolutely different fields of life, but is this really the case? From the post-colonial perspective, Stephen Frosh (2010), following Hegel and Foucault, has shown that resistance often repro-duces and entrenches the power relations that have brought it about. Addressing itself to the master, i.e., the colonial oppressor, resistance derives the subjecthood of the colonized from the recognition of the colonizer. In that sense, resistance, especially in its total forms, subverts its own liberating power at the very same time as it realizes this power. Looking at the psychoanalytic side of resistance, it transpires, if we read

Freud's technical writings attentively, that for a long time he thought that the therapist's task was not to dig into the unconscious by offering deep interpretations, but rather to allow the unconscious to be stirred, to rise and bubble into consciousness. He thought that if the patient managed to divest himself of the oppressive part of his consciousness (manifested in repression), the unconscious material would rise to the surface due to the strong impulse that informs it. There is no need for the patient to go out 'angling' in his unconscious – the latter will 'come' to the patient of its own accord. What prevents this from happening in normal life is the very anxiety that relegated the repressed material to the unconscious in the first place. This is what Freud called 'resistance', referring to the particular forms in which it appears in the analytic process. The therapist's prime task, Freud thought, was to neutralize resistance, and the way one does this is by means of interpretation. In his technical writings, Freud indeed argues that *all* the therapist needs to do is interpret the resistance. This should suffice for therapy to move forward. And what if there is no resistance? Well, if there is none, then there is nothing the therapist can do. **There is no analytic psychotherapy without resistance.** This was the main reason why Freud believed it was impossible to conduct analytic psychotherapy with psychotic patients: they lack resistance. Not that they have no problems – on the contrary – but when these problems manifest themselves without resistance they do not allow analytic psychotherapy. Resistance in Freud's theory is effectively what holds the ego together while, at the same time, the ego maintains resistance. Ego refers to a structure for which the energy comes in the form of resistance. In psychosis, ego and resistance get jointly fragmented, leaving the psyche without the basic conditions for analytic therapy. To conceive of resistance as a barrier to therapy, therefore, would be erroneous. It is the absence of resistance that constitutes the real obstacle. Analytic psychotherapy builds directly and wholly on resistance. Resistance is the therapist's ally – this is what is interpreted, this is the *sine qua non* of therapy. It supplies therapy with the ladder for progress. Thus, a re-examination of Freudian resistance that holds the post-colonial notion at the background brings about a different understanding of the concept. In both contexts, identity requires resistance. Setting out from the gap between the post-colonial and the psychoanalytic understanding of resistance, my analysis shows the manner in which each can enrich the other. Such conceptual convergences form the central theme of Chapter 7.

If, as Fanon thought, liberation from oppression is similar across the social and the psychological domains, then psychotherapeutic theory and practice may offer significant insights for resisting the evils of colonialism, as well as in ameliorating the destructive dynamics that oppression or colonialism bring about. If this is the case, psychological activism may have a particular meaning, that is, the struggle against oppression and its results by means of tools that rely on psychological analysis on the whole, and on therapeutic lessons more specifically. Such an effort is indeed underway, and impressively so, in different places worldwide and in Israel too, particularly within recent decades. This is the subject of Chapter 8. Psycho-political activism implements ideas which I present in earlier parts of the book – from the central role of *action* in subjecthood and its development, through the liberating nature of *turning to the other*, to the key position of the notion of *injury* and the need *to move out of the role of the victim*. In Israel specifically, because of the region's conditions of living, organizations that are dedicated to the struggle against the occupation have been in existence for years, and some of them have rallied together under a psycho-political banner. Most recently, the latter evolved into a unique group called *Psychoactive*. The activities of this organization are analysed in Chapter 9, along with the activities of two other organizations similar in some ways, but very unlike it in others. The discussion of the modes of operation of these organizations articulates the possibility of a new type of community which, not unlike a religious community, is guided by moral objectives and mutual solidarity, but which unlike the latter, is not religious and does not subject the individual's life to its own set of values. While the individual's participation in the group does help to create a group identity and a sense of mutual commitment, it does not require the individual to sacrifice her individuality and favour the group demands. This activism, which I call *post-ist*, suggests a different order, the *activist community*, with a wide range of ethical relations between individual and group, whose features I discuss in Chapter 8 of the book.

It is my belief that this book offers a choice of new thoughts regarding psychoanalytic theory like, for instance, the idea that action and interpretation are not essentially different (Chapter 2); the notion that triangulation is an extension of the concept of identification (Chapter 4); the idea that the therapeutic event develops around experiences of injury of the patient (Chapter 5), or the idea that resistance promotes therapy rather than being an obstacle to it (Chapter 7). The book also includes some practical contributions such as, for instance, the idea that confrontations with the patient, when appropriately modulated, can be extremely valuable, therapeutically speaking (Chapter 1), or that political discussions can be therapeutic (Chapter 10). But for me the book's major contribution should be in elucidating the interface between psychotherapy and social involvement (Chapters 6 through 8). The existence of this interface should not be taken to mean that psychotherapy leads necessarily, or *should* lead, to therapists' social involvement, but that it *can* lead there. If the therapist wants, there is a simple but rich way of understanding social situations, as well as of acting in relation to them, by using her professional knowledge. And it is this possibility that allows the therapist as such to be a subject in the social order – it is this possibility that links therapeutic theory to the times and conditions in which we live.

1
The Subject

Being-a-subject

There are different ways to be happy, healthy or fulfilled. One can make money, one can be active in the community, be invested in a valuable relationship, in parenthood or family life; one can be an achiever in some activity, say in sports, art or public life. But psychotherapy sets its aims elsewhere. Psychotherapy, in a sense, could be said to deal with another dimension of happiness or health altogether. This is to say, psychotherapy is concerned with the way in which the individual experiences himself while going about the various activities of his daily life. I would like to refer to this reflective dimension of life, in which the individual constitutes her or himself both vis-à-vis and within the sum of her or his actions and activities, as 'being-a-subject'.

This being-a-subject, for me, is the fundamental perspective of psychoanalysis – not merely of the therapeutic approach, which is at the focus of the present book, but of psychoanalytic personality theory as well. While it is marginal in the present context, personality theory cannot be wholly left aside when we come to explain and describe the perspective of being-a-subject. What is required, first and foremost, is a discussion, even if brief, of what it means to be a subject – a question that philosophers have been looking at throughout modern history.

It is obvious, already from my opening remarks, that while, in my perception, being-a-subject involves reflectiveness – i.e., the individual's consideration of her or himself – it cannot be reduced to this reflectiveness as such. Being-a-subject, as I consider it here, at the outset of my discussion of the concept, is reminiscent of how it is conceived of by phenomenologists like Heidegger (1927/1962) and existentialists like Sartre (1943/1958) – namely, a general mode of being in the world, a certain way of going about things, including mental things (like thinking thoughts or having fantasies). Being-a-subject bears a resemblance to Heidegger's notion of *Dasein* – something which is borne out by the central role of reflectiveness in it, since *Dasein* is defined as a being that is capable of understanding – or of attributing meaning to – its own being (ibid.). Similarly, but with a significant difference, nevertheless, I consider it critical for being-a-subject that we should be able to perceive the things we do, or the situations in which we find ourselves, as things and situations that are ours, as things and situations that carry our personal imprint or name. What distinguishes between this and Heidegger's approach – and what links it, by contrast, with Sartre – is that here being-a-subject turns to the world. For Heidegger, the subject is more immanent, directs itself more inward (see also Chapters 1 and 11). In the ideal being-a-subject, the individual experiences her actions as the outcome of her choice, something she or he has chosen to do. However, I formulate my notion of subjecthood more tentatively than being-able-to-make-choices, in such a way as to make being-a-subject possible also when a person does not carry out or experience a choice. One could substitute 'making a choice' by the softer notion of 'taking responsibility', which is to say seeing oneself as responsible for the acts one has committed or for the situations in which one is or has been. This predication of the subject is better than predication through acts of choice because it enables us to conceptualize being-a-subject also for those instances where we did not choose to do something or to be in the situation in which we find ourselves. In this conception, a person can take responsibility for things he did not choose to do (or indeed, decline responsibility for things he did elect to do). Still, the notion of responsibility does not embrace important meanings of being-a-subject. So it can occur, for instance, that while I do not feel responsible for my condition, I do nevertheless feel that it is part of me and I perceive it as an inherent part of my life and my identity, even if I would much rather not be in this situation or be the person who did this thing, which I may not hold in high regard and due to which I may even suffer. At the same time, I recognize that this deed or this situation is part of who and what I am.

Being-a-subject is inherently tied up with *negativity*, which may be expressed in the experience of negative feelings such as threat, anxiety, or distress. Though these feelings may be different from each other in some crucial ways, they always concern the possible loss of subjecthood- its erasure or annihilation. This is especially striking in

Sartre's work (ibid.), in which being-a-subject always emerges in the face of death, or of nothingness. The radical human freedom which Sartre propounds is only possible from this position – of being versus nothingness – because any constitution in the face of positivity is always already marked or shaped by this very positivity. When facing nothingness, by contrast, the individual is free to choose without the constraints of what he is already. It is by rejecting Sartre's notion of absolute freedom that my approach is not existentialist – though I do call it *ex-sistentialist* (see Chapter 11), a term I borrow from Lacan (1973/1998) to refer to the manner in which some aspects of our being escape mentalization in a total way, even beyond the escape that is implied by the Freudian notion of the unconscious. This elusive aspect of being, which Lacan calls 'the Real' (ibid.), is what for me constitutes the subject as negativity. Being-a-subject forms itself against a background of a Real of which she has no positive knowledge. This introduces into being-a-subject an inexorable element of *absence of freedom*, by contrast to Sartre's notion of the subject. Negativity plays a formative role in being-a-subject not only in my *ex-sistentialist* approach, but also in psychoanalysis as a whole, where negativity appears in the various forms of suffering, especially anxiety, but not only. In psychoanalytic writings, this is sometimes mistakenly thought of in terms of disease but, as I show throughout the book, the notion of disease neglects to appreciate the ethical nature of being-a-subject.

Much like in Sartre, for psychoanalysis being-a-subject is logically impossible in the absence of a threat to its very existence. In psychoanalysis, the two most general threats are those of corporeality on the one hand, and the dependence on the recognition of another subject, on the other hand. First, the subject is irremovably attached to a body, despite the fact that this body is never directly constitutive of being-a-subject; the body always remains alien to it (see Chapter 2). In some cases, the body limits, constrains or even obstructs the being of a subject, but even when it does not, it remains a threat to it. Second, being-a-subject is reliant on the recognition of another subject – a recognition which is never simply secure. The other, as Sartre said, is always a bit of a hell for the subject. Chapter 3 deals extensively with this aspect of subjecthood. From these two threats, it follows that the whole ensemble of concrete conditions for being-a-subject is marked by experiential negativity, by suffering. This is one reason why the analytic therapeutic context offers us a privileged field of investigation where it comes to being-a-subject. The patient arrives in therapy with the visiting card of the threat, of experiential negativity. Analytic psychotherapy operates by directing itself towards this negativity.

Let me give a brief illustration. A woman friend in her sixties lost her husband after a long illness. The first two years following his death were very hard. She was in constant pain due to her partner's absence and suffered from an unbearable sense of futility and grief. Gradually she found her way back to a life that resembled her previous life, which was active in all respects (work, family, learning), but without the desire she had felt before. She was low spirited, most of the time, especially when alone at home, and even though she was as active and dedicated as ever with her grandchildren, she experienced them like a burden no less than a pleasure. In one of our conversations, at some point in the third year after her husband's death, I asked her whether she would not like trying to take anti-depressant medication. '…in a low dose', I said, 'you can take it for long stretches of time, there are no side effects'. She laughed in response and said, 'Oh Uri, it wouldn't enter my mind. It's hard. I am no longer enjoying things the way you used to know me, but that's my life. That's the sense I make of it, the pain and the pessimism included. When I take a look at my life, it seems to suit the picture as a whole. I would have liked to be in a different place, experience more joy, but I wouldn't dream of doing it by force, by medicating myself'. Given her situation, this woman's response, for me, exemplifies being-a-subject. It contains the discomfort of facing an absolute negativity, the death of her life-long partner, his absence, the continuing experience of him missing, of missing him. From within this absence, she now constitutes her position in the world, she cannot imagine herself without it, she does not want to. She does not try to cover up or to deny the absence; she makes no attempt to pretend and is instead determined to stake out suffering as her proper mode of being for the time being. At other times she was different. There is no inner self here that is more truthful than her earlier life-loving self, but nor is it less truthful. The central place of suffering in this dialogue of ours indicates how a therapeutic perspective may be relevant to the life circumstances of this woman, even if she rejected the manner in which I suggested therapy to her – in the form of anti-depressants. This rejection underscores the *psychic* nature of the type of therapy that directs itself at being-a-subject, as well as the way in which insistence on the psychic nature of any possible therapy actually constitutes the woman as a subject in the circumstances that make up her life. She lives her particular life. It is this life that is hers.

Being-a-subject forms a focal point for therapy in all psychoanalytic approaches, though the terminology used may differ (awareness, responsibility, maturity, etc.). The nature of the process by which it is attained, however, has been variously described. On the one hand, there are the objectivistic approaches of which ego psychology is an excellent representative. According to this approach, general balances in the mental economy allow the individual's optimal functioning, whether emotional or social. Ego psychology has a fairly specific image of the psychic normativity which allows the individual to occupy her place as a subject within her mental makeup, as well as in society and, as it happens, these two coincide. This image involves a notion of a person who works, has a family, and views reality soberly and with a degree of detachment, as something that does not depend on her interests, actions or aspirations. A person's ability to promote such functionality is called 'ego strength' and it is the task of psychotherapy to promote this strength. A strong ego is apt to help a person control her feelings, be a good citizen, maintain her health and the health of her loved ones, be pleasant in social intercourse and to her surroundings, look after her property, make a good living and so on. The basic motto of psychotherapy that is based on ego-psychology, therefore, is 'Where Id was, there will Ego be' (Freud, 1933, p. 80), which effectively states the objective of the analytic process. The Id in this formula represents everything instinct-driven inside us, whatever pushes for instant gratification and eludes the demands of culture or of due consideration of the other. For Freud, being psychologically healthy and taking one's place as a subject is crucially bound up with controlling one's impulses and adjusting them to the social and cultural reality. This reality, of course, is not easily represented and does not unfold its demands in anything like an univocal manner. On the contrary, in fact, in certain cases. According to Freud (1930), however, social reality is constituted on the basis of three fundamental prohibitions, the prohibition of taking another person's life; the prohibition of eating human flesh; and the prohibition of sexual relations with members of one's closest family (i.e., the prohibition of incest). For ego psychology, a person can be psychically healthy or, to put it more precisely, take her place as a subject, to the extent that she observes these three basic prohibitions – even if she entertains impulses and fantasies whose sole aim is to break these rules. Because there is a wealth of extensions of these prohibitions which generate a large collection of social norms, being-a-subject, for ego psychology, manifests in social conformity.

Freud's message, however, is not just one of conformism, normativity and social conservatism (Frosh, 2010, pp. 6–13). It also recognizes human drives and the passions, which also inform his being-a-subject or, even in a stronger formulation, his mental health. Psychoanalysis has left its profound impact on Western culture as the catalyst par excellence of sexual liberation – initially as a result of the recognition of the universality, the naturalness and the omni-present nature of sexuality, and subsequently because it recognized that sexual oppression comes at a high cost in functional terms, to the point of mental illness. This led to the insight that being in touch with our desires, including the sexual ones, striving to satisfy them, as long as this does not obscure or obliterate the desires of others, actually contributes to mental health and social functioning, as well as to cultural pluralism. Ironically, given the conservative nature of psychoanalysis, it was often accused of promoting sexual permissiveness, mainly on account of theories like that of Wilhelm Reich (1936/1951) who, in his later writings, celebrated sexuality as the prime dimension of being human. Such theories, however, did help to put into proportion the functional objectivism of ego psychology. From the point of view of this book, it is significant that Reich started out, theoretically speaking, from opposition to fascism and the attempt to conceptualize this opposition in psychoanalytic terms.

In recognition of the liberating potential of psychoanalysis and being faithful to the original formulation in German of the aim of psycho-analytic therapy, Lacan (1955/2006, p. 347) re-translated Freud's words.[1] Instead of 'Where Id was, there shall Ego be', Lacan put it, 'Where it was, there shall I come into being'. He argued that while Strachey (Freud's first, official English translator who coined the terms 'Ego' and 'Id') used 'Ego' and 'Id', in Freud's original wording the regular personal pronouns 'Ich' and 'Es' ('I' and 'It') had featured (see also Hadar, 2010a). What is impressive about the difference between these translations is that with the minimal theoretical tools of translation Lacan creates a crucial shift in meaning, from the objective to the subjective. The thematic shift is from the vision of a person who fits in with a certain normative ideal to a vision of a person who strives towards being-a-subject. Therapy aims to allow a person to be whatever she chooses or wishes to be (as long as it is within the limitations of the possible and the lawful). The ideal suggested by Lacan's translation is, of course, similar to my definition of being-a-subject, that is to say, the ideal of a person who stands behind her actions and thoughts, who perceives and experiences them more as

---

[1] Immanuel Berman drew my attention to the fact that both Morris Eagle (1984) and Thomas Ogden (2001) proposed translations similar to those of Lacan. I choose to conduct my discussion with reference to Lacan, nevertheless, for reasons of precedence.

an 'I' and less as an 'it'. This implies a clear conception of what constitutes, in the eyes of psychoanalysis, a good choice in a person's daily life. It is this choice that optimizes the being of a subject, the one that allows the person to put herself behind the choice as best as she can. The measure I propose here for being-a-subject is a matter of experience in the first place, although it implies a fit between the chosen course and the pre-existing tendencies of the subject, her desires, which is not an easy issue and may be circular in its reasoning at times.

Nevertheless, this formulation allows me to state that the interest of therapy is to identify domains in the life of the patient in which she feels robbed of selfhood, a stranger to her actions or milieu, and then make possible and initiate, where possible, a psychological process that will let the patient recognize herself in those places too. She may then connect with them, be more active in them and not just bear them, suffer them or, worse, be a victim to them. Such a process may involve a change in the subject's experience of the area of life that is under discussion (work, family, etc.), to the effect of making one feel better at home with it, less alienated or, if this is too much to ask, less tormented by her sense of alienness. In the latter case, the unease can come to feel and be thought of as fitting with the subject's sensibilities, as in the previous example. Much of this book is dedicated to a detailed examination of this work, but before I continue, let me remark on a certain fundamental 'ill-at-easeness' associated with being-a-subject, an ill-at-easeness that is irremovable, I believe. This is what one has to learn to live with.

Subject to a body

Being-a-subject, it would seem, emerges in a paradoxical field. It is perceived and conceived of as a non-physical sphere of life, a challenge to the physicality of existence, a protest against it, or even an indication that existence grows human where physicality is constrained, where the physical is no longer merely physical. Yet, the subject, on the other hand, is firmly welded to a specific body, an entity which is physically defined, positioned in space and time and marking a mobile territory. While my approach acknowledges forms of subjectivity that are not attached to a body (see Chapter 3), it nevertheless cannot make sense of purely disembodied subjectivities. In fact, the present approach is non-religious in precisely the sense that body-less subjectivity is perceived as derivative to embodied subjectivity, or is perhaps even parasitic upon it. Body-less subjectivities act in the world through bodies that are not directly attached to them. This idea considerably complicates our notion of being-a-subject.

The individual relies totally on the experience of his body in order to forge the platform on which his feelings of ownership, of belonging, and so on, rest. Such feelings originate in the ability to determine that a certain part of space belongs or does not belong to the subject's body. For instance, healthy people decide very expertly whether the body they just touched is theirs or someone else's, or whether a body part they see belongs to them or not. In ordinary states of experience, this is done with such skill that people are not aware that this is not trivial. Brain injury or sophisticated experimental manipulations can easily cause the individual to lose these capacities and, along with them, the entire experience of self integrity (Salomon, 2011). Similarly, in all experimental approaches, the very core of self experience inheres in the individual's ability to tell when a motion of one of her limbs is caused by an outside force or by her own will – something which is the basic foundation of the possibility of agency. Things are not self-evident here either even if most of us experience them as such. Again, these experiences are easily unsettled as the result of brain injury or planned experimental manipulations (ibid.). These two basic abilities – to identify body parts as our own and experience bodily movement as self-initiated – make up what experimental psychology calls 'the minimal self'. Its extension to other domains of experience and cognition is considered the hard core of self functioning. To the extent that being-a-subject is related to the experience of self, it is also related to these body-based experiences.

In addition to functions that are related to the minimal self, the body also serves as the metaphorical field in which subjecthood is expressed and articulated. For example, the notion of the *face*, especially in the wake of Levinas (1985, 2000), powerfully illustrates the subject's rootedness in the body. Similarly, in the Jewish priestly blessing, *birkat hako-hanim*, the divinity casts its being-a-subject onto the recipient of the blessing by positioning his face in relation to the recipient, 'May God turn His face towards you' and 'May God light His face to you'. As I show in Chapter 2, the specular or imaginary distinction between the subject and the other relies on the distinction between in-front-of and behind, between face and rear. Expressions involving the face like 'to face' (a situation) or 'to lose face' usually define the state of subjectivity in a particular context. A similar metaphorical indication of subjecthood also originates in expressions involving the *hands* – including their important role in the previously mentioned priestly blessing.

Clean-handedness is another word for guiltlessness, and even-handed-ness refers to impartiality – qualities that also define the individual qua subject. Of course, the human body offers metaphors for a whole range of themes, of which subjective states are only a part, but within the metaphorical field of subjective states, the body holds a singular position as a source of metaphors.

Finally, in modern society and in its legal underpinnings, being-a-subject is most determinately acknowledged through the subject's ownership of her or his body. Indeed, the individual's body is uniquely protected by the law from any external infringement, as long as the individual does not break the law. Even then, the law takes care to protect the individual's rights over her body much more than her property rights or civil rights. For example, in the case of the individual's regular property rights, they can be mortgaged, impounded, expropriated, sold, or bought. The body, by contrast, does forever belong to the one subject who is defined by it, or even: It is the body that defines the singularity and the continuity of the subject as a legal entity. So central is the body in the law's definition of the subject that the law forbids even the very subject who is associated with the body to inflict offenses against it. A subject's imminent attack on her or his own body constitutes one of the rare conditions when the law allows the other access to the subject's body. In such a case and under these circumstances, the other gains the right, if not the duty, to take limited authority vis-à-vis the subject's body. The psychotherapist, for example, is allowed and even, in some juridical systems, obliged by law to prevent the possibility of the patient's committing suicide. In most countries, professional ethics requires that a mental health worker (like other professionals) should physically prevent a person from inflicting damage to their own body. I am not sure whether I fully agree with this position. True enlightenment, it seems to me, should allow us to accept the possibility that a person may not want to go on living, that the continuation of life may not be the preferred choice of the subject. This would extend the individual's subject rights into a domain which to me seems duly hers or his. Giving the subject the right over her own life, I believe, would assert the enlightened balance between subjectivity and its body, but this is not the place to discuss this issue in depth.

Having observed the central place of the body in the definition of the subject allows us to understand why contemporary therapies that turn toward the subject – psychoanalytic psychotherapies – derive histori-cally from therapies of the body, i.e., from medicine, even though the former are informed by principles that are very unlike those of the latter.

Still, psychoanalytic thinkers since Freud, especially Lacan, have tried to maintain views of the psyche and its healing that were not subservient to the medical model. The body has kept its central role with regard to subjectivity, but without imposing biological reasoning. This is achieved by means of the notion of *desire*, by virtue of its mediating position between body and mind. The body is present in desire because it is always a bodily experience, with its often measurable correlates. And the mind is present because of the *absence* that is inherent in desire. It is always addressed from the corporeal here and now to the intentional then and there, to otherness, usually inflected in a future tense. This is what renders desire a category of the subject, a category that can be pivotal in establishing subjecthood and which has been singularized for this purpose by those psychoanalytic theories that aspired to preserve the centrality of the body in the understanding of mental processes. Desire, then, is that part of subjectivity that connects mental life with bodily experience on one hand, and with other persons, on the other. As such, desire is realized through or is organized around those aspects of the body that allow linkage between inside and outside (and vice versa), the erogenous zones. It is this quality of these zones, their placement between inside and outside – their topological duality – that is possibly the most crucial in how they join between body and subject. Due to the paradoxicality of the physical grounding of the subject, the body is simultaneously external and internal to it. Hence any form of bridging between them must of necessity be marked by this topological duality. Lacan's contribution here is two-fold: First, he disengaged the interface body-subject from its anatomic stability and allowed it to occur at any site whatever on the body (though the erogenous zones kept their privileged status in this regard). Second, he brought into prominence the ambiguous topology of the zones of desire by situating them between self and other. I discuss this now in greater detail.

Lacan called the body-subject interface *objet petit a* – a term not less awkward than Freud's *erogenous zone* or Klein's *part object*. In an attempt to simplify the use of these concepts while, at the same time, preserving some components of both Klein's and Lacan's terminology, I call the body-subject interface an *objecta* – and in the plural (for there are many of them) *objectas*.[2] The objecta is a mental entity which situates *jouissance*

---

[2] Terms like *parta* or *organa*, in my opinion, could be more precise in their anatomical overtones, but lose the root of the object that is prevalent in earlier psychoanalytic terms that address this issue. Here I preferred a terminological continuity, partial as it may be.

(enjoyment or excitation) on one of its sides, thereby marking, or even creating, the inside of the body. The inside of the body is where bodily jouissance takes place and it is always signposted, so to speak, by an objecta. In this way, the objecta defines a bodily sensation which relates to the body envelope but does not remain there. Instead, it resonates inward and is engraved in memory. The positioning of the objectas on the surface of the body underlines the manner in which this surface defines, both for the other and for society, the place of the subject. Rather than body part, the objecta is a mark, a mark of something that is *not* there just as much as it *is*. As a mark, the objecta is wholly determined by the bodily environment in which it is situated; it constitutes an imagined entry into that environment. In Figure 1.1, I illustrate this idea. Here the body envelope is represented in the form of a Möbius strip in order to show the duality between inside and outside in the corporeal environment of the objecta.

The drawing illustrates how the objecta, by appearing in an area of transition between inside and outside, marks the region around it as a zone of linkage between subject and other. This precisely is the point of drawing the objecta on a Möbius strip, namely, to distinguish between my topological ambiguity and the more ordinary positioning of the erogenous zone as an opening, which maintains the clear distinction between inside and outside. In the topology of the erogenous zone, there is no choice other than making the subject an internal entity. In

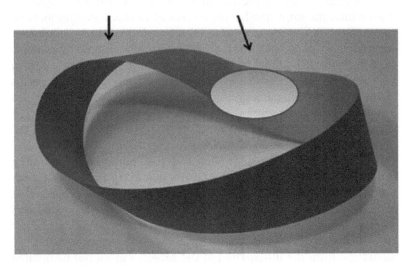

Figure 1.1 Situating the objecta on the body envelope

the objecta version, by contrast, the topological ambiguity of the site implies the ambiguity of being a subject (see also the last section of this chapter, 'Subject and Self').

When we consider the anatomy of the human body with the aim of identifying areas of potential linkage between subject and other, regions of attraction, one possibility quickly dominates the imagination, namely, that there is a bifurcation here between convex and concave regions. For one, the topology of attraction, a term that has a clear topological definition, also divides into areas of positive and negative attraction, the former being convex and the latter concave. But of course, my present formulation refers primarily to the facts of imaginary attraction (desire), where the ability of protrusions and cleavages to fit into each other is formative (Forrester, 1991). Despite the formal similarity of the preceding to conventional gender distinctions, topology offers us the chance to undo the predication of desire on gendered properties. Our anatomy, irrespective of sex, has both protrusions and cleavages and they can fit with each other in whatever combination allowed by our topological imagination. Desire, in that sense, is always polymorphous. Given this nature of my definitions, I see as an asset the abstract continuity between traditional notions of sexual attraction and the present ones. Reinventing the wheel is not always the worst option.

In terms of the imagination, because the subject is rooted in the body, the situation in which the subject is linked to the other by the fitting of a cleavage around a protrusion constitutes a symbiotic situation from which she must free herself – the way to reach an autonomy of personality must involve, on one level or another, the separation of body parts. Here we can think of the infant who removes its mouth from the mother's nipple (this is the illustration that Lacan offers in his 10th Seminar (1962/2001), which serves as a model of the subject' s move toward functional autonomy). After this separation, the objecta is imagined as belonging to one side only – either that of the subject or that of the other. An act of separation of this type, which results in the objecta's being perceived as belonging to one side only, is called a *cut* by Lacan, a notion which, for him, has concrete implications for ending the therapeutic session. Here the idea is that every parting is a separation. This means every cut reconstitutes the subject's separateness from the other. If we want the separation to be as clear as possible – as we shall see, it stays locally blurred in the best of cases – then the cut must be trenchant, namely, such that it does not occlude the subject's separation from the other. Though the subject cannot but be defined by the other, she can attain a degree of autonomy nevertheless, and this is achieved by the clear break, the cut. This is what the truncating of the analytic session purports to do – to render patient and analyst as sharply separate as possible. The Lacanian wisdom here is the very inverse of its Kohutian counterpart. Rather than acting as a selfobject, as an internal agency in the patient's mind, the analyst positions herself as clearly separate from the patient as possible. How does this sharp cut affect the subject's imagination? In theory, it allows the subject (the patient) to imagine the objecta as belonging to only one side, either that of the subject or that of the other (the analyst). In the previous discussion, I defined the sharpness of the cut in precisely this sense, of situating the objecta in only one side of the self-other divide.

At this point, after the sharp cut, Lacan makes one of his less known, but more exciting contributions. He says that if the objecta is imagined on the side of the other, it generates desire – a fantasy, that is, that seeks re-connection with the other. If however, it is imagined as located on the side of the subject, the objecta begets anxiety. This affective bifurcation between the poles of desire and anxiety is the outcome of the ambivalent ownership of the objecta, of the way the objecta – unlike any other part of the body – eludes unambiguous ownership. The objecta, after all, is not a solid thing, it is not some thing, but rather the mark of an absence, a site of potential linkage between subject and other. That is why it can always belong to either the subject or the other. Its belonging to the other does not negate the possibility of its belonging to the subject, and the other way around, its belonging to the subject does not negate its possible belonging to the other. Thus, if the objecta is imagined as belonging to the other, the other is imagined as someone who holds on to parts of the subject, not unlike what happens in the Kleinian projective identification. This arouses the subject's desire. By contrast, when the objecta is imagined as situated with the subject, it still does not lose its connection to the other, so the subject experiences herself as containing an alien element. It is as though something other than herself has attached itself to her body, giving rise to a basic discomfort. In this sense, again like in the processes Klein described in relation to splitting, the anxiety caused by the objecta will always have a paranoid aspect, a sense of a foreign, alien presence. This anxiety does not only attach to the body but to the immediate surroundings as well, to one's sense of being-at-home – something which Freud captured beautifully in his paper on 'The Uncanny' which, in the original German, *das Unheimliche*, includes an allusion to the sense of home. One major consequence of the objecta perspective is that the subject realizes her inter-subjective embodiedness not just in the form of desire, but also through anxiety. These two experiences enter the world of analysis in a state of entanglement. The business of therapy always includes the disentanglement of the two emotions. Though this can already be observed in Freud's writings, it only becomes explicit in Lacan, and especially so in his seminar on anxiety (Ibid). The dualism desire/anxiety of human embodiedness returns eternally and at times from surprising corners. As a dimension of experience, it deeply resonates with the eros/thanatos dualism, or that of sexuality/aggression, which are all central axes along which the present book orients itself. Anxiety/desire is where the duality of being-a-subject, to the extent that this duality has any explanatory power, attaches itself most closely to the body.

Psychotherapy and being-a-subject: basic assumptions

For me, the most salient thing about a therapy inspired by the Lacanian reformulation of the therapeutic objective (transforming 'it' into 'I') is that it is an open-ended project[3] because, as we saw in the previous section, even only embodiedness already implies that there will always remain elements of a person's life that are not 'I' and which thereby offer themselves for work. There are other reasons for which some mental contents may be excluded from one's perception of oneself, for instance because they involve suffering or because they are unconscious. Suffering almost always is met by its disowning by the subject, as a strategy of reducing it. As if disowning is part of what should make us suffer less. As a result, we tend to conceive of suffering as externally imposed upon us, as never the result of an act of choice. Part of how Lacan's notion of *jouissance* serves us is in admitting suffering as a subject-constituting experience, as a choice. We are all masochistic at times, some more, some less. Likewise, mental events are unconscious inasmuch as they are experienced as not-us, as foreign (even when we speak of them in the first person, as in dreams). Having discovered ways of rendering the unconscious conscious, psychoanalysis mainly addressed itself to the unconscious. It so happens, as psychoanalysis soon found out, that making the unconscious conscious often – and

---

[3] The fact that promoting being-a-subject is an open-ended project does not imply the unendingess of therapy, though it might. The finitude of therapy for Lacan, for instance, and as opposed to myself, was very important and something into which he put much thought, precisely against this background of the open-endedness of promoting the being-of-a-subject (Lacan, 1958a/2006).

perhaps even in principle – goes hand in hand with a reduction in suffering. Consequently, psychoanalysis' main method has become that of making the unconscious conscious. In the following discussion, I argue with Lacan that this therapeutic perspective is too narrow if we want to fully articulate the processes that aim to facilitate being-a-subject. I start my theoretical investigation here with the questions of suffering and (un-)consciousness.

For Freud (1937), the therapeutic project is never-ending because the unconscious is inexhaustible, because there are repressions that are prior to the individual's biography. Early on in his work, Freud had held a different view. He was more optimistic about the possibility of a total analysis and assumed that the whole of the unconscious came into being under the pressures of social conventions (or of the super-ego, at a later stage in his thinking). With time, and to no small extent under the influence of Jung, he came to believe that the origin of many repressed contents was evolutionary rather than personal. In *Totem and Taboo* (1913), for instance, he argued that the deepest regions of the unconscious are associated with aversion to smells and tastes related to the sexual parts of the body, i.e., the rectal and urinary parts. In the times when the human ape walked on all fours, according to Freud, its social senses were informed by rectal and urinary stimuli, and these stimuli were perceived through the senses of taste and smell, much like what we can still observe with dogs, for instance. In the transition to bipedal locomotion, a shift that occurred over a period of millennia, the senses of hearing and vision took over from the erstwhile perceptual processes of the human ape, processes initially driven by strong survival instincts. In order to allow hearing and vision to rule over taste and smell in affecting perception and cognition, the nervous system inhibited the latter whenever visual and auditory information was available. This inhibition took the shape of a negative experience of taste and smell, of nausea. According to Freud, the inhibition of smell and taste appears primarily in the form of disgust of urinary and rectal smells, which become especially troublesome in relation to sex, when urinary and rectal regions come into the focus of attention. These basic disgust responses to sex, he says, form the most primal layers of repression, which can only be undone by the extraordinary mental forces that are mobilized during sexual excitation.

For Lacan, the unconscious is inexhaustible in a more far-reaching way than for Freud. For him, the intimate relation of subjecthood to speech causes conscious and unconscious processes to evolve in tandem, as the two sides of the act of speech (Hadar, 2001). Here the unconscious is not merely inexhaustible. Any practice that aims to transform it into consciousness only further enriches the unconscious and renders it more subtle. The value of nurturing consciousness and self-consciousness is not in reducing the unconscious. Rather, a richer consciousness also refines the unconscious and expands the individual's ability to realize her or his ambitions (what Lacan calls their 'desire'). Lacan's first step in explaining this state of affairs resembles Freud's construal and rests on the identification of a mental capacity which appeared at the point in evolution that constituted the transition from ape to man. For Lacan, the critical mental capacity is not vision, like for Freud, but rather the *linguistic ability*. This development is what shifted man from a transparent and static form of social organization to a complex and dynamic one, from a mental order dominated by fantasies to one ruled by the production and examination of diverse hypothetical possibilities. The crucial contribution of language, for Lacan, lies in the ability to represent things and situations that assume a third subjectivity, in addition to those of the addresser and addressee. It is this ability to represent a third subjectivity that allows humankind to conceptualize a social order, because this is what makes it possible to (mentally) conceptualize the implications of a certain communicational dynamics. I consider this more extensively in the following paragraphs and in Chapters 4 and 9. Here I only explain how it is that language produces, at one stroke, both the possibility of being a subject and the boundaries of that possibility. In this respect, it would be helpful to appreciate the particularity of human language. Bees, for instance, are capable of describing to each other the structure of the surrounding territory and to circumscribe, within that territory, the particular place in which nectar is to be found. But one bee lacks the capacity to tell another bee that a third bee, whom they both know, believes there is nectar in some place. The bee's communication relies totally on the principle of presence – indeed it is more like a *demonstration* than a representation, and in the logic of demonstration there is no way of representing a thought whose subject is not present. This is something that human language achieves effortlessly. Lacan believes – and in this he refers to the leading linguists of his time – that the main feature that allows human language to represent non-present minds is the ability to produce complexity through iteration, namely, by a systematic repetition of the same rule of construction. On this – in contrast with other issues – Lacan's way of seeing things is very similar to that of the leading linguist of the second half of the twentieth century and maybe of all times, Noam Chomsky (1956). What is unique about human language is not its vocabulary – many other animals have an impressive vocabulary – but rather its structure, and more specifically its iterative structural rules, which enable cumulative construction by means of the repetition of the same syntactic rule. Paradigmatic, here, is the case of clause subordination, a syntactic construct that is universal for all languages. For example, in the sentence 'Alex says that there is honey north of Canterbury', the clause 'Alex says (something)' is the formative clause, within which is subordinated the clause 'there is honey north of Canterbury'. This construction can be repeated within the sentence to include subordination within subordination, for example, in the sentence 'Alex says that, if we wait until spring, there will be honey north of Canterbury'. Here the subordinate clause itself includes another subordinate clause (the conditional clause), leading to the general structure, 'Alex says that (there is honey north of Canterbury on condition that (we wait until spring))'. In principle, setting aside the computing constraints of the human brain, subordination can be continued ad infinitum. Rules that are similar to the subordination rules also appear in the construction of social order. Considered on an abstract level, these also encapsulate the potential for unlimited extension over number of people and degree of complexity. Because of this structural similarity, Lacan thought of language and the rule-governed aspects of society as establishing the same order of mental life, the Symbolic. We can say, then, following Lacan, that both society and language construct themselves by reference to similar combinatorial principles which, in general, constitute the Symbolic order. The most basic social rules that are analogous to subordination rules in language are those of the prohibition against taking a person's life and the prohibition against incest. It is fairly clear that these rules allow any person or group of persons to reach outwards towards other persons and form a principle of social expansion (although, of course, they do not guarantee expansion. For that we need other, constructional rules). Let us, then, have a look at the subject as it emerges in the Symbolic order – in the rule-governed order – and let us do this, for the sake of the argument, from the point of view of possessing language, or, in Lacan's terms, of being a 'speaking being'.

The feature by means of which being a subject in the symbolic order is best observed derives from what Descartes presented as the principle of the *cogito,* namely, the principle articulated in the statement, 'I think therefore I exist'. What we witness here is the subject as she does the things that most fundamentally define her as a subject (thinking, for Descartes; speaking for Lacan). In this logic, we uncover what it means to be a subject by observing the formative act that makes its performer a subject. As we can see in Descartes' maxim, there is a logical gap between the contents of the subjective act (thinking), and the kind of subjectivity that this act generates ('existing' in Descartes maxim). For Lacan, the contribution of psychoanalysis to the Cartesian story resides in showing that, while there is a gap between the act and the ensuing subjectivity, the two are not unrelated and the relation between them is a thematic relation, a relation of signification. Thus, when I think (or speak), the thought necessarily has a content; indeed, there is no thought without content, yet the conditions of being a subject for the one who does the thinking are of a logical type that differs from the content of the thoughts. In order to think a certain thought I need some knowledge and intelligence – in the first place, that is, I must be a thinking being. This notion along with its implications is more easily grasped when we replace the act of thinking with that of speaking. Using the same basic principle, when a person says something there are certain conditions that make it possible to say it, and these conditions are unlike the content of the statement, though they do relate to it. The tension between these conditions and the content of the statement is especially palpable when the statement is formulated in the first person singular ('I'), and this special status of the notion of 'I' in connection with being a subject is one of the bonuses of Lacan's reformulation of the objective of Freudian therapy. Let us look at a few examples. 'I think it is time to go home', implies that the speaker is in a position of authority, without which it would be hard to understand why such a sentence would be enunciated (although there are, of course, other discourse conditions in which this statement can appear). Similarly, 'I told him to stop nagging', puts the speaker in the position of someone who is fed up with the other and, more or less, annoyed with him. It is not difficult to see that certain conditions of speaking will clash with what is being spoken. 'This job is killing me', poses a clear gap between the self of what was being said (the one whose job is killing him) and the speaking self (who is rather alive and possibly even angry). Now, when we say something (in the first person) we are unaware of the conditions of speaking, even if we might become aware of them a moment later. For Lacan, this gap between the subject of the statement and the speaking subject constitutes the basis of the unconscious. The subject of the statement (appearing in the content of the statement) is the conscious subject, while the speaking subject ('the subject of enunciation') remains – at least for a while – unconscious. I return to the time interval between these two moments in the speech of the subject but, for now, I only wish to stress that speech engenders both consciousness and unconsciousness. Also, there are many examples of this throughout the book.

As we have seen, the unconscious is grasped by Lacan as those conditions of speaking that constrain the being of the subject but, of course, these are not the only constraints on being a subject. The unconscious conditions may be the ones that are most rewarding to identify, those which can be transformed by an interpretative move, which may bring immediate gains such as expanded knowledge. Being a subject, however, also suffers from certain limitations as a result of conditions whose presence is more obvious and familiar. When a person speaks, she already is a particular individual, with a particular history and certain competencies which are all typical of her. None of these were of her own making: they depend on when she was born, on her biological sex, on her particular parents and so forth. The speaking subject may be healthy or ill, may have suffered the loss of a loved one or maybe of a part of their body. All this belongs to the individual's conditions of speech. They are part of the things that will affect how we understand what she says, the way she tends to think about things, and so on. Still, this whole, crucial collection of factors that have influenced the individual's life and that influence how we understand what she says were not of her choice and she might well have preferred to do without them. How can a person position herself as a subject in the face of these things, and what does psychotherapy say or do about them?

Psychotherapy and being-a-subject: positions

One widely circulating truth about psychotherapy is that it does not change the conditions of the person's life but only her attitude to it. This is obviously inaccurate and although a change of attitude is the prime therapeutic vehicle, therapy often in many ways also affects the circumstances of the patient's life. Analytic psychotherapy does, however, in a sense, stand out for the way the person's psychic conditions change without this necessarily requiring significant change in her life circumstances. The relationship between internal change[4] and external change, therefore, is complex. In therapy, the external change is a by-product of the internal change, while the latter, the internal change, is the immediate objective. Though a person's being in the world, the way

---

[4] I use the term 'internal' in a purely colloquial manner. As we see later, 'internal' may mean that some event could not be perceived by the observer, but it does not mean that the mental forms an internal space.

she lives her life, her interpersonal relations, and so on, remain the ultimate business of the therapy, its main tool is that of inner change. It
is inner change that is supposed to make outer change possible, but
this inner change is actually best achieved when external manifestations are set aside, when one manages to be free of them. The praxis of
analytic psychotherapy, one could say, envisions the individual's release
from the iron grip of reality. However, this takes place while the external
manifestations continue throughout to mark the place of the subject,
like the hidden notes in the common children's game 'treasure hunt',
in which a 'treasure' is hidden somewhere and the search group sets
out with a note – a sign – that directs them *not* to the treasure, but to
another sign, which directs them again to another sign, until eventually the last sign directs them to the treasure. In this way, the process
of finding and deciphering the direction sign repeats a number of
times before the treasure is reached. The signs need to be followed, but
the route between them can be anything. By analogy, the therapeutic
discourse can and should free itself from (external) reality, but it must be
cognizant of the signs that indicate the existence of factors that are not
particularly impressed by internal processes. Something analogous also
appears in psychoanalytic psychotherapy, serving to direct the patient
in the reality of her life events. In the context of therapy, I refer to the
reality signs as 'subject positions'.

The subject position is a very specific stance that the patient takes
vis a vis the things about which she speaks. To use the language of the
Lacanian definition of the therapeutic objective, it is the act of introducing the 'I' into the picture of 'it'. When a person takes a subject
position she attenuates the externality of the contents to which she is
relating, the contents about which she speaks and which she expresses.
She inserts herself into the picture or into the situation about which
she is talking. One can think of representational acts other than speech
by means of which the subject may define her place, but because
the medium of analytic psychotherapy is speech, I refer to the act of
speaking as the major route along which the subject takes her position.
When a person speaks, she can describe a state of affairs that bears
absolutely no relation to her, a condition that stays identical to itself
regardless of what she says or how she looks at it. In the subject position, however, the speaker presents herself as someone on whom things
depend to some degree or another. So, a person may describe in great
detail an apartment she viewed the other day as she was looking for
a place to rent. She may elaborate on the spatial organization of the
apartment; where the kitchen and sitting room are in relation to the

bedrooms, and on the different sizes of the rooms – and all this without putting herself into the picture. In the subject position, the speaker will put herself into the picture, for instance, by telling how she felt when she was looking at the apartment and what she thought about it (Did she like it? Did she feel it may serve her purposes?). Once the speaker puts herself into the picture, it is no longer the same as it was before. The taking of a subject position, in and of itself, affects the state of the spoken affairs, the state of the subject. Of course, the external situation might not be altered in any way as a result of the fact that some speaker expresses her attitude about it or her position in it. In the case of describing the apartment, for instance, its structure will not change because the speaker took a subject position. What does change as a result of the subject position is the subject herself. Let us take a look here at a few more examples.

Suppose a person describes a political state of affairs. She might do so without expounding her own attitude to these things in utter objectivity. Such and such forces are at work in the political field, the personalities who are in charge of these forces are so and so, and the events that have recently been taking place are a, b, and c. She might bring off this description without even once using 'I', without marking a subject position. When she adds her beliefs and thoughts about these things, with an *awareness of their subjective nature*, then she actually takes a subject position regarding the political story. While nothing may have happened to the external state of affairs denoted by 'the political situation', for the subject who describes the political situation something therapeutically meaningful has happened, something – if you care about the medical side of things – healthy. The phrase 'with an *awareness of their subjective nature*' (of her thoughts and attitudes) is quite important here. From contemporary work on the nature of political knowledge or historical knowledge, we know that even at the level of description, things are already hermeneutically saturated, replete with the subjectivity of the speaker, the observer or the researcher (Gadamer, 1976). The 'subject position' is not about the uncovering of this inherent subjectivity, but rather comes to acknowledge the fact that the person who speaks or describes it is, in one way or another, present in her description, and that she chooses to put herself in that place not necessarily because her thoughts or attitudes are more correct or better informed than those of another, but because she is ethically impelled to take such a position. Because taking a subject position is healthier. Because this is how one may live one's life to the full or, at least, better approach such fullness. In taking a subject position, the individual says, 'This or that is the situation, and I feel so and so about it, and I think this and that needs to be done for things to get better'. It is the aim of therapy that the patient should not settle for the mere description of things and instead define her place regarding them, that is, occupy a subject position. From the sociological or historical points of view, the taking and holding of subject positions also has, in the long run, an indirect political impact. Later in the Chapters 7 and 9, I examine the notion of psychotherapy from the perspective of its possible political impact.

Therefore, it is possible to take a subject position by becoming knowledgeable and by having an opinion, but this is not the only way. One can also become aware of what one feels and chose to say something like, 'This or that is the matter and it angers me or makes me happy', without thereby expressing a 'position' in the narrow sense of the word. Here the speaker situates herself qua subject in a softer manner than when she would have said that this or that is what she thinks about the matter in question. In this case, the person enacts reflectiveness, supports a psychic state which is divided into a level of speaking and a level of self-awareness. In our context, being self aware, being able to say what one feels, does not just aim to expand knowledge, but constitutes an attitude, a form of (self-)realization. The therapeutic value of knowledge expansion is related to the manner in which such expansion generates conditions of being, creates a subject in the broad sense in which I use the word. A patient, for instance, tells me that he came late for our meeting because of a traffic jam. In this description, he may feature as a total object, victim of the circumstances or the road. Nothing he might have felt or thought could have altered this. If, however, he managed to say how important the meeting was for him, how dismayed he was at the delay, how helpless it made him feel, and how this reminded him of his childhood, and so on, then something therapeutic actually occurred. He put himself in a subject position even in this unpleasant situation.

Someone once said to me that analytic psychotherapy does something strange and confusing. Initially it tells the patient, 'Looks here's your dad, and here's your mom, they are who made you into who you are'. Later it says, 'It's not your mum and not your dad, it's you, it's your life. You are what you make of yourself'. This seems to me an accurate description. In therapy, when we are dealing with a particular issue, we start with trying to discover the constraints that limit the subject, those moments and situations when the patient loses her place as the subject of her own life, those points at which someone else – say her mother and her father – influenced or even determined who she would be. They could be the ones who decreed whether she would be weak or strong, fearful or happy, an outcast or an achiever. It is only then, and from this position and experience, that a move can be initiated that may possibly re-position the patient as a subject. Such a move could be one which examines and formulates the manner in which even the most impenetrable life situations could be the result of the patient's own actions, or – should this be implausible – evoke in her feelings about her situation. Therapy could then enable the patient to assert whether or not she is happy with that situation, whether or not she disowns it, or accepts it under protest. The first part of this maneuver might be viewed as the unveiling of the truth, while the second part involves an ethical positioning. We can say, therefore, that an analytic move consists of a first stage which stands in the sign of discovering the truth, while a second stage involves an ethical positioning. It is probably the case that therapeutic theory hitherto has tended to focus primarily on the first stage. In Chapter 5, I describe a third step which I call 'symmetrising', in which the subject repositions herself in a place that is different from that of the initial reflectiveness.

This logic is especially pertinent in the analysis of emotions. Intuitively, we tend to think that feelings are not in our control: if we were hurt, we were hurt; if we were moved to tears, then we were exactly that; if we fell in love then we fell in love, and if we didn't then we didn't. These things are not up to us (and if we think and act as though they are, then we are considered as cold people, robots). Usually, people pitch feelings against thoughts and opinions, as we seem to control the latter. I myself am not sure where we have more control – over our thoughts or our feelings – but control is not really what's at issue here, in the context of therapy. What matters is the subject position, and here things are the other way around. Opinions and thoughts might easily be rendered in an objectivistic manner, as independent truth, as choices whose focus is external. Emotions, by contrast, cannot easily be captured in this way, because they are always *someone's* feelings, hence always subjective, always declaring the subject position, always presenting their 'owner' in relation to the issue at hand. This is why therapy so often turns towards emotions, encourages awareness of them and facilitates their articulation.

Something similar, but perhaps even more dramatic, happens in the case of dreams. Here the dreamer often is required to take a position regarding things about which she doesn't even know what they are. She finds herself talking in the first person singular about events of which she does not know for sure how they connect to her life. A person may

dream that he is walking in an unknown street, in an unknown, desolate city, when suddenly there appears an old, white-bearded man in a
carriage pulled by two brown horses. The old man stops and offers the
dreamer a ride, and when the dreamer asks 'Where to?' the old man
replies, 'You know where'. The dreamer has no idea what place the old
man has in mind. He takes fright, begins to sweat and refuses to climb
onto the carriage. Though he knows nothing about the place, the old
man and the destination that appear in the dream, the dreamer tells
about them with utter confidence in the first person singular since he
experiences the man of whom he tells in the first person singular, as
absolutely himself, someone who could not possibly be anybody else.
Here the dreamer happens to be in an intimate first person position
in regard to events of which he cannot make sense. The process of
analytic psychotherapy involves tying the dream phenomena to things,
events, people or places which the dreamer knows from his own life.
Thus the analytic work extends the boundaries of being a subject in the
patient's life.

The use of the terms 'position' or 'positions' reaches some way back in
the history of psychoanalysis. It appears in a formative and somewhat
subversive manner in Klein's (1975) perception of early infantile development. For Klein however, the position is not a subject position, but
its opposite. It is the mental logic which the infant and the child cannot
escape. At the same time, as Kosofsky-Sedgwick (2003, pp.128–138)
argues, the point of the Kleinian position is to free the analysis of the
child from the conceptual rigidity of notions like 'personality structure'
or 'character'. The position is more time-dependent, given to change,
and can occur side by side with another position. When contrasted with
notions like personality or character, the Kleinian position is a close
relative of the perspective of being-a-subject.

Subject and self

Thus far I have described the concept that constitutes the ethical
in therapy inconsistently, mostly as the being of the *subject*, but also as
the realization of *self*. I suppose it has been obvious that in the current
context, the first is the more appropriate notion – but what, in fact,
distinguishes between them? The answer to this question requires
a significant change in our understanding of what makes therapy
therapeutic, of what is the therapeutic element of therapy.

In the analytic approaches that discuss the self, and especially those
in which the self has a special status, the self is seen as pre-existing

the therapeutic process, which engages in revealing it. For Jung (1971), for example, the self represents the point of equilibrium of the forces and contents that act upon the individual, and mental activity that originates in the self (and is regulated by it) is always on a higher level of integration than mental activities that derive from another inner agency such as, for instance, the ego or the super-ego. In Winnicott (1965, pp. 140–152), similarly, the true self represents motifs and modes of imagination and action which are better attuned than other parts of the psyche to the individual's inner world and her most coherent and creative places. Thus the self represents a sort of centre of the personality, a kind of essence whose realization optimally expresses the individual; expresses her in a way that is more fully responsive to her natural inclinations than would be achieved by meeting social demands. The subject, by contrast, is an agency that is re-generated for as long as the individual takes her positions. The subject defines itself at the moment of its manifestation. In that sense, the subject has no existence prior to its action, to its choice, or its position. Levinas's philosophical perspective is radical in this respect: The domain of the subject is not one in which we clarify whether or not something exists; it is not the domain of ontology but that of meeting or answering certain demands or principles. Consequently, the subject is constituted without the need of being true or attuned to inner voices or to other tendencies that are immanent to the individual's personality. To become a subject one needs to perform an act of subject formation which, as we see in Chapter 3, is an act of facing the other. The externality of the subjective act appears also in some psychoanalytic thinking, but here the subject is, in addition, constituted by reflectiveness or self-definition, attained by a withdrawal from the content of the statement to recognizing the conditions that enable the speaker to articulate certain contents (in the first person). In this context, the difference between Descartes' philosophical understanding and Lacan's psychoanalytic one originates in the procedural difference in deriving the specific enabling conditions of the spoken contents. This gives rise to the difference between the ontological and the ethical investigations regarding the subject. While the ontological investigation purports to clarify the conditions under which the subject exists (or may exist) regardless of the context, in the ethical investigation the enabling conditions of a statement are always context-embedded, even if certain invariants in the individual's life conditions create an experience of continuity and are predictable. These invariants, however, are always open to subversion through radical change in the conditions of the subject's life, something that will always be accompanied by some distress, by an experience of self-alienation, when the individual may feel a stranger to herself. The following are a few examples. Consider my conversation with the woman whom I presented in the section on being a subject. As you may recall, the woman told me about her depressed state of mind and when I suggested she might take anti-depressant medication she rejected my idea, saying, 'It wouldn't occur to me, Uri. I'm having a hard time, I don't feel joy in the way you remember me doing in the past, but this is my life. This is how I make sense of it, including the pain and the pessimism. When I take a look at my life, it fits the picture. I'd gladly be in some other place, but I'd never consider getting out of it by force'. I do not think that the subject formation in this statement, which manifested in her objection to taking medication, was more in tune with the woman's personality (and hence somehow more true) than other possible responses. Rather, her subjecthood resided in the very taking of a position and standing behind it, in her explicitly connecting between the understanding of her life and the position of not forcing herself out of depression. As I know her, she might just as well have said, 'That's a good idea, actually. Maybe I should try to take medication. I always seem to believe that I must cope with everything in the most strenuous way, not avoiding any difficulty. Maybe at my age I can already do things the easier way. With less sweat and tears'. Indeed, if I could not have imagined this type of a response as being in line with the woman's personality, I would probably never have offered to take anti-depressants in the first place. This illustration bears out that there is a whole variety of very different responses by means of which a person may take a subject position, but this does not imply that any response would achieve this equally successfully. What, for example, about the following response, 'What a great idea, Uri. Why should I be suffering so much. That's exactly what pills are for. That's why I live in a modern world. Strange I did not think of it myself. You see, that's why it's a good thing to talk to people – to hear what they say. A really good idea. Would you also know a doctor to refer me to?' A response of this type would raise my suspicion, I would feel that something might not be quite in order. Not that this response might not, in different circumstances, have seemed a convincing subject position. And not that openness to the ideas of other people does not settle well with this woman's person-ality – on the contrary, it suits her very well. It's just that the tone is too light-hearted, too content, and this does not cohere with the mood of our conversation up to that point.

Let me give another example. In the previous section I described a dream in which a patient finds himself 'in an unknown, desolate city, when suddenly there appears an old, white-bearded man in a carriage pulled by two brown horses. The old man stops and offers the dreamer a ride, and when the dreamer asks "Where to?" the old man replies, "You know where". The dreamer has no idea what place the old man has in mind. He takes fright, begins to sweat and refuses to climb onto the carriage'. How can this dream be processed in a manner that promotes being a subject, and how would this be different from a rendering that envisions authenticity with one's self? On the face of it, and especially from a Jungian angle, the dream invites interpretations of self-realization since it described a situation in which the patient is aiming towards something – something that is represented by the place to which the old man offers him to travel and concerning which the patient has absolute knowledge, even if this knowledge is not accessible to him and fills him with fear. The old man who is steering his horse-drawn carriage might represent a wisdom which the patient holds inside but with which he cannot connect, either because it implies a type of thinking which the patient is not prepared to recognize as his own and which he perceives as 'old' or ancient, or because this knowledge is stored away deep inside his psyche and he cannot reach it even if he wanted. Either way, a self-oriented therapy would try to discover and describe this different knowledge which the dream suggests; follow the routes whereby this knowledge perhaps revealed itself in the patient's past and draw his attention to how he is avoiding it in his action. Analysis may allow the patient to become connected to this knowledge in a more purposeful and in a fuller manner. A further assumption of this type of therapy would be that, to the extent that the patient adopts this different knowledge, his fears will also subside. By connecting to himself he will achieve a better balance.

In contrast to the interpretative move of self discovery, a process directed to being a subject could prefer to pause at the dream's suggestion of a yearning for change, the patient's sense of a need for significant change in his life and his fears concerning such change. This interpretative line might note the dreamer's feeling that, for change to happen, he must first know where this change will lead and the way in which uncertainty paralyses him. Here the analyst might point out the vicious cycle of inaction that leads to uncertainty which itself again feeds into further inaction. A 'solution' for such a dilemma cannot, of course, be derived directly from the dream, for there are always many good interpretations and change must occur, if at all, with the knowledge that the chosen path is not the only best one. Therefore, the cycle of passivity, of 'itness', can only be exited by means of action. This forms the main rationale for Lacan's truncated therapy session. The multitudinous field of interpretations must be cut at some point or another because it will not exhaust itself. Ethical interpretation, aimed at being a subject, might draw attention to the fact that while it could be exciting for the patient to be wandering through the foreign city of life, it also makes him feel uneasy, threatened (*unheimlich*, as Freud (1919) would have called it). In acknowledgement of Sartre, we might also talk about the patient's feeling that his life is passing (the old man and the hinted fear of death) while he is not doing enough. But then, what does 'not doing enough' entail? For life does not exactly propose a certain goal which it is then upon us to attain. A further interpretative option with a view to being a subject could be associated with the patient's search for a father figure who might support him and show him the way. Is this, perhaps, what he is looking for in therapy (and what he rejects by refusing to embark the carriage)? If therapy itself plays out his conflict of autonomy in such a way, how can it hope to resolve this? Again we can see that the ethical perspective must keep in mind that the interpretative chain is endless and must lead to a choice, an act that has personal arbitrariness built into it.

What is crucial in both of the previous interpretative options does not lie in the identification of a singular truth, i.e., the truth about what the dream tells the dreamer, but in the way they construe the dream contents in terms of the patient's life. In the case of self-related interpretations, the interpretative process comes to lay bare the dreamer's inner essence, while the mode of interpretation which I called 'ethical' addresses the possibilities for the patient's improved positioning as a subject that are raised by the dream. Needless to say that, with more information about the patient's life, one is better placed to conduct a fuller interpretative investigation – one that might well be very different from the two possibilities I mentioned. By raising the possibility that good interpretations may remain unarticulated without seriously hindering progress I do not deny the relevance of truth to the evaluation of interpretation. Rather, I would say that there is a kind of therapeutic pragmatism that imposes ethical limits on the search for truth (see Chapter 11). The notion of truth, in the sense in which it obtains in hermeneutic theory – i.e., in the sense that any theme that arises in analysis has a plethora of links to the patient's biography – still allows extremely significant differences between diverse interpretations and diverse interpretational options (see also Hadar, 2001). From an ethical point of view, however, truth values are not always critical. What is critical is the ever-present need for a balance between thematic connectedness in the subject's narrative and the pressure of being a subject, of making choices, of asserting oneself. The latter is of an ethical nature, the pressure to take a subject position. In this context, we might also understand Winnicott's idea that the interpretations with which a patient comes up are preferable to those that the therapist offers, simply because self-interpretation, by way of a therapeutic act, answers the need to take a subject position more, even where it might be less 'true' in terms of its wealth of links to the patient's life. In Chapter 11, I analyse in some detail the tension between the true and the ethical in the context of analytic hermeneutics.

2
Interpretation and Action

Enactment and analycity

I already had occasion to mention one of Lacan's more far-reaching insights, namely, that interpretation alone, due to its infinitude, cannot exhaust the therapeutic impact of analysis (Lacan, 1958a/2006). One can always go on interpreting and the idea of reducing the unconscious in this manner does not hold, because the unconscious also grows with interpretation. Whereas interpretive processes carry the benefit of growth and enrichment, they lack something fundamental because the self is consolidated on a different plane, which I call the ethical plane. This relatively simple insight, reiterated in both Lacan (1958a/2006) and Schafer (1976), reframes in a radical way the psychoanalytic bias toward interpretative interventions. Classically, the psychoanalytic process is characterized by the contrast between understanding and doing, *analyzing* and *enacting*. The latter, enactment, is conceptualized as a form of resistance, maybe even its paradigmatic form. This idea is guided by the principle whereby, 'In analysis, that which does not appear in the form of memory or interpretation will appear in the form of enactment or of resistance'. To evaluate this truism, one needs to understand the critical difference, subject wise, between analyzing and enacting. In my mind, what is crucial here is that memory and interpretation are always about something else whose existence precedes its appearance in analysis. In the case of memory, the originary event is something that happened to the patient beforehand, while in the case of interpretation the originary event is something that the patient said earlier. By contrast, enactment always involves something primary. In some sense, it is always only itself. It always subverts the analytic 'afterwards-ness', as Laplanche (1993) called it. Laplanche captured what he

42

considered the formative trait of analysis in this term 'afterward-ness', namely, the idea that an event is analytic to the extent that it refers to another event, the 'original' event, which is represented, translated or reconstructed by the therapeutic event. In the simple case (and the paradigmatic one, for Laplanche as well as for Freud), the original event happened much earlier in the history of the subject and the analytic event recalls or reconstructs it. But unlike in memory or in reconstruction, the enactment never refers solely to the earlier event it represents. It always includes something that is original, *sui generis*, to itself. It is exactly this trait of the enactment that stands for its privileged nature vis-à-vis the positioning of the self, from the ethical perspective. This suggests that the vitality of enactment as a therapeutic event is not less than that of remembering or interpreting, which is strange to classical theory and in need of a serious elaboration.

No professional practitioner, of course, assumes that it is only by means of contents that the therapy advances, only by making the unconscious conscious. There is a gamut of rituals: the patient's arrival to the clinic, sitting or lying down, first greetings followed by a silence during which both therapist and patient collect themselves towards the point of speech. There is the point when the patient says something from which the first theme of the conversation evolves. Some therapists sit down and observe silence, others may ask, 'How are you?' or 'How do you feel today?', or some other introductory question. Then there are closing steps at the end of the session: a quick glance at the clock, a statement about the end of the session, with or without warning. The patient, from her side, might get up and leave immediately, nod her head and stay lying or seated, or even go on speaking a bit, completing her line of thought. She may leave and say 'Goodbye', or without saying anything, she may turn around at the door or she may not. None of these moves are analytic, yet they leave an important mark on the therapy and, as such, much has already been written about them. They are traditionally considered enactments, but what about the analytic or classical interpretation which forms the opposite pole of enactment? Does it not also carry aspects of enactment?

Let us consider the classical, paradigmatic analytic manoeuvre, the one that constitutes the opposite of enactment, recollection. From the point of view of the analytic process, of 'afterward-ness' (which for Laplanche defines the role of memory in analysis), there is an important difference between the first appearance in therapy of a certain content and subsequent appearances, which will always resonate the first occurrence. The first articulation demands a decision and marks a possible hesitation. It involves transforming something internal into something external and this is not easy, especially when it comes to things that were kept inside for a long time. It is uncertain what may happen to spoken things when they reach another person's ear. How will they be heard? How will they be met? This is actually not only the case with 'another person's ear'. The patient herself might find that when she says them out loud things sound different from when they were only images or thoughts in her mind. It is in this sense that the first articulation of a memory will always tend to resemble an enactment more than any subsequent mentions. Similar considerations hold for the therapist's response: it also cannot constitute a simple interpretation, but always also involves a counter-enactment. In the present chapter and section, I return to the logic of enactment and interpretation but, for now, let me examine this in a more concrete manner. Suppose, for example, that a patient has recounted for the first time something difficult that happened to him – perhaps, he tells about how as a child he went lost and then was overtaken by anxiety that he might not find his way back. What could be his prime need after telling this story for the first time? Surely, it seems to me, this must concern the therapist's recognition of the traumatic nature of the event. When the story of losing his way is told for the first time, the patient might very well be unsure about the nature of his panic as a child. Was it real or did it only happen in his fantasy? The first thing he probably wants is recognition of the reality of the panic. Recognition is, of course, a kind of interpretation ('This was really a very frightening event'), but it is also a kind of enactment, an act of confirming the validity of the subjective position of panic – a subject-instituting act. Any reaction to the initial presentation of a memory or a current event will thereby also constitute a validating or invalidating act, even where we, analysts, have been trying hard to be interpretive. I think that the following vignette exemplifies the inescapability of the enactment-logic of some things that emerge in therapy.

His relations with his father were a great source of distress to Samuel, a well-educated man in his early forties. In fact, I did not quite perceive to what extent, because Samuel was so capable at most things. Usually, I would give rather associative interpretations to what Samuel told me, and he appreciated the flow, the freedoms. But when he told me about events involving his father, the conversation tended to turn problematic. Reacting in my usual way, I would draw attention to what the event about which he had just told might suggest about himself, my patient, rather than about his father. This often hurt Samuel, sometimes deeply so. He claimed that I always identified with his father and refused to see things from his perspective. I could reply by saying that he identified me with his father, that in his relationship with his father, he tended to play a zero-sum game: either you are with him, or you are with me and there's no middle ground. Thus, for instance, Samuel once told me how, as a child, he went on a stroll along a Tel Aviv boulevard with his father and stopped to watch a juggler who was giving a performance. About five minutes passed when he looked and saw that his father had vanished. Samuel was overtaken by a great fear. I said something like, 'Only in the presence of your father was the jungle on the boulevard a safe space'. Samuel responded, 'Is it on purpose that you don't understand or what? It's exactly the opposite. I could never, but never, trust his being present'. I thought, then, how alive and in what a state of fermentation things with his father were for him, as if they had happened only now, as though only now he had told me about them for the very first time. I think it was then with Samuel that I saw that when a patient tells something for the first time, it is an occasion not for interpretation but for action, in essence, an act of recognition. Something other than interpretation, I felt, had failed to occur between us, something that precedes interpretation, and that might have allowed him to assume a position regarding the story, regarding his father and regarding me. In the absence of that something, Samuel was stuck with the primary nature of the story, with his lack of receptiveness to an interpretive approach.

The relationship between interpretation and action resembles that between the subject of the statement and the subject of enunciation, respectively, something I discussed in Chapter 1, in the section, about the basic assumptions of analysis that is oriented toward being-a-subject. In that sense, interpretation and action, analycity and enactment, are the two sides of speaking. In every therapeutic act, therefore, aspects of action as well as of interpretation are involved. The traditional notion according to which enactment does not promote therapy and is the square opposite of interpretation or analysis does not render the variety of ways in which the discursive encounter between people may be therapeutic. This stance, moreover, does not allow us to understand the inner logic of interpretation. Every speech realizes different forms of action and acts of speech. It is the choice of both therapist and patient, at any given point in the therapy, whether to tend more to the action-related aspect or alternatively to the interpretation-related one. Freud's (1914) initial position, paradoxically, to the effect that only the resistance was to be interpreted (with the aim of clearing the stumbling blocks on the way to analysis or recollection) actually holds that the therapist always interprets the action-related aspect of what is said. This is really a kind of implied definition of the analytic asymmetry: In analysis, the patient is trained to focus on the content of what is being said, whereas the therapist interprets its action-related (existential) side. The patient sees herself in the statement, whereas the analyst shows her in the mirror of the enunciating act. By implication, the unconscious in analysis is, to a large extent, a division of labour. In a more mutual situation, the unconscious may play a much smaller role. Unsurprisingly, Freud (1937) noted in his later writings the paradoxical core of this distribution of roles. This is what the notion of 'the impossible profession' (ibid) means, namely, that it is the analyst's task to look at the existential conditions of the patient's speech. The Freudian position is quite consistent, though not always entirely transparent, and it is based in a reconstruction of parenting relations with the aim to advance the subject formation of the one who occupies the place of the child. Unlike Freud's approach, the one I present here is part of the more general effort of inter-subjective approaches to promote the symmetrisation of the patient's and the therapist's involvement in the analytic work (Aron, 2001).

Speech as action

In discourse analysis – a subfield of linguistics and philosophy – during the second half of the twentieth century, much attention was called to the fact that speech is always also a type of action (Searle, 1969). This insight supports the ability to understand the wealth of possibilities of therapeutic speech beyond the interpretation of content. It is therefore useful to pause, I believe, at the philosophical-linguistic side of speech as action. This line of thinking started with Austin's (1971) distinction between *constative* and and *performative* statements. Classical constative statements are regular information-carrying sentences such as 'Tel Aviv is the city with the largest population in Israel', or 'The earth circles the sun in 365 days'. Classical performative statements are those in which speaking introduces a new fact into the discursive field. For example, in the suitable context, uttering the phrase, 'I hereby inaugurate the Polish immigrants' center' determines that the Polish immigrants' centre, hereby, has been opened for use. Similarly, when contextually suitable, uttering the phrase, 'I hereby pronounce you husband and wife' determines the social and legal status of two people as a couple. There are some obvious differences between these two types of statement. Constative statements, first of all, do not at all require a subject that is human. They might appear from outer space and still have the same effect: their content.

Classical performatives, by contrast, must have a human subject, as they are performative exactly because the statement is that of the subject. Should someone who is not invested with the proper authority, declare 'I hereby pronounce you husband and wife', this annuls the performative nature of the utterance and turns it into something else, perhaps a quotation or a joke. The subject of a performative statement must be an agent who has the authority to actualize its content. If the coordinator of a therapy group says, 'I would like to ask for silence and to open today's meeting', she makes a classical performative statement, but if, after some moments of silence, someone then says, 'Right, so I'll be the first today', this latter person is in no need of authorization other than being a member of the group. Still, this is a performative statement to all intents and purposes, a statement whose very articulation forms the action to which it refers. This last example, nevertheless, slightly pulls us into the constative direction. When someone announces that he will be the first today, the speaker also conveys something informative. His statement would not really work if someone else had spoken before him. Here, then, we see a further condition of performativity: the statement must be spoken in the present-future tense – what Lacan called the *future anterior*, in the sense of 'from now on ...'. Performatives are always 'from now on', all the way to a possibly unspecified point in the future. Though this lack of specification does not need to involve a large duration, its role is important. If we consider, for instance, the coordinator's statement, 'Let's take a break until a quarter to twelve' then, while the announced break will take exactly – more or less – until a quarter to twelve, the statement about the break, which is what constitutes the performative utterance, is valid from the moment it is made until a short while later. Thus, it may happen that the group actually gets up for a break (and maybe even until a quarter to twelve), but there may be another coordinator who responds by saying, 'It looks like a good idea to keep going until twelve thirty, so we can combine the break with lunch'. The first statement is still performative, but one with a relatively short span.

Now, let's examine the statement, 'I want to go home', assuming it is uttered by a person who is in company and who really wishes to go home. Even if this is so, the speaker here does not simply report her wish to return home – which would amount to a constative statement – though it is clearly true that the speaker wants to start returning home, this is why she says what she says. Yet, the utterance may not merely report the speaker's state of mind, but actually hope to change the course of events by its very enunciation so, in this sense, it is rather performative. The statement constitutes the axis of (hoped for) change. In the psychoanalytic approach I am promoting in this book, however, the sentence 'I want to go home' is performative in an actually more far reaching sense. Until it is articulated, there is a range of possibilities concerning the subject's wish to go home. She can ignore it or change her mind; she can forget about it or, for some other reason, not utter it – possibly leading, in that case, to growing bitterness. Once something is said, it acquires a different, more solid, undeniable quality. It is the speech act that made the wish into what it now is. This is true in general for the expression of feelings. Saying them causes them to be represented to the other, creating an echo (and possibly a response) which is not merely constative, not merely stating the feeling of the speaker. Only by availing itself to an other, a feeling comes into being, acquires a subject; the spoken statement creates subjectivity as an act that directs itself to the other with the aim of gaining recognition of the speaker's mental state (Kosofsky-Sedgwick, 2003).

Does a performative statement have to be in the first person? This is an important issue if we want to maintain that performatives have special value as a subject creating act. If, indeed, performatives are always in the first person, then this, in and of itself, puts them in a particular position with regard to subjectivity. We may look at some examples. Let us consider the following sentence, for instance, 'You are no longer allowed to enter this house'. Since the statement itself here functions as the act of prohibiting entry, it is thoroughly performative. The subject, however, is in the second person whereas the first person only seems to make a marginal appearance. The assumption, though, that the speaker has more authority over the house than the addressee is crucial to the performative valence of the statement, and in this sense it is equivalent to another statement which more adequately reflects its performative character, that is, 'I forbid you to enter this house'. In that sense, still and in principle, it is a first-person statement. Let me consider another example, that of an announcement by an army officer who addresses olive pickers[1] in say Hebron's Tel Rumeida, 'This is a closed military

---

[1] Settlers often violently stop Palestinian olive pickers near their settlements. Tel Rumeida hill in Hebron has a settlement on it, whose residents try to prevent the Palestinian dwellers of the area from picking olives. Israeli and international activists are in the habit of joining Palestinians for olive picking, in order to defer some of the settlers' violence. Usually, the Israeli police and army end up removing the olive pickers, rather than the violent settlers. They do this by issuing a decree whereby the area is closed for military reasons, which authorizes them to remove anyone who is not officially a resident of the area. My wording of the hypothetical 'military closure' decree is arbitrary – the numbers I mention are totally invented – but it imitates the real decrees.

zone. You must leave immediately'. Again, the act that institutes performativity here goes by way of the quotation of another act under which the military command signed an order to the effect of 'military closure'. Such an order usually details something like, 'Authorized by Section 4 of military emergency law, I declare zone 458 in the Hebron District a closed military zone as of signing this order until the end of the Sabbath etc., etc.' So, even here it seems performativity does not depend on an unidentified agent, but on one that is indicated by the first person (see also Yaffe & Hadar, unpublished). All in all, we witness a very tight connection between language performativity and subject formation. This does not imply, of course, that all first person statements are performatives in the strong sense of the word. Constative statements of the type, 'I will be 18 tomorrow', or 'I'll be on holiday until Monday', are not particularly performative.

The linguistic notion of performativity entered cultural criticism and social philosophy by extending the range of symbolic acts to which this idea could apply. This extension allowed a whole range of acts other than verbal or linguistic to encapsulate performativity. The common denominator of these acts was, first, that they were all symbolic and second, that they positioned the doer of the act as a subject with regard to a particular addressee who was not in the second person position. What this constituted was a growing circle of cases to which we could ascribe the intention to influence the subject positions of the agent, as well as of a host of potential addressees. In historical terms, our understanding of the illocutionary force of statements and other speech events became enriched when they were first understood as actions. Then, with a backward loop, we grew aware of the way in which non-speech acts can also effect changes in subject positions, acting as messages to addressees (which often included the actor herself and thus transformed her subject position). One example, which gained classic status in cultural history, is that of Antigone's action, intended to enable the proper burial of her brother's corpse in defiance of the edict of King Creon, her uncle. In her *Antigone's Claim* (2000), Judith Butler interprets Antigone's act of burial as one that encapsulates female resistance to sovereign masculine authority while also, with the same performative gesture, subverting the ethos of the unity of the (ruling) family. Because of the exemplary position that this particular family holds in cultural history, with Oedipus in its nodal points, subverting family unity amounts to the subversion of the position of the masculine in determining subject positions.

The parallels between my approach to action and interpretation in analytic psychotherapy and the description of performativity in language and culture are quite obvious. In both cases, the heart of the matter is the manner in which subject positions in some social domain are transformed by symbolic acts. In both, the objective is the positioning of the individual as a subject in relation to the social domain that functions as the field that institutes subjecthood. In the case of therapy, this involves mainly the patient's circle of close friends and family, while in the case of culture, the social domain may involve a particular community such as the workplace, the residential area in which one lives, the consumers of a particular media, and so on. Of course, 'culture' here does not define a social domain, but only the means of performativity. These may be quite different between culture and therapy. Whereas the former may consist of a very large number of performative procedures, the latter involves primarily speech and language or rather the range of devices that originates in the use of personal pronouns in speech. It is precisely the latter that is the focus of the present chapter. Still, some features of performativity may be common to culture and therapy, probably because of the linguistic interface. Of special interest in this book, and I return to this in various places, is the fact that, in the field of performativity, negativity has a special, perhaps even privileged, status. Thus, performative moves are often acts of resistance, criticism, or protest. This is because in the social field, negativity characterizes the turning of the subject towards the other. Of course, performative negativity is particularly pronounced where the subjectivities involved, either as agents or as addressees, are in a state of conflict. In this regard, there is particular affinity between the field of analytic psychotherapy and the field of post-colonial theory. In both of these domains, the negative nature of performativity constructs itself around an event of injury, as I show in Chapter 5 of this book. This central role of injury creates affinities that are closer than usual when comparing the individual and the social domains.

Positions revisited

It is generally assumed that there is no point in conducting arguments or discussions within therapy because such debates only express and escalate resistance. The received idea is that doing therapy means to interpret the contents on which therapist and patient disagree and not to enact them in an argument, which represents a discursive practice that is more on the action side of the spectrum than on that of talk. But if, as I argue in the following, enactment is therapeutic and if all speech is also enactment, then argument or discussion may be more therapeutic than hitherto acknowledged. Indeed, they may occupy a special place in the therapeutic process, marking a midpoint on the continuum between interpretation and action, between the power dimension and the content dimension of subject formation in the course of analysis. As such, debate could play a respectable and singular role in the therapeutic discourse, a role which deserves clarification.

From the perspective of the speech act, when a person debates she does not merely come up with arguments about the issue at hand. She also makes a kind of declaration about the nature of her speech, something to the effect of, 'Just so you know: this is where I stand'. A person might be an interpreter – an interpreter of interpersonal relations, for instance – and never once articulate her stance; indeed, she might for some reason or another even prefer to keep that stance concealed. When an argument arises, however, when the conversational praxis is that of the debate, the person forgoes her role as an interpreter and declares, whether or not directly, that what she says is not only a matter of truth, but also a matter of choice; she says what she says because this happens to be where she chooses to position herself, according to her personal predilections. In the analytic therapy literature, however, argument would seem to have no overt place and when it does – something that happens from time to time – it does so clandestinely and is likely to be denied. In Freud's technical writings (1914), interpretation always has an argumentative dimension. It envisions to shift the patient away from a position of resistance. Freud often mentions the need to persuade the patient to let go of perceptions that reflect resistance in exchange for perceptions of cooperation with the therapeutic process (say, free association). True, in Freudian analysis, explanations and persuasions are not considered a proper part of therapy. They are regarded as ancillary to free association and recollection, but they play an important role, both at the start of therapy and at points of stasis, points which carry special significance for Freud. So argumentative episodes and incidents of persuasion make recurrent and necessary appearances in analysis – and if this is how things effectively are, then why not let them enter by the front door rather than have them sneak in through the window? It may be better to think of the role of the argument as a proper therapeutic engagement and to theoretically ground this in our understanding of the therapeutic process.

The most general justification of debate as part of therapy, naturally, derives from the justification of action and enactment in therapy which, in turn, rests on our understanding of ethics, as I argue in this book. The general reason, that is, in favour of the therapeutic acceptability of debate is that it may, in certain conditions, promote being a subject, or promote the patient's subject positioning. When I formulate it this way, it may make one feel, 'Sure, but isn't it a tautology to claim that debates have a way of enabling a person to take positions? Even in the intuitive definition above, this is exactly what happens in them'. As is the case so often in analytic theory, though, things are not as simple as they seem. First, in the therapeutic situation the therapist occupies a position of power and there is a danger that debate will cause the patient to relinquish her own position rather than hold and express it. At times, the patient invests considerable effort and thought in how she might please the therapist and gain her empathy or sympathy. To the extent that it risks the love of her therapist, debate might cause the patient to abandon her position, give up on it or hide it. Second, conducting a debate changes the therapeutic discourse because it generates a confrontational atmosphere, which is not conducive of free association or of the reverie that analysis aims to engender as the first, indispensable condition for the analytic process (Ogden, 1998). No analytic therapy is possible without the free flow of thoughts and their expression.

As for the first apprehension, debate in therapy really does demand that the therapist be extremely cautious and be thoroughly experienced in avoiding rhetorical moves that are dismissive or contemptuous of the patient's stance. It is usually pretty difficult to argue without attacking the (subject) position of the person with whom we are arguing, especially when the discussion is emotionally charged (in principle, debates always develop into emotionally pressured exchanges). It seems to me that, if the therapist assumes the possibility that the other side will maintain her position and accepts the possibility that she herself may change hers, then two things will happen. For one thing, the discussion takes a very different course from what we usually witness in the street or on TV. The therapeutic debate must be more respectful and flexible than its common counterpart, even where differences of opinion are serious. Second, from time to time, the therapeutic debate should shift gear and reflect on the discussion and what it represents for the patient, including the therapist's interpersonal dynamics. The discussion can yield important materials for the analysis of the transference (and the counter transference, of course), materials that might not have become available without the debating dynamics. In my experience, when a discussion is conducted on these lines, the patient not only does not surrender her positions vis-à-vis those of the therapist, but actually tends to reinforce them, at least on the behavioural level, though another level may emerge on which the patient identifies with the therapist's position. There are always 'additional levels', of course, no matter what is at issue in the therapy; in this, the praxis of debate is not unique, and these additional levels may be worked through in the usual ways of the analysis of the transference.

As for the impact of debating on the atmosphere of the therapeutic conversation and on its envisioned freedom, I set great store by reflective, ruminative discourse and its liberating qualities. As Ogden (2001) has so well articulated, this kind of talk, which he calls 'reverie', seems to be one of the most therapeutic parts of what occurs in the analytic process. This implies, at least, that debating practices should not make their entrance before the reflective discourse has sufficiently settled in, a point of timing which requires attention and judgment on the part of the analyst. Once, however, reflective discourse has been achieved and maintained – I do not wish, and cannot, determine criteria for what exactly would qualify as such – debating maneuvers may not form a threat and, moreover, may actually deepen and further stabilize the reflective discourse. Even though the purely reflective discourse brings about an internal release and facilitates the flow of association and imagination, it simultaneously instils a sense of disconnection from reality and, with it, insecurity and anxiety. While the patient may experience its liberating effects, she may also feel that the analytic process is not relevant to her actual life, does not seem valid outside the clinic, especially where the extra-therapeutic conditions of life include a variety of risks and dangers, actual or imagined. In a more forceful conversation, 'reality' may find its way into the therapy, informing the assertion of self and creating a sense of competence. I present two illustrations of these ideas.

I start with Shlomo, who was in his thirties at the time. Some years into the therapy, Shlomo found himself deeply involved in a new love story, in which the woman took a role somewhat like the femme fatale, she was interested and enjoyed the relationship but did not commit. Shlomo was the one who maintained the relationship, who expressed his feelings of love and showed commitment. At the same time, Shlomo's parents suffered a serious financial setback, which affected Shlomo because he largely depended on their financial support. In terms of the family morale too, things deteriorated severely and here it was the family that relied on Shlomo to look after its emotional balance. While these problems were going on, in his conversations with me Shlomo chose to focus on his romantic life, and this allowed us a wonderfully reflective conversation, metaphorically rich and fluent. Therapy was both pleasurable and useful. Still, aware of the family problems, I felt somewhat uncomfortable, so that eventually I tried to draw some attention to the family issue as well. Shlomo said there were enough people with whom he could talk about that business, something which was not the case with his romantic problems. Hence, he preferred to focus on the latter. I accepted his explanation. About two months later, though, Shlomo started accusing me of not being sufficiently involved in our conversation. He said that I seemed out to enjoy it while leaving the work to him. I commented that this strangely resembled his issue with his girlfriend, whom he also experienced as insufficiently involved. Shlomo replied that here I was again, dodging responsibility, throwing the ball back to him. After some more meetings during which Shlomo's complaint lingered in the background while we continued talk about his romantic relationship, Shlomo repeated his dissatisfaction with my lack of commitment. I responded saying that the things that were happening to and around him were arousing a lot of aggression and that he did not know what to do with this. Shlomo became very annoyed and said that it was bad enough that I was not doing my job. It became even worse when I pointed my finger at him! Was there no limit to my self-righteousness? I felt that Shlomo was looking for a confrontation with me. Something in our imaginative wanderings did not suit him and he needed a stronger mode, probably to feel that the therapeutic setting could offer reliable holding in his family travails. I answered with as much determination as I could summon, yet – it seemed to me – with a controlled degree of aggression. I argued that therapy was about understanding him, not me. That it felt to me like we both were working quite hard, though that wasn't the point; the point was rather to understand his anger with me against the background of his frustrations at home and with his lover. I said that I could see that he was going through a difficult time, but that this was no reason to be so aggressive with me, and that this moreover did not improve his situation (of this I was not convinced at all, but I nevertheless argued it with conviction). For the whole duration of a session – nearly, it took some time to warm up – we were on the brink of yelling. We said goodbye in a tense mood. Shlomo said he just couldn't believe this was happening here, in therapy. The next session began very stiffly. Shlomo said it was hard for him to talk after last session's animosity and I said something like, 'Yes, we're not used to that'. Slowly he began talking about the situation in his family which had continued going down the slope. Initially haltingly, then with more and more determination, we talked mainly about his family.

In subsequent meetings, these issues came to occupy much more space than they had done at any time in the foregoing period. A window had opened, a way that had not been manifest hitherto. I would like to stress that it was neither reflectiveness nor averted anger that helped to open this window but rather the mutual enactment of the argumentative situation. Paradoxically – as Shlomo's experience was the opposite – it was confrontation with me that allowed him to feel solid enough to relinquish the modes of talking we had become used to and to get connected to the difficult 'reality'. This made it possible for him to be reassured about his ability to sustain and survive the difficult family situation.

Another example is that of Merav, who was an analytic psychotherapist herself. Merav thought very highly of me, especially as a theoretician, but she kept a safe distance from me for several years during which she spoke carefully and painstakingly, often concentrating on a variety of theoretical issues regarding her own patients and therapy in the general sense. In her first years, she clearly used therapy for learning. She brought in carefully measured materials and stayed focused around them, which allowed her to continue in therapy without exposing herself too much, without bringing in her more vulnerable sides. On a more theoretical level, though, Merav would, from time to time, engage me in a passionate debate about one issue or another, something she contrived to do in a way that tended to make me forget, temporarily, what we had been talking about before we slipped into theory. It always surprised me how, momentarily, I would feel confused and hurt when she did not agree with me. For one thing, was it not exactly in this context, that of theory, that she most admired me? And, for another, I sounded so convincing to myself! I just couldn't see how I did not come across like that to her. Our theoretical debates never went out of control to become heated or unaccepting, even when they aroused strong feelings in me. On the surface, they were always well contained. I wondered for a long time what was going on in our discussions, from a dynamic point of view, but whatever insights presented, they did not seem to warrant sharing them with Merav, so that we never got to do any reflective work on this pattern. Years later, still in therapy, I mentioned these arguments to Merav, arguments which, during our first years, had been a real issue for me, but no longer so by the time I mentioned them. Merav did not remember these episodes as remarkable in any way. Perhaps, she thought, she did not always agree with me about certain things in the first years, but she remembered no intense discussion. In fact, she said, she did not think it ever happened that she really did not agree with me on some theoretical point. It seemed totally impossible. This was when I understood the value of these past discussions: In her experience, Merav was so impressed with my ideas and argumentation that almost the only way in which she could experience intellectual autonomy as a professional was by debating with me. The problem was that all this took place on a rather dissociated level and hence did not quite register as such. To make things worse, I had not been quite conscious of this dissociative nature of our debates, which is why, for years, I did not comment about them as an object for analysis, even though my own emotional response to them always bothered me. It should also be noted – I find this strong evidence in favour of the analytic value of enactments – that even though, at the time, the debating pattern did not get analytic attention, the complications they brought in their wake, as they emerged in the transference, seem nevertheless to have been worked through. Argumentativeness as such did almost completely vanish from our discursive repertoire, which only underlines the subtle dialectic between interpretation and action in analytic psychotherapy. Enactment and the absence of analytic reflection did not cause this pattern to remain unworked through.

These two illustrations have to suffice for now and I hope that they bear out how debate, a type of discourse that entertains a close relation with enactment, may promote the therapeutic process and the being of a subject.

Interpretation, enactment and ethics

The formation of the subject has occupied a central place in modernity's pursuit of truth, beginning in the seventeenth century with Descartes and continuing to the more recent formulations of the twentieth century and especially, for our purposes, those of Husserl and Freud. These latter thinkers – in the fields of philosophy and medicine, respectively – though full participants in the project of modernity, also signal the end of an era because, more or less against their own will, they exposed the internal contradictions of the project, and thus the paradoxes of rationalism. In Europe, the social-political contradictions of the modernist project led to an outbreak of violence on a scale hitherto unparalleled in the annals of humanity. On the plane of theory, subjectivity eroded and clashed with scientificity, issuing in a deep rift between the humanities and the social sciences, on the one hand, who were not prepared to renounce the centrality of subject and subjectivity, and the exact sciences, on the other hand, who had no way of dealing with subjectivity and preferred, in the end, to ignore it (Gadamer, 1976). If Freud and Husserl had something in common that, more than anything else, hastened the demise of modernism in the humanities and the social sciences, it is interpretation and its theoretically crucial role in negotiating the relations between the human subject and truth. In the work of both of these thinkers, interpretation (under different terminological guises) takes to the extreme a notion of truth that evolves mainly as the result of a subjective effort. For both, interpretation constitutes truth, on the one hand, and the subject, on the other. The traumatic events of the mid-twentieth century, however, caused their followers to experience an irreversible disarray of the notion of truth – whether it was due to their loss of faith that the true and the good would eventually coincide, or because they realized the relative and plural nature of any truth. These developments led, in the good case, to a radical pluralism and, in the bad case, to a hypocritical form of liberalism (see Badiou (2001) on the hypocrisy of Western talk about human rights). Interpretation, and its attendant therapeutic benefits, formed the centre around which the analytic approach formulated its achievements until the 1960s. From then on, an accelerating theoretical dynamic took over which pointed at the limitations of the hermeneutic turn, a dynamic initially driven by therapeutic approaches that were not analytic (e.g., cognitive-behavioural therapies) and later by analytic approaches that were not therapeutic (e.g., some schools of cultural theory). In fact, Lacan elaborated a para-hermeneutic (and in certain of its versions outright anti-interpretational) psychoanalytic theory as early as the 1950s, but his perceptions were hard to digest for the psychoanalytic establishment, with the exception of professionals working in South America. From the late 1970s, however, para-hermeneutic approaches started to burgeon in analytic circles that were clearly not Lacanian (in contrast to the South American schools that strove to integrate Lacanian notions with the more central psychoanalytic streams, especially, though not exclusively, the Kleinian). Roy Schafer (1976) and Donald Spence (1982), representing self-oriented approaches, and Jay Greenberg and Stephen Mitchell (1983), coming from interpersonal psychotherapy, drew the major part of the profession towards the insight that interpretation does not generate truth, certainly not one truth, though it is still good, or good enough, to contribute to the development of the subject and of subjectivity in analytic psychotherapy. More recent years have witnessed the recognition that interpretation has limited capacity in constituting the subject – a way of thinking that evolved from modern and postmodern reasonings. The modernist element we can see at work here is related to the fact that in constituting a subject, some externality needs to be addressed. Modernity had hoped to buttress the subject with the truth (Hadar, 2001), and the coming apart of this vision left the subject dangling without a grip on reality. Post-modernism found the subject's external anchoring in ethics (Levinas, 1985, 2000; Derrida, 1998), but here too, the subject is formed distinctly apart from interpretation – or rather, with an awareness of the limits of interpretation, where truth is substituted for an ethical positioning of the subject. As things came to be in the group of relevant theories, those that ranged under the post-modern, ethics can under no circumstances be posited without reference to hermeneutics, if only because we cannot understand either what is ethical, or what is the question of ethics given a certain state of affairs, without reaching for interpretation. At the same time, though, interpretation being infinite and boundless, it is never sufficient for the constitution of the ethical, because the ethical demands decision, one way or another. The subject that is constituted on a purely hermeneutic basis is a subject whose ethical positioning is extremely flimsy. This insight offers a prime impetus for the writing of this book. It forms the horizon against which I formulate and illustrate the basic principles of an analysis that is geared towards being a subject.

Yet, at this point we reach a new dilemma regarding the project of a therapeutic psychoanalysis, a dilemma that was brilliantly formulated by Rina Lazar, a leading Israeli psychoanalyst, when she spoke about the ethical dimension as a possible register of failure in psychoanalytic therapy. She conceptualized this through the notion of 'reflectivity as an ethical failure', which she articulated in the course of a session dedicated to a discussion of the film 'Waltz with Bashir' at the conference of the International Association of Relational Psychotherapy and Psychoanalysis, held in Tel Aviv in June 2009. The hero of this film suffers for many years from guilt concerning his imagined part in the 1982 killing of Palestinians in the Lebanese refugee camps, Sabra and Chatilla, during the so-called First Lebanon War. Though racked by this guilt, the hero is not impelled to engage in social activity that addresses the violent aspects of Israeli society, which he himself identifies as a major contribution to Israel's complicity in the slaughter. These feelings do, at the same time, lead him into a significant, ongoing conversation with a gifted friend who happens to be knowledgeable about psychology. The main insight their exchanges produce is that the protagonist is not to blame for the massacre in the refugee camps because, for one thing, he was not directly involved, and for another, he would have been unable to do anything to prevent the bloodshed. What the conversations with his psychologist-friend eventually clarify is that the relevant context for the hero's feelings of guilt should be sought in his parents' survival of the Nazi concentration camps, and not in the murders of Sabra and Chatilla. This is a great source of relief for the protagonist, and it eventually allows him, among other things, to create the very film we have been watching. What preoccupied us at the Tel Aviv conference was the problematic state of affairs when people have severe feelings of guilt yet they do not, at the same time, act to redress the injustice involved. With regard to the film, the viewer has a sense that the concrete refugees of the camps are never quite present: the Palestinians never quite take their positions as subjects. The Israeli subject that thus evolves is a subject that wraps itself in the Jewish narrative and remains blind to Palestinian subjectivity. The protagonist's guilt is a matter between him and his Holocaust branded superego. As a result, the film develops its themes by forms that are classical in the Israeli narratives of heroism and warfare. These forms always convey a pride, a boast. It is this state of affairs that yielded the notion of 'reflectivity as an ethical failure'.[2]

So far, the solution I offer for this ethical failure is to resign the approach whereby action is seen to negatively affect analysis for the sake of one in which enactment is part of the therapeutic processes of analysis. The perspective of action which I argue is so sorely absent from 'Waltz with Bashir', may push analytic psychotherapy towards approaches that are fundamentally more attuned to the ethical. Yet still, something is lacking. I have already suggested that this something is similar to what Emmanuel Levinas proposes, along with many other people working in contemporary continental philosophy: the concept of the *other*.

---

[2] Stephen Frosh (2010, p.11) presents a similar idea where he tries to understand psychoanalysis' failure to oppose fascism, even though there were those, like Reich – as I previously mentioned – whose struggle against fascism was informed by psychoanalytic considerations.

3
The Other

Enactment and the positioning of the other

When we take a step back from the *content* of a statement and look at its *existential conditions* we make an interpretative move, but are also carrying out an action. Such an 'act of interpretation' always puts the patient's words vis-à-vis a certain otherness, something that is not exactly what he said. This is what makes for the fundamental challenge that interpretation poses. It invites – and perhaps even forces – the patient to live with a statement that relates to something that resembles, but is not wholly identical, to what he said. Again, as was the case with the dream, the patient cannot but perceive the interpretation as something that relates to what she has been saying, and yet the interpretation always significantly diverges from it. Psychoanalytic 'working through' precisely implies that the patient has to hear his own words as something different – more or less – from what he himself said. Consider, for example, the differences between a number of interpretations of the statement, 'My sister always comes to visit me at the most inconvenient times'. Many are the ways in which we may respond to or interpret this statement. We might (1) choose to try and gain more information, 'Could you give me an example of such an inconvenient visit?'; or (2) make an interpretative move a la Rogers, 'You really don't feel like her coming over'; or (3) follow a more daring line of interpretation like, 'Could it be that exactly the fact of her visiting turns it into the most inconvenient time? Perhaps her presence is too demanding for you?'; or again we might venture (4) a wild interpretation, like, 'You love her so much that it overwhelms you emotionally and upsets your equilibrium'. I don't think it is very difficult to make out, in these rather schematic illustrations, a function of distance or of otherness that separates between the patient's statement and the therapist's interpretation. In my examples, this distance grows from (1) to (4) in the sense that the patient who has to assimilate (4) will have to cope with a greater degree of semantic difference between his own words and those of the therapist's response (Hadar, 1998). As such, this matter of degree is obviously not at issue here; what matters is the formative need in therapy to instill a relatively large degree of otherness, manifest in the analytic interpretation in general, and in the therapist's specific interpretations. I emphasize the therapist's interpretations because a process of *personification of otherness* necessarily occurs in the course of analysis, giving rise to the various phenomena of transference. What I mean by this is that people obviously come to therapy to hear something else, something about themselves that is different from what they usually hear through internal speech. There would be no point to seeking therapy otherwise, but the presentation of this 'something different' in analysis happens via words, in contents, as statements. Over time, the representation of the therapist comes to inform unconscious processes, which is partly why Lacan described the unconscious as 'the discourse of the other'. The patient's relations with this other subject – who exists both internally and externally to the patient – then produce the transference. This, indeed, is how becoming aware of the unconscious is constituted as the process whereby the analyst's otherness is assimilated.

Lacan (1960/2002) has discussed transference as the two-way process of, on one hand, personification of the unconscious and, on the other hand, the de-personification of the analyst. His deductive reasoning unfolds, more or less, as follows. The unconscious is what the subject has not assimilated as part of his self and as a result it stays resolutely 'other' in the manner that it is experienced. 'Other', that is, exactly in the sense of not being self, but – as well, and with no less salience – the contents of the unconscious are not some absolute 'not self', a 'not self' which lacks any connection with me, a 'not self' that does not affect my life. It is in this sense exactly that the Lacanian other is unlike its Levinasian (Levinas, 2000) counterpart, which is indeed absolute in his otherness. In psychoanalysis, by contrast, the 'not self' that is represented by the concept of the unconscious is part of my life in a manner that rouses my protest. Protest, because the unconscious always unsettles the being of a subject, reminding the subject that even in his own home, he is not always master. In that home, moreover, there is another agent who may take over in certain circumstances, who does take over in certain circumstances (such as, for example, during sleep). For Lacan, the related logic concerns the use of language and speech.

The possibility of words to mean something, to have a meaning, in and of itself, encapsulates intentionality and agency; it therefore implies a subject that is assumed as the source of meaning, a subject whose intention creates the meaning (presenting as a linguistic sequence). This is somewhat attenuated with regard to consciousness where meanings, in principle, may emerge as probabilities of either accidental or causal processes. Consciousness can ascribe or derive meaning in an objective mode, in a mode that is subject-independent. In the unconscious, by contrast, this cannot happen. As Lacan (1973/1998) formulated this with one of his brilliant inversions, consciousness, using causal deduction, may state that 'Where there is smoke, there is *fire*', but the deductions of the unconscious are those that are marked by associating the property of meaning with the property of having a subject. Thus, the unconscious says, 'Where there is smoke, there is a *smoker*'. To reiterate, unconscious contents undergo personification and assume the existence of agents. Thus it happens that the resolutely (though not absolutely) other contents of the unconscious appear as the contents of the other, of a personality that is other, different, though not wholly so. Lacan concludes this analytic sequence with his famous aphorism, 'The unconscious is the discourse of the other'.

In the context of therapy, I would like to note that the otherness of the therapist is not of the same order as the otherness of all other individuals in the life of the patient. Usually, people do not engage in relations whose main purport is the otherness of the other, relations, that is, which they enter exactly in order to hear something different. On the contrary, they get into relationships with people with whom they find it possible to identify. It is via the corridor, as it were, of identifications that we enter relations, especially intimate ones. That is one of the great sources of frustration and heartache when we fall in love, namely, the fact that *we fall in love by way of the* **corridor** *of identification in order then to discover a great* **hall** *of otherness*. The therapeutic relationship, however, is entered precisely for the sake of otherness, with a view to what is going to be hard to digest because it is other, alien. This conceptualization is diametrically opposed to Kohut's reasoning. In Kohut's (1977) approach, the notion of empathy is the fundamental principle of interpretation that informs the therapy; it is geared towards the confirmation of the patient's identifications – on the assumption that the latter are injured to some extent or another. I am not sure to what extent Kohutian therapy actually is done differently from any other type of analytic psychotherapy, but I think that the underlying theory errs with regard to the identifications that are brought into play in therapy and how they operate (see also Green, 2001). Let me put this in the language of the analysis of the transference. Because of the principle of otherness – which I explicitly pit against the principle of empathy – the basic therapeutic transference is always negative, at least in part. The other represented by the therapist, the other of the unconscious, is not any other. It is the other that reveals the self's insufficiency, the other whom we accept under protest. If therapy does not forge a connection with the negative core of the transference, a vital therapeutic component remains inactive (see Chapter 5). Clearly, the human states and processes generated in and by therapy are very complex, and some of them are only very partially therapeutic, but owing to the resistance that the unconscious necessarily evokes – together with the positioning of the therapist as other – negativity must be present in the form of negative transference. To this, Kohutian theory remains blind, and it is a blindness which I would qualify as 'ethical'. I consider the outcomes of this ethical blindness, and ways of dealing with it, in Chapter 5.

The personal other

In Chapter 1, I discussed the ethics of therapy as being directed towards self realization. So far, what I have suggested is that therapy attempts to put the patient behind the conditions of his life and to allow him to speak in the first person and in an active language about an ever widening range of his experiences and his surroundings. I have asked, on several occasions, whether this does not issue, then, in a therapeutic ethics that is tantamount to an all-out egotism, verging on a Sadean imperative, one that squarely opposes its Kantian counterpart and whose key injunction would read – in terms of the present text – something like, 'Do everything that you experience as authentic to yourself: don't relent and don't allow your identifications to be distracted by the objects of your actions'. This formulation includes one critical juncture, what the subject experiences something as his own as against the unsettling effect of relating to his object. I have already argued several times and in diverse places (e.g., Hadar, 2001) that a personality theory can only be considered psychoanalytic if it rejects the totality of the distinction between subject and object, if it conceives of the subject as something that cannot be constituted without the object. One can argue this in semantic terms, the concept of the subject is unintelligible without recourse to a concept of the object – but that is insufficient for psychoanalysis and leaves us with linguistic semantics. Object relatedness can also be understood in the most general developmental terms, roughly in the manner articulated by Hegel (1807/1967). In his dialectical logic, a conscious system reaches a qualitative developmental change, involving an increase in the level of the system's complexity, only when subject and object trade places, when the object of consciousness itself becomes a subject (of consciousness). In this way of thinking, any change in the complexity of a conscious system involves the – at least temporary – conversion of the object into the subject and of the subject into the object. In this move, consciousness becomes embodied in matter and – at the same time – makes possible the emergence of a different kind of consciousness out of matter. This approach, however, is not psychoanalysis either, of course. What is missing here, for our purpose, is the specific way in which a human individual develops who is capable of exercising will, responsibility and choice. This, according to psychoanalysis, cannot emerge in the isolated individual, as it were, out of himself alone, but must evolve on the basis of interaction. The most emphatic psychoanalytic versions of such a way of thinking are represented in interpersonal approaches, namely object relations, relational, or intersubjective approaches (Mitchell & Black, 1995). But in Freud, too, this insight appears clearly and in various guises. Examples can be found in the definitions of the distinction between the libidinal and the death drives, between sexuality and aggression (Freud, 1920), where the former are associated with modes of relating to the other – Freud even defines them as object oriented (or object seeking) drives – as opposed to drives that aim to preserve the self and ensure its survival, which are tied up with aggression and revolve around death. In this view, seeking the other's recognition only inheres in sexuality and eroticism, while survival constitutes a domain of mental life that opposes both culture and sexuality. The drives of survival are ready to sacrifice sexual and social existence in favour of the preservation of self. In this terminology, what I have so far presented as the ethics of psychotherapy accords better with aggression than with sexuality, an ethics that still clashes with (the outer limits of) the categorical imperative. It would appear that only in the domain of the erotic, object drives will concede the needs of self for the sake of connection to the other. On the face of it, this is a resounding contradiction which takes us back to the clash between the classical and the Lacanian translations of Freud's definition of the objective of analytic psychotherapy. In ego psychology, analysis comes to boost erotic and social forces at the expense of egocentricity. In the Lacanian model, by contrast, therapy is about the ability to insist on the subject's condition of desire, about the ability to maintain desire. Lacan (1959/1992) does not regard this as morally objectionable but, on the contrary, as the very essence of the ethics of psychoanalysis. This comes about because Lacan does not adopt Freud's opposition between sexuality and aggression. For Lacan, they do not denote separate domains of mental life, they do not define different fields. Every step the subject undertakes, every motivational factor consists, at the most fundamental level, of two components: one erotic and one aggressive, one of pleasure and one of death, one of the subject and one of the other. Once we move, in our purview of the psyche, beyond the pleasure principle, we lose the ability to describe homogeneous psychic entities and are doomed to dual modes of thinking about any sphere of human behaviour. This is what is encapsulated by the notion of 'jouissance' or enjoyment, the irrevocable duality of mental life, of what always involves both *eros* and *thanatos*. Lacan's reading projects Freudian constructions onto a Hegelian plane, where subject and object are mutually dependent. Various psychoanalytic approaches reflect this idea in their different ways.

To begin with, the child is not born as a subject but as its parents' object in the sense that his or her subjectivity is a manifestation of their subjectivity. This holds in all psychoanalytic theories, even those in which the subject's page is not initially blank, where the child comes into the world with a general outline of its internal structure like, for instance, in Klein (1975). For her, there is a basic 'ego' structure which from the start distinguishes between the sphere of the self and the sphere of the other ('object' in Klein's terminology). In this structure, the domain of the ego is marked and experienced as 'good', while that of the other is marked and experienced as 'bad'. For Klein, this dual asymmetric structure- self/other, good/bad- is the most fundamental psychological ethics of the subject-less individual. From here things develop in a Freudian direction, that is, in a direction that symmetrises between self and other and, through the same process, balances between good and bad. The Kleinian subject starts out from the greatest amount of splitting between these dual categories and development always implies that the self has assimilated increasing levels of otherness and that good and bad become increasingly mixed up. For Winnicott (1965), the picture is even more 'other-oriented'. The infant does not have any inborn subject-object differences and only starts its way as a subject through the internalization of a subjectivity that is not his own. Immediately after his birth, the infant only distinguishes between pleasant and unpleasant and experiences a limited variety of intensities. He reacts to discomfort by complaining, but knows that he is tired (rather than hungry or in pain) because his mother tells him he is tired, and he knows he is happy (and not satiated or wakeful) because his mother tells him he is happy. When he starts out as a subject, he cannot be himself without his mother's presence, because her absence immerses him in anxiety. Only gradually does he acquire the ability to go on feeling 'himself' in her absence. In Winnicott's approach, we could say, the other (the mother) constitutes the infant as a subject. One's initial subjectivity derives directly from that of the mother. This situation in which subjectivity is generated by the other remains preserved in the subject in the form of its fundamental object-directedness, the basic need for an object in the formation of subjectivity. This kind of other-dependence reaches its zenith in Benjamin (1988), where the subject continues throughout his life to constitute himself in relation to the other, to need and aspire for the other's recognition. Indeed, being a subject stays devoid of meaning so long as it does not relate to another subjectivity, to the subjectivity of the other. What the subject looks for, she believes, when he addresses the other – on the sexual plane as much as on that of communication – is another subjectivity who may recognize his own subjectivity. *Without the other subjectivity **he** cannot be an **I**.*

The subject and the personal other

Ever since Freud's (1905) first discussion of sexual development, the individual has come to be seen as someone who reaches subjectivity as a function of a whole system of identifications with the object. Freud argued that the child – always, paradigmatically, the male child – accedes to selfhood only when he gives up the competition with his father over his mother and becomes ready to delay ownership until when he will have become like his father, an adult. Until that moment arrives, the boy has something to strive for, to be like his father. And what about girls? The situation of the girl is complex. She must somehow contrive to transform the sex of her object – from a woman to a man, an exigency that leaves her with a not altogether clear cut identity as a sexual subject. In spite of its formative status, the Oedipal narrative was always and still remains rather schematic, almost wholly lacking a psychology, but it does present the child's subjectivity as deriving from that of its parents. It is, in Freud's version, always both parents who take part in this process and they create the difference between subject and object in a system (the family) in which *the gendered subject is constituted on the basis of identifications and the object of desire is constituted on the basis of the suspension of ownership or the delay of gratification.* Herein lies the formative importance of the Oedipal narrative (see the following discussion and Chapter 4).

Klein (1975) adjusted the Freudian scheme. For her, the same inborn functions institute – simultaneously – both subject and object. She conceives of both subject and object as strata that exist from birth as internal representational systems. The subject, therefore, does not have to emerge from nowhere, through a formative mental action (identification), as it does for Freud. In addition to a basic structure (subject-object or self-other), the child is also born with two basic mental functions: *projection*, which transfers a representation from the domain of the subject to that of the other; and *introjection,* which moves a representation from the domain of the other to that of the subject. Which of these two basic actions will be the one to operate in the case of a certain representation depends on how that representation is experienced. If it is experienced positively, then it will be introjected but if it is experienced negatively, it is projected. This is how the domain of the subject gets built as the representational domain of what is good and that of the other as the representational domain of what is bad. In that sense, the good is a mental extension of pleasantness, while the bad extends unpleasantness. This is the paranoid-schizoid reality on the basis of which personality evolves. Within a relatively brief period of time (two to four months) a whole texture of representations emerges relating to body control and body functions, some pleasant and some unpleasant. These are then mapped onto, or get superimposed upon, the sphere of interactions with the object, especially with the mother. This realm of representation is also divided into good and bad. The former gets introjected and creates a circumscribed domain within the representational field of the subject, that of the 'ego'. Put slightly differently, the ego emerges in the field of the subject as a stratum which he can know and control better than other strata. Compared to other events that are experienced in the first person, it is easier here for the subject to take responsibility and to make choices.

In the Kleinian scheme, once the ego has emerged, another function is added to the earlier two basic ones, which comes to recognize the similarity between the self and a whole cluster of features in the other person (the object) – but now introjection does not immediately undo the exteriority of these features. This function can be conceived as a simultaneous activation of introjection and projection. While projection marks the cluster as external or objectal, introjections marks the cluster as similar to the self. *Similar but not identical.* This is how I conceptualize identification. It allows the subject to construct an intermediate stratum, between self and other, between subject and object, a collection of features or experiences which are both one's own and the other's. They are features of oneself, yet this does not nullify their otherness, and they belong to the other, yet do not immediately arouse the need, or greed, to make them one's own. Now, together with identification, there are three functions which constantly produce and reproduce the field of the subject (and the most accessible part within that field, the ego) as well as the field of the other, including the cluster that has undergone identification, the desired part, which Klein calls the object. Because both ego and object grow large and complicated in the course of the infant's intensive mental activity, each becomes more and more stained by the other, the ego includes an increasing amount of negatively charged representations, while the object comes to contain more and more representations with a positive emotional charge. Before too long, the ego then undergoes a splitting, the negative part gets separated from the main body of the ego and undergoes projection because if it stays in the domain of the ego, it will threaten to break it apart. But the fact that it has undergone projection does not remove the marking of the split-off part as belonging to the self. As a result, there is now a part ego which resides in the field of the object. The problem is that, through identificatory relations, the ego does not stop being attached to the projected, split-off part. It becomes of vital importance to the self that the external object, i.e., the other, will hold on to its split off part and to the behaviours it instigates. The subject starts to behave in a manner that will force the other to embody the split-off part, a complex referred to, since Klein, as 'projective identification'. It is, in a sense, with the emergence of projective identification that subject and other become full players in the field of object relations. Now they continue getting refined and more evolved, but the character of the field no longer changes substantially.

Similar to Klein, for Lacan, too, it is the story of the reciprocal conditionings between subject and other that forms the main narrative by which the other enters the scene of psychoanalytic theory. Lacan, however, tells the story in a somewhat different manner because for him the relationship with the other makes up only one out of three orders of mental life, namely, the Imaginary. For Lacan, the set of relations between the subject and the other comes about as a result of mental activities that resemble those described by Klein, but he conceives of these as acts of a *visual* intelligence that generates iconic representations,

representations that preserve the unity of their object and which, by a totally unconscious determination, are called 'projections' in mathematics. I mention this for its curiosity value, but also by reference to the manner in which Lacan often uses mathematical metaphors or 'mathemes', as he called them. For Lacan, mathematical metaphors are important because they best encapsulate the manner in which the Symbolic incorporates arbitrary elements of signification.

The critical moment in the development of the Imaginary, when the child discovers what it means to be a subject, is when he looks in the mirror and sees his image (Lacan, 1949/2006). This specular situation, or rather, specular metaphor, generates a number of important insights. To begin with, the mirror obviously is always there. But for it to function as such, the child's Imaginary intelligence must be sufficiently developed to be able to identify the relationship between her own body image and the image that is reflected by the mirror. This is not so trivial as it may seem. Clearly, it is not very difficult to identify the reflected image as a human figure (a few days' old child can distinguish between human and non-human figures) – but it is a lot more complex to recognize that this figure is his own reflection. The child does not know how he looks from the outside. There is no simple correspondence between how he looks and the bodily sensations to which he has access (effort, self-locomotion, pain, sense of heat and cold, of hunger and satisfaction, etc.). Though he may be familiar with parts of his body – his hands, his legs, his clothes – of the most important part, the face, he has no idea. In fact, the initial impact of his encounter with the face, due to its alienness, may take him even further away from self-identification. So what is it that eventually allows the child to identify himself in his mirror image?[1] First, the simple, obvious things, like the aforementioned hands and legs and clothes. Let's call these *part subjects*, to resonate Klein's part objects. Second, alien though the face may appear, it is right there whenever the child finds himself facing the mirror; thus, whatever is not identified as part subject is identified as a result of the iterative nature of its appearance (I return later to this matter). Third, the child picks up the unusual control he has regarding the image in the mirror: if he wants it to move its head, the image moves its head, and if he wishes for its cheeks to inflate – its

---

[1] As I mentioned in Chapter 2, experimental psychology (as well as Winnicott) assumes that self experience derives from, predominantly, kinesthetic and tactile information, a type of information that is, of course, wholly absent from the mirror image.

cheeks inflate. And in symmetrical fashion, the mirror image will not do anything that he does not want it to do, in that the mirror image has hardly any will of its own (though it does, nevertheless, manage to surprise the subject in various ways, for instance, when the mirror is concave or convex). Finally, there is an entire dimension the child experiences with his body which is lacking from the mirror image. This is the dimension of depth, glaringly absent from the two dimensional image. Depth is a prime determinant of the subject experience of his body, for example, the child can put things into the body and take them out of it, which cannot be done with the mirror image. As a result, the subject is radically associated with three dimensionality. For example, the self is conceived of as the innermost part of the subject, as something that is entirely internal, something that marks the three-dimensional nature of the subject. In Lacan's Imaginary order, the self is always internal, something which cannot be said about the Symbolic order where, as I have already mentioned several times, the subject is constituted by turning outward to the other, no less than by turning inward. I develop this point below.

In the dialectic of reciprocal definition, the other is the subject minus (at least) one dimension. This is the key truth about identification, about recognizing one's self in the other. I already mentioned that the mathematical function called 'projection' happens to be exactly characterized by removing one dimension from the form on which it operates. If you look at it in this manner, psychological projection too could be regarded as an act that removes one dimension, a removal that transposes the projected image from the subject to the other. As previously said, the missing dimension in the other – missing in relation to the subject – may be a dimension of depth – at least at the level of specular experience, and this defines subjectivity as an internal characteristic. But the missing dimension can also be a dimension of the will, on the motivational plane. Wherever a subject has direct access to the experience of will, it always is self-will. It isn't as though the subject has no access to the other's will, but this is never direct, always derivative. The result is a motivational asymmetry. The specular subject prefers his own will to that of the other. The specular subject, in this sense, is unable to see the large extent to which the other is part of himself. For Levinas, this is the message of 'Love your neighbour as yourself', or the subject's inability to transcend the specular positioning of the other. In this frame of mind, loving the other 'as yourself' is the best we may hope for. But there is always the possibility to transcend the specular position of the other towards positioning him as such, as an other.

There are other things missing from the mirror image, in addition to the third dimension, for example, the ontological dimension, i.e., the continuity of existence. If the subject moves his head slowly to the side, then the mirror image disappears at a certain point, and a very slight movement back will cause the image to be restored. One can disconnect from the mirror image and link up with it again, it can appear and disappear, at the subject's will. Yet, on the one hand, the mirror image is always possible, one can always return to it. Whilst it does not determine the existence of the subject, it is always ready to be restored. These features of the experience of the mirror image generate corresponding concepts of subject-other, namely, Imaginary subject-other relations (as opposed to Symbolical ones). I call the respective (Imaginary) agencies 'specular subject' and 'specular other', and would now like to describe their relations and (specular) dynamics at greater length.

The specular subject, to begin with, is always what is *here* while the other is always what is *there*. This could offer a possible frame for Freud's (1920) discussion of the *fort/da* episode, where a child invented a game of disappearance and reappearance, drop over a reel tied to a string over the side of his curtained cot, saying 'fort' (gone), and then pulling it back saying 'da' (back). The child's ability to mentally represent the reversibility of the other's absence, the transition between presence and absence, depends on the ability to construe *da* or *there* as the place of the other. Therefore, the grasp of presence-absence implies the conceptualization of here and there – which is mainly an imaginary conceptualization – and these dimensions are, again, related to the consolidation of the imaginary distinction between self and other. These three mental dimensions- self/other, present/absent and here/there- mutually and synchronically constitute one another and we cannot determine logical or temporal priority in their relations. Once the infant makes distinctions in terms of one of them, it will also involve processes that are related to the others. Thus, knowing the difference between here and there will soon enough imply the understanding of the difference between present and absent, as well as that between self and other. This forms, in a way, the psychoanalytic fundamentals of space and time, the psychoanalytic equivalents of Kant's apriori categories, but in psychoanalysis they are not apriori.

The marking of 'here' as the site of the subject allows us to gain some further insight into the way our imaginary notion of the *home* comes about, along with the sense of intimacy that attends being at home. It is possibly the construal of the image of home that allows for the marking of 'there' as the place that may house a subject (and not only the place of the object), and this then makes possible the subject's imaginary venturing out into the world in such a way that the subject does not need to experience it as overly threatening, as involving the loss of subjectivity. The difference between the home and the body as entities housing subjectivity inheres exactly here. While it is not possible to leave the body without completely losing subjectivity, leaving home is possible. Seen in this manner, agoraphobia – the fear of leaving home – may be the result of an over-identification of the home with the body, leaving home triggers the imaginary danger of a total loss of self.

The preceding characterization of the imaginary dimensions of experience also implies that the imaginary subject is always present. If it is not present – conscious, thinking, talking – then it does not exist. This has been the predominant Western-modern perception of the subject ever since Descartes, in the seventeenth century, first construed it as a central issue in the understanding of consciousness. Jacques Derrida (1998) and the postmodernists criticized this approach, which they called 'logocentrism', with its hierarchy of presence and absence, where the former is metaphysically prior to the latter. Derrida thought that logocentrism had irresolvable inner contradictions and, moreover, immense destructive influences. Irrespective of these criticisms, psychoanalysis always preserved the intimate connections between presence and consciousness. This is the case even in Lacan, who regarded the subject as irredeemably split between presence and absence, both of which are enacted by representation or rather, by signification. In the Imaginary, therefore, the subject is restless, its disappearance is always total. The object, by contrast, may vanish, but this also implies its ability to return, and when it returns it does so as thing-ness, as *das Ding*, in Kantian-Lacanian terms (Lacan, 1959/1992). The absence of the object, in this sense, is always relative; it is an absence for the sake of a return. This is the logic behind the very unflattering public relations that return or repetition has enjoyed in the history of psychoanalysis. Repetition, on the one hand, was the basis of pathology as it is reflected in the notion of the 'return of the repressed'. On the other hand, it underlay the death drive, as it was conceptualized in the definition of aggression as compulsive repetition. These construals derive from the repetitiveness of the object, in contrast with the ongoing presence of the subject. Hence, in psychoanalytic theory, repetition has always been regarded as the negation of subjectivity. But clearly, when subject and object do not maintain their distinct status – in an approach where the object, too, has subjectivity (while the subject has thing-ness, a body) – repetition and continuity may also trade places.

What makes the object into what it is, its thing-ness, is formative, though it never is all there is to it. This is why we can talk about part objects (Klein) and the *objet-petit-a* (Lacan) – which I call the *objecta*. It is in these part objects, these entities, that thing-ness embodies subjectivity.

One feature of the specular plane derives from thing-ness and unfolds in the dynamic of the part objects. This dynamic arises as a result of the question: To whom do the part objects belong? On the one hand, they always belong to the other, because the object, due to its externality, its basic situatedness, always is associated with a certain thing-ness. And yet, on the other hand, the analytic object is never wholly external and the thing-ness of the subject is the pole around which the unconscious is formed (Lacan, 1959/1992). This is why deciding where exactly the part object is located always involves a certain arbitrariness. It may equally be related to the subject as to the other. However, where we actually locate the part object between these poles creates totally different mental results. If the part object is perceived as belonging to the other, it will arouse desire, yet if it is felt as belonging to the subject it will arouse anxiety (see Chapter 2 and Hadar, 2009).

From the other to the Other[2]

When earlier on I presented Jessica Benjamin's approach to the manner in which the subject needs the other, I wrote by way of a summary, '*Without the other subjectivity **he** cannot be an I*' (p. 70). This sentence includes two personal pronouns referring to the same entity, namely, the entity that is trying to constitute its own subjectivity, the subject in its ongoing emergence. Initially I refer to this entity as 'he' and then I call it 'I'. This formulation anticipates Lacan's approach to the role of the other in the formation of the subject, a role which we may initially understand in terms of how personal pronouns contrive to outline any subjectivity. Any subjectivity, any agency, always occurs as part of an entire constellation of agencies. Any 'I' comes about in the vicinity of a 'he' and a 'you'. For Lacan, a critical moment in the development of the subject occurs with the acquisition of language because it is only then that a person develops sufficient mental ability to allow him to engage

---

[2] Hebrew has separate words for the personal and the impersonal other- /zulat/ and /acher/; the former is derived from 'in addition', and the latter from 'different' and 'behind'. Here we assume the Lacanian notation of capitalizing the impersonal other (Other).

in the basic operations of subject formation and to realize their potential of being a subject. It is only then, with language acquisition, that the subject grows capable of separating between volition or wish ('desire' for Lacan) and its fulfilment, to represent to himself diverse options of choice or to project the mental act of attributing ownership of an act or a condition towards another plane which is marked by the assumption of responsibility for that act or condition.

Language has a variety of expressions that convey agency and define the acting entity in relation to other acting entities. Always, the subject is constituted with and through them. These expressions are the personal pronouns, words that manifest themselves in a diversity of combinations and derivations (mine, they, me, ours, himself, and so on), but their core is formed by three (or four) persons: I, you, and she or he (and it). These words always make up a complete agential environment so that it is impossible to speak of 'I' in isolation from 'you' or 's/he'. Interestingly, the expression that encapsulates being a subject, 'I', emerges relatively late in the process of our evolving understanding of personal pronouns, only after we have a thorough understanding of 's/he' and 'you'. In its earliest uses of personal pronouns, the child calls itself by its own name, that is, he uses the third person (Yaffe & Hadar, Unpublished). This tallies with psychoanalytic theory when it argues that we are unable to create our own subjectivity in the absence of an other's subjectivity. If we can talk of 'precedence' in this context, then surely it must be that of the other, at least developmentally. Everyone is initiated into subjectivity through his mother. This is why the existence (both prior and simultaneous) of other subjectivities is a necessary condition for subject formation. How many other subjectivities we need here is, I think, an interesting question.

Lacan thought that the specular dynamic, which arises between the subject and a specular other (the mother) is depleted after a relatively short time, no longer offering a source of enrichment – in relation to both the subject and (m)other. But the result is not an end to identifications and an ensuing separation between child and mother. This is impossible due to the psycho-logic which I explored in the previous chapter, which requires the other in order to maintain self consciousness. In addition, of course, the child would not be able to physically survive alone at this stage. This is where a process of decline in the tolerance of one towards the other sets in. Because they have already gone once or twice through a round of introjection, projection, introjection, splitting, identification, projection, etc., the differences between them – in character or behaviour – stop being a source of enrichment.

After some such cycles, both subject and other stay with what turned out to have suited their character and temperament and the remaining differences generate a type of 'empty work'. The cycles of identifications and projections do not achieve any change in the perception of the self or of the other. Yet, these cycles do exact some mental price. If we do not profit from them, they arouse repulsion, start being an annoyance, they may even cause people to feel uncomfortable with what they have internalized and appropriated. The troublesome challenge of difference may intensify to the degree of becoming absolutely intolerable. Every difference questions the validity of self, rather than recognizing its source of renewal. From this point onwards, thought Lacan, it's an either or game, either me or the other. A struggle for life and death. This situation I call 'the ethical depletion of the dyadic setting'. Here the possibility to exit the ethical deadlock depends on the appearance of a third subjectivity in the field of subject relations. This subjectivity, which psychoanalysis refers to as 'Third' ('First' and 'Second' being 'subject' and 'specular other' respectively)[3], has been there all along. It is part, even, of the bio-logic of children's coming into the world. In some way, the Third is present in the field of object relations, though it does not have to be in body or in the form of a person, indeed, it may occur as a mere sign, 'the Name of the Father', as Lacan called it. Despite this minimalism of presence, the Third is not required to do anything to enter the dyadic setting, because the ethical depletion of the dyadic setting will draw it in, willingly or not. Life in culture as we know it and in which we partake leaves open large margins for what is not so willed. Fathers, for example, are not always in a rush to enter the ethical squalls that arise between mother and child. Yet, there are those who do come of their own volition and with a view to being a subject. In terms of an ethical perspective, that is always better. Fathers of their own free will are preferable to fathers in spite of themselves. In any case, the Third joins the specular dyad from a place of psychological minimalism, from 'the name of the Father', yet it must, from there on, evolve into a fuller presence, that of a specific person, with wishes and expectations that are directed towards the child. The reason for this need is simply because the psychological means that underwrite the Third's entry into the dyadic scene go on containing, critically, specular

---

[3] Henceforth, I capitalize the ordinal terms whenever they refer to agencies in the ethical consideration of subject relations (First, Second and Third) in order to distinguish these concepts from the colloquial, ordinal use of the terms (first, second and third).

dynamisms as well. Beyond a first step, the ability to fully function on a higher, symbolic level requires a fuller presence of the Third; fuller, that is, than serving as a mere pointer at an additional ethical position. In fact, 'father' may be thought of as different from 'Third' precisely in offering a fuller presence and in a way that does not depend on the parent's sex.

The introduction of the Third entails far reaching changes in the basic dynamics of object relations. First, though the initial appearance of the Third into the dyadic setting is the result of a need that is immanent to that setting, it nevertheless comes about through a mental operation that is neither introjection nor identification. What this requires is the child's ability to use a presence which is in principle not bodily, a symbolic presence, the name of the Father. Second, by 'interfering' with the specular processes, the Third transforms the basic processes of object relations themselves. Thus, projections, introjections, identifications and projective identifications do not continue to act in the same manner as they did hitherto. Since this latter point has received little attention in the psychoanalytic literature (though it has been discussed more in the literature on the systemic psychology of the family), I would like to dedicate a chapter to it, which I do in the following discussion.

Let us briefly pause at the ethical logic of the basic family setting of child, mother, and father. I write 'the ethical logic' to emphasize that my main interest is in the dynamics of being a subject in such a setting. From the way Lacan presented it in his discussion of the mirror stage, it is obvious that the dynamic of the dyad requires a physical presence because dyadic actions operate on images (even if this then is extended towards a specular intelligence, which acts on *internal* images that become, with time, increasingly free of external physical presence). The Third is outside the ethical setting, not only because it is physically not present[4] but also because specular intelligence does not easily manage with differences of the second order. The child can manage the difference between himself and the other, but not the difference of differences such as the one between him and father as opposed to him and mother. The trigonometry of the comparison between three bodies, their

---

[4] I do not, at this stage, want to enlarge on the question of the various types of physical absence or bodily presence, but I would like to note that there is a whole continuum of presence and absence in which the breastfeeding presence of the mother always features as being of a higher order than that of the father, even when he is present by touching or embracing (Hadar, 2010a).

differences, projections and identifications, we may say, is simply too complicated for a child in the first year of its life, which is dominated by specular intelligence. What eventually allows the child to bring a Third factor into the story – not even in the form of a subject to begin with, only as a factor that depends neither on the child himself nor on the other – is the unfolding of a new function which played no part in the ethical game hitherto, namely the faculty of language. It is this ability that the child uses to mark the Third and retain its image for when he will be needed. Indeed, the child is not obliged to use him just because he is present. The child can rather easily suspend the Third from the ethical game, as linguistic marking makes this possible without having to concede its representational power. In this, it is remarkably unlike the actions that constitute the specular or the Imaginary order, which requires iconic presence. Thus, the entrance of the Third is neither necessity nor temptation, merely an option to be taken if and when the need arises. And when the need arises, the Third enters the scene as the mark of possibilities, as a word, as a word that designates a subject, that is, as a name. One can describe it like the moment when, somehow, a question is dropped, something like 'Hey, and what about him?'. From that point on, there occurs an enriching, a filling up of the Third in the shape of answers to the question 'What about him?' or 'Who is he and what is his role in relation to myself?'. The child gathers more and more materials of signification, that is to say, words. What takes place here is what I have already described in the context of the therapeutic situation. Once a critical amount of material concerning the absent presence (the Third) has accumulated, it becomes an agent in the field of the subject, a carrier of a will of its own. This requires no decided act of recognition as such, no declaration on part of the subject or demand on part of the Third. The Third takes its place as an agency via the child's wish to know how this absent presence, this symbolic presence, affects his own positioning qua subject. It is elegant, theory-wise, to consider the first phase of the Third's emergence as relying on the child's acquisition of proper names relating to the Third, while the second stage would then be informed by the acquisition of verbs, verbs of action perhaps – but I have no empirical support for this conceptualization. There is a lot more work to be done on the manner in which language acquisition informs the development of subjectivity.

An additional linguistic factor in the incorporation of Thirdness involves the acquisition of syntax, and more specifically of the ability to generate subordinate linguistic structures like, for instance, 'Can anyone who is ready to do so please come to help me'. The sentence is composed of one sentence ('anyone who is ready to do so') being embedded within another sentence ('can anyone come to help me'). The fact that 'anyone' can have an agency of its own is represented in the embedded sentence, thus forming the Third. For Lacan, this ability shifts the subject to another level of being a subject, namely, to the Symbolic level, which depends on the acquisition of the third person – not just in the regular sense of personal pronouns (she, he, it), but also in the less obvious one of the specific syntactic structure of subordination. On the one hand, this ability allows the subject to represent a presence that is not present – a feature that is, as we have seen, crucial to grasping the Thirdness of the Third, to understanding the manner in which the 'Father'[5] bides the time when he will be required to appear on the family stage. I use the word 'bide' not in order to justify or advocate a father's passive attitude toward the nurturing of his pre-lingual infant, by no means. From the perspective of familial functioning, fathers can and should take their place as actively and fully as possible for reasons of social participation and sharing (and not specifically child develop-ment). But their presence qua subjects for the child will be on hold regardless of how involved they are in the child's life. Only when the cognitive abilities that allow the assimilation of another subjectivity have emerged – with the development of language – will the possi-bility marked by the father's presence transform into a fuller presence. It is from that moment on that the Third presents itself as an agency that differs essentially from the subject (the child) and the other (the mother) – different in the sense that his presence is of another order, an absent presence, a negotiated presence. This negotiation is conducted mainly via language, but this does not mean that it is negotiated only through the father. The mother is equally involved inasmuch that she also practices, always already, symbolic modes of interaction. Here we encounter some controversy regarding the role of the mother following the father's entry on the stage of familial agencies. By one approach, advanced most prominently by Julia Kristeva (1982), the child must reject the mother's involvement with the forging of his subjectivity in order to gain sufficient freedom to adopt linguistic and cultural modes of subject formation. If this fails to occur, then the emotional intensity of the relationship with the mother will again and again drive out the Third, at every renewed surging of desire and identification. As I see it, however, the father's agency will not make its full impact on subject formation if it remains only symbolic, only a name. For example, the

---

[5]   In Chapter 4, I discuss the gender-related aspects of the Third in greater detail.

father must also be grasped by the child in his corporeality, as somebody who acts through his body, and this requires the mother's involvement, as we see in the next chapter.

However this may be, the introduction of the Third not only resolves the deadlock of the dyadic system, it also connects the child to a whole world of other agencies. As I have already argued, the specular dynamic of comparison between persons – if it requires entire cycles of projection, introjection and identification – becomes critically compromised once additional persons are added. Specular mentalization cannot sustain this complication. Linguistic representation, however, thanks to its hierarchical structure, has the capacity to represent additional agencies with relative ease. Hence, it is by gaining command of language that the child achieves the ability to understand the social order. The addition of the Third to the family scene of subject formation allows the child to recognize wider social circles.

The manner in which I have chosen to present things in this chapter suggests a parallel between the constitution of the Third qua subject, and the acquisition of language. In the domain of language acquisition, the developmental sequence consists of the learning and cognitive assimilation of (1) proper names, (2) nouns, (3) verbs, and (4) syntax (clausal subordination). The analogous progression in the formation of the Third would be (1) marking the possibility of an additional subjectivity (the name of the Father), (2) the grounding of this possibility in a personality (the father), (3) the father's becoming an agent in the familial field, and (4) extension of the familial field to the social field as a result of the Third's pointing in the direction of other subjects' involvement. Again, what we witness here is the Lacanian correspondence between the lingual and the social fields, a correspondence which issues in the symbolic order. Before addressing the manner in which the social field affects being a subject, though, I would like to devote some attention to the influence exerted by the Third on the specular field. This entails some important yet under-researched implications for psychoanalysis.

4
Thirdness

The specular Third

How can the Third's entry into the ethical setting (the setting of subject formation) be presented in terms of specular dynamics in general and identification in particular? The question is crucial here because Freud (1920) already marked identification as key to our understanding of the positioning of the subject in the social setting. Much theoretical work has already relied on this notion, a reliance which – by the approach this book offers – has by now exhausted its explanatory power. In a recent article (Hadar, 2010a), I described the entry of the Third into the dyadic setting by means of the idea of inserting a mirror into the specular setting, an idea that extends Lacan's discussion of the mirror stage. This additional mirror, though, is not placed in front of the subject but behind him, so that its reflections can be perceived by the subject indirectly, in the mirror that faces him. The metaphor of the additional mirror creates a model for understanding how the Third joins the dyadic system, where the front mirror represents the Second (the mother) and the hind mirror represents the Third (the father). This model preserves the conceptual benefits of the dyadic specular model, where the structural features of reflective (mirror) relations provide a skeletal structure for the understanding of the triad as a familial-social setting.

The first thing afforded by the second mirror[1] is a view of parts of the subject which he could not have seen without the Third. What

---

[1] The 'Third' in the family setting is the second 'other' and is reflected in the second mirror, that of the father, in addition to the first, the mother's mirror. In order to avoid this numerical confusion, I refer to the father in terms of his position as a subject (the Third) rather than in those of his position as other (the second).

becomes visually available to the subject is his 'other' or back side.[2] This underlines the fact that the other and the subject are inextricably linked, so much so, in fact, that the other is always part of the subject. There is no otherness in and of itself. This metaphor of the other or hind side (of the subject) renders well the crux of my understanding of the unconscious as something that most intimately belongs to the subject but which cannot be observed directly, as this is something that requires the intervention of a Third, perhaps even of an analytic psychotherapist.

Second, the place defined by the Third's position behind the subject is not unique. Many hind positions allow the posterior mirror to reflect the subject's back side in the frontal mirror. This type of reflection can be afforded by a whole assortment of positions and angles, thus generating a variety of positions that are potentially Third, all doing the specular work of the Third well enough. Still, not each and every point in space will do. What is needed for back reflection to occur is a certain relationship between the subject, the frontal mirror and the hind mirror. If, for instance, the additional mirror is placed to the side of, or behind, the first mirror, then there is no reflection at all. In fact, in this case, nothing in the subject's self-reflection will change. This leads us to the conclusion that there are certain conditions of specularity that must be met for Thirdness to come into operation and these conditions can be defined, on some level, according to the 'geometrical' relationship between the subject and the two mirrors. These Thirdness conditions have entered the relevant discourse under the notion of *orthogonality*. Orthogonality can be viewed as a negatively defined property of the two mirrors, namely their never being on the same line and at the same angle relative to the subject. It can also be perceived as specular independence between the frontal and the hind mirror. This may be teased apart into two sub-properties: (1) not being situated on one line, which makes it impossible to reduce the reflection in the Second to the reflection in the Third (and vice versa), and (2) a certain frontality or oppositeness of the Third as he turns to the Second, in such a way that what is observed in the Third will also – even if only partially – appear in the Second. Geometrically speaking, it is not difficult to determine when there is orthogonality between two mirrors, but it is not at all very simple

---

[2] In Hebrew, 'other' and 'hind' derive directly from the same root (/acher/-/achor/).

to metaphorically pull the concept towards the social constellation. I discuss this in the next section.

The third feature implied by the specular geometry is related to the way in which the Third, as a mirror, not only affords a view of the backside of the subject, but also issues in a proliferation of mirror images of both frontal and hind sides of the subject. The additional mirror transforms the specular field into a hall of mirrors in which figures may be distinct in terms of perspective and distance, but it is hard if not impossible to point at any one reflection as more authentic than another. They are all manifest with a certain degree of familiarity but never through their immediate presence, not at a level of familiarity that could be called 'intimate'. I would say that what this suggests is the Other's fundamental plurality. This is where the difference between the other and the Other inheres. The other who faces the subject is singular. There may be another other, and yet another, but at a given point in time, the other is singular. The Other, by contrast, is always plural, always represents a whole community of individuals, excepting, perhaps, the infinite Other, whom both Levinas (1985, 2000) and Lacan (1973/1998) sometimes call God and to whom they ascribe a certain uniqueness. To conclude, the critical effect of this dimension of the added Third is that it links the subject not just to another person, let's say the father, but to the whole group of individuals with whom he has only limited acquaintance, who are not fully present as subjects, but rather offer an impersonal support of the subject's subjecthood. In that sense, the Third negotiates between subject and society and, developmentally, initiates the subject into the social order.

This conceptualization of the Other as formative of the social subject has non-trivial implications, both theoretically and clinically. From the point of view of theory, the metaphor whereby the second mirror constitutes the Third clashes with the importance Levinas (1985, pp. 86–89) attaches to the notion of the *face* in the constitution of the Other. For Levinas, what is important about the Other is the possibility to face her or him, to meet their gaze, to see, to recognize and accept the ineradicability of the Otherness of the other (see the last section of the Chapter). This is effectively the definition that Levinas offers for the Other, that is, the Other is the call, or perhaps the demand, to face otherness without blinking at its stubborn difference. In my construal, by contrast, and like in Lacan and Klein, the room for the Third is created by a certain despair with the ineradicability of the difference that constitutes the spectral other. This despair is the first harbinger of the Third's emergence – the

Third whose development constitutes the Other. The Other requires a triangular setting and generates the dorsal, posterior gaze; it is only through that gaze that it affects the face. From this point onward, the dynamic that enriches the field, the field of the subject, is always a posterior, 'afterward' (Laplanche, 1992) dynamic. It is always negotiated by mediating representations and reflections. It is always of the second order or beyond it, given to interpretation.

As regards the clinic, the specular model carries a number of implications – but we take, by way of an illustration, the implications for the therapeutic difference between whether the therapist is seated facing the patient or behind him – the latter, usually, with the patient lying on the couch. In terms of geometry, in the face-to-face situation the therapist positions himself in the place of the other or Second, whereas sitting in the back of the patient puts him in the position of the Third. Of course, the concrete communicational dynamics has its own influence on the positioning of the analyst and may pull this way or that, toward the positioning of the analyst in the Second or the Third position. I discuss these concrete effects in various places in the present book. Still, the spatial arrangement of the seats has a constant, gravitational pull towards one positioning or another and this pull is always there, even when the concrete dynamics create stronger interpersonal dynamisms. In that limited but consistent sense, the specular setting will be more direct and democratic in the face-to-face situation, while when the therapist sits behind the patient the setting will be rather more formal and authoritarian. The former, therefore, allows less tension between fantasy and reality. The therapist is always more present than in the couch situation. Face-to-face seating, therefore, affords the lifting of defences and the disclosure of fantasies to the extent that the analyst's speech also tunes in to an intimate discourse. In the couch setting, by distinction, regression and the articulation of fantasy does not require a suitable discursive reality because the formality of setting itself offers imaginary defences against intrusion. The disclosure of fantasy may then run on the potentialities of the patient's imagination alone. This creates the effect of depth, of the disclosure of hidden mental contents, but at the expense of the ability to generalize the analytic achievements to ordinary life situations. I suppose that this brief characterization coheres with most analysts' intuition and may emanate directly from analytic experience, in which case the specular geometry adds little beyond complicating the picture. If these would be the only implications of my model then, it would seem, the whole thing would not be worth the effort. Anyway, by way of a start, it is encouraging to see that such an obvious conclusion of such complex considerations aligns with intuition as well.

Orthogonality

From its inception, psychoanalysis evolved as an attempt to describe and explain the subject's emergence in the setting of the family. It did so by attributing different and complementary roles to the mother and the father. Orthogonality, under the more traditional heading of Oedipal dynamics, captured the way in which the mother and the father assume their irreducible roles vis a vis the child's subjectivity. Since its early formulation by Freud, orthogonality purported to explain the issues of desire and identity as they arise in the presence of the object, with a logic in which the subject faces one object, even when this object transforms, say, from mother to father or vice versa. This explanatory frame gives rise to a fundamental problem. In all versions of psychoanalysis, desire is conditional on and nourished by the object's difference, the manner in which it is unlike the subject. Identity, by contrast, depends on and is nourished by the object's similarity, the way it resembles the subject and allows identification with it. Identity is the result of identification. This is the most basic meaning of the subject's dependence on the Other. In this logic, subjectivity evolves in relation to two others who are different from each other in some crucial way. One acts as the object of desire and one as the object of identification. This reasoning explains well the ethical depletion of the dyadic setting, where the same other acts in both roles. It is this ethical depletion that leads to the transferral of one of the subject functions (desire or identification) to the other parent. In the Oedipal story, the son transfers the identificatory function, while the daughter transfers the function of desire. Orthogonality explains not only the dynamics of subject development but also the astonishing persistence of the institution of the family. In the Oedipal narrative, the family's vitality is the result of its providing the minimal conditions for the development of the subject as one who is constituted by identity and desire.

Kleinian theory proposed another solution to the question of identity and desire. The same object is not appropriated in its entirety – rather it is split by the subject due to his structural duality, a duality which exists from birth. The Kleinian subject is divided into 'good' and 'bad' on the basis of the distinction between pleasant and aversive experiences respectively. This duality is projected onto the object so that part of it (the 'good' part) comes to act as the object of identification, while another part (the 'bad' part) functions as the object of desire. Though Klein never actually said so, the splitting of both subject and object removes the need for orthogonality since the same object can take both roles. Indeed, the rise of interpersonal object-relations and relational approaches had the effect of gradually removing the need for Oedipal explanations, thus introducing deconstructive, perhaps even subversive, elements into psychoanalytic discourse. But the problem is that though Klein's approach, by making it structural, takes care of the subject's functional duality and allows for a great deal of development on the basis of a dyadic or specular dynamic, it has no explanation for the radical change represented by the social order or, in Lacan's term, the Symbolic order. What the Kleinian approach also fails to address is the question of how the subject evolves beyond the paranoid-schizoid position; beyond the point, that is, at which subject and other become mutually destructive. Lacan's approach, by contrast, while preserving the theoretical gains made by the splitting of object and subject, does not attribute this to the self's inborn structure, as Klein did, but rather to the assimilation of language and the Symbolic order. I think that Lacan allows for a more coherent understanding of how the dyadic – or specular, as he saw it – setting enables the unfolding of the subject in the pre-split experience, but becomes wholly insufficient once language emerges. For Lacan the splitting caused by the Symbolic affects both identity and desire. The father's admission into the family setting has the effect of opening the subject's horizons without negating the inner split, that is, without separating between the object of desire and the object of identification. Both are perceived as split (in the Symbolic order). Rather than distinguishing between identification and desire, Lacan's orthogonality facilitates the transition of both from the impasse of the specular to the split of the symbolic. The Third is the lynchpin in the transition from a specular dynamics of desire and identification to a Symbolic dynamics.

Though apparently simple and easy to imagine, geometrically speaking, orthogonality becomes remarkably complex when one considers it in the social-familial sense. The key question here is how to translate this property, orthogonality, to the sphere of life at home and the family: What would account as the positioning of two people in different and complementary places in relation to the subject, as well as in a particular relation between themselves? How exactly does this positioning unfold and express itself? What causes the Third, who was present around the infant right from its birth and influenced – perhaps – the position of the Second, to suddenly take an orthogonal position vis a vis the Second and the child – a role which she or he did not occupy until then? The answer to this latter question, in the Lacanian specular logic that I have been following so far, holds that the Third emerges after the Second has become internalized by the subject and the dyadic setting has become ethically saturated. The former part of this understanding is shared, to the best of my knowledge, by everyone who referred to the triangular setting in child development, from Freud to Andre Green. They all construe orthogonality as something that is created only after the place of the emergent subject has been defined and the child, as a result of its interaction with the Second, has already entered the domain of the subject. The latter part of this understanding is not shared by these theorists, namely, not all psychoanalysts believe that the inclusion of the Third involves the ethical depletion of the dyadic setting. In Freud, for instance, the mother goes on functioning as primary object throughout life and is, hence, never exhausted or rejected, even when her subject positioning is repressed.

Assuming the dyadic maturity and some basic linguistic knowledge, what features of the interaction with the child determine the ethical positioning of the two people who are closest to the child? Is it imperative for the new person who has entered the picture to occupy the position of the Third while the one who has been there already stays in the position of Second? A similar problem, in a sense, presented itself to Freud when he pondered the apparent need for the girl to transfer her sexual object from the mother to the father. In classical theory, orthogonality is, of course, tied to the Oedipal setting and hence to gender difference. The mother constitutes the Second and the father the Third, but this Freudian-Lacanian dogma is actually far from obvious. My own distinction between the Second and Third agency refers to the tension between presence and absence of parental agency, a tension that corresponds, on the one hand, with the physical nature of the parent's presence and, on the other hand, with the child's evolving linguistic ability. The physical aspect of parental presence has an extremely complex gendered bias, one that may not have received sufficient attention so far. At one end of the other's physical presence is the interaction with the breastfeeding mother, an interaction that has acted as an ethical and aesthetic ideal throughout cultural history and has inspired a huge number of artistic and theoretical works. This ethical ideal can also be presented in sensory and psychological terms – in addition to cultural terms – since the breastfeeding interaction takes place on many levels of sensual and emotional experience of both baby and mother: the exposure of the skin, the contact with extensive skin areas, the special structure of the oral stimulus and the manner in which it affords the rhythm of sucking, the sensory-motor multidimensionality of the difference between nipple and milk, the spreading inward of fluid warmth from outside through the mouth and down into the inner space of the stomach, and so on. In psychoanalysis, all these have made breast feeding the ultimate source of metaphors for specular processes (or object relation processes). I cannot tell how remote bottle feeding is from the breastfeeding experience because I have not sufficiently studied the issue, but it would be logical to assume that breast feeding goes further in terms of the sensory-motor wealth of the experience of feeding. It is from such an angle that the ideal of the Second is a feminine one, but bottle feeding may allow the other to drop her feminine bias without unduly distorting – perhaps without distorting at all – the primary positioning of the Second. In that sense, the bottle feeding interaction creates the other with a physical presence that is, in the present conception, lesser than that of the breast-feeding woman and might not distinguish between the sexes, but is still very powerful in its positioning of the other as Second. At the other, distant end of physical presence is the subject who is only perceived through one remote channel of perception – auditory or visual – and who interacts with the child in a highly symbolic fashion, namely, in a linguistic mode. The analyst in the couch situation seems to me para-digmatic of this distant mode of physical presence. My description hith-erto gives rise to a continuum of levels of physical presence, one end of which is constituted by the adult female who breast feeds, followed by one who bottle feeds; next, perhaps, the one who plays physical games, fondles and tussles; after this comes the one who chats, sings and shouts and then the one who is quietly present and then the analyst in the couch setting. Finally, at the absent end, there is the adult person who is not there but who may come in for dinner and, surely, for a goodnight kiss, though he may again not be at home by the time the child wakes in the morning. Still, he has a name, the name is there. We can try to imagine how this construal would apply to a family situation of two adult women, the one who is physically more present takes the position of the Second whereas the one who is more absent takes the position of the Third.

The manner in which physicality, absence and presence are forma-tive in creating the orthogonality between Second and Third is further emphasized by the role of language in the definition of Thirdness. For Lacan, language generates the Third in its quality of being rule-governed. This translates, in the social domain, into the order of the Law, where rule and Law together form the Symbolic. Although the Symbolic is generated by a set of arbitrary rules – rules that lack natural motivation (unlike, for example, in biology) – these rules nevertheless encompass agency that manifests in the various concrete forms of Lacan's Other. In language, the Law is represented mainly by the rules of syntax, as I have already had occasion to explain in the chapter 'From the personal other to the Other'. These rules entail a substantial degree of arbitrariness – but then, arbitrariness is a formative feature of language as such, both on the level of syntax and on the level of phonology. Lacan (1958b/2006) thought of the arbitrariness of the Law as a phallic function, that is, as something that is produced by the juxtaposition of presence and absence. The phallic function singularizes each presence, creates a signifier of it against the background of a relative absence, of castration. As a result, phallic presence is always formal, tending more toward form than toward substance, being more symbolic than real. This property of language, whereby each presence is in some way empty, is probably rendered better in writing than in speech and is very well borne out by the nature of punctuation marks. While mostly meaningless in their own right, they do critically affect meaning and they are directly linked with syntactic functions. They operate at the level of sentences. Indeed, Lacan refers to the speech of the analyst – who, for him, always acts in the role of the Third – as punctuating the speech of the patient rather than as presenting any contents as such. In this sense, interpretation is an act exercised on the patient's words, an act that re-organizes them, puts them into a slightly different order than the one in which the words appeared in the patient's initial speech. By distinction from the Third, the Second is more 'physical' even when it is considered as a system of representation – an Imaginary – because it is generated by iconicity, namely, by a morphological similarity between the sign and its meaning, like in onomatopoeic words. Here again, the Second relies more heavily on presence and physicality than the Third, who is constituted by arbitrariness and with whom absence is always around the corner.

Gender, then, is not prescribed by the logic of orthogonality as such. Rather it emerges in the context of normative family functioning in Western societies, a scenario in which the mother stays at home and the father is at work. The gender of the Second and of the Third derives from presence and absence from the domestic space, with absence from the domestic sphere being perceived, in and of itself, as presence in the social sphere. The fact is, however, that children create a Third for themselves in other family constellations as well, ones that do not come under the normative definitions, like single-parent families (in which case the Third is not even embodied in home life) or gay and lesbian families. So that, again, if all settings in which children are being raised generate a Third, what is the point of talking about orthogonality at all? This indeterminacy applies not only to considerations of physicality, but also to social considerations. Thus, in my construal, the Third links the child to the community, something which also follows from the ethical structure of the Oedipal setting. To the extent that one of the parents is more fully defined by their social situation, then it will be this parent who assumes the role of the Third. Still, in conventional socializing, whereas the father may occupy his place with reference to work, the mother will do this via activities like shopping, PTA meetings, meeting with friendly families, and so on. Connections with social environments occur in either case so that, again, orthogonality is not easily captured in a manner that is coherently gendered, unless the family setting is rigidly traditional.

Now, if orthogonality is so relative that any adult person in a parenting situation will immediately orient himself according to it (one in the position of the Second, and the other in the position of the Third), does it actually ever occur that two people somehow fail to take these positions in regard to the subject? Is this a possibility? Of course, the linguistic system of personal pronouns – the difference between the second person and the third person – may allow language to create all of the orthogonality that is necessary for subject development. If one caretaker is present, then the linguistic function of the third person may take care of the Third, although this purely linguistic Third feels somewhat depleted in its own way. Perhaps there is some advantage for subject development if the child grows with two adults in its closest vicinity, when Second and Third can be enacted by different persons. Without further empirical research on orthogonality, it seems to me, it is hard to say anything more specific.

Triangulation and identification

As far as I am aware, it was Abelin (1980) who introduced the term *triangulation* into the psychoanalytic jargon. He did so in an attempt to fuse between Lacan's and Mahler's (1972) approaches to separation and individuation. By means of the notion of triangulation, Abelin tried to offer an up to date angle on the child's Oedipal development, an approach which purported to make sense of the father's contribution to the child's subject formation within a classical and normative family setting. Triangulation was supposed to enable the child to define its place in the family in a way that is relatively independent of the mother's recognition and the father's approval, thus allowing greater clarity in the child's familial positioning, as well as the autonomous definition of his selfhood in the familial context – which may be difficult in this sense, due to the parents' dominant presence (Pines, 1985). Later, the term was adopted by the system approaches to the family, at which point, however, it accrued a pathological connotation according to which triangulation occurs as an alternative to direct communication with any one of the members of the family (Bowen, 1978). The manipulative potential of triangulation is, of course, very important, yet it is not, and not as a rule, pathological. My use of the term is rather germane to Abelin's, yet I do not tie it to normative gender identities as does Abelin. Because the concept of *identity* tends to be dyadic in principle, I believe that the concept of triangulation constitutes a strong triadic alternative to it. This is the idea I would like to develop in this section.

Freud (1921) tried to sidestep the dyadic logic of identification and to take the concept further into a manifold of social situations. For this purpose, he added another dimension of identification – we shall call it horizontal identification – which is plural in principle and operates on those who are situated at the same social level as the subject. This contrasts with classic identification which is singular (i.e., involves only one person) and operates vertically by being directed at someone who is on a higher social level (parent, leader, employer and so on). Such a differentiation between a mode of identification which is fundamentally singular – because it does not simultaneously operate on a number of people – and one which is plural, communal, or group-oriented seems pertinent to me because the two dynamisms to which they refer are qualitatively different – even if, as Freud noted, they act in congruence, at least in the social context.

Freud's distinction between two types of identification is reproduced in the notion of triangulation, but triangulation has three features that distinguish it from horizontal and vertical identification. First, according to triangulation, both types of identification already make their appearance within the family and only jointly do they fully facilitate the child's positioning as a subject. Freud's horizontal identification only appears later in life. Second, in triangulation, plural identification (which, as said, already occurs within the family) also operates vertically with regard to anyone who is placed higher in the social hierarchy (a parent, for instance). Third, in triangulation both types of identification are at work at the same time and in coordination, and the child activates – and is in turn activated by – both for the sake of the definition and the preservation of his place as a subject. This is how the concept of triangulation expands the notion of identification to an approach in which subject formation requires three independent agencies (Hadar, 2010a) rather than two, as most psychoanalytic theories assume. While I have already discussed how the Third acts within the family structure, I would now like to elaborate on the integrated way in which the Second goes on taking an active and necessary role in the subject's development. Triangulation in fact would be meaningless without this continued activity in relation to the Second; otherwise we would be left with two distinct types of identification.

Some of Lacan's followers (Weber, 1991, for instance) argued that in order to open up to the Symbolic order – the order of language and society – the child must disconnect from his mother and reject her. Unless this happens, specular dominance and the intensity of identification do not leave room for any other agency, least of all to a new and different dimension of subject functioning, namely the formal-lingual-social function. The most prominent among these theoreticians, Julia Kristeva (1982), coined a new term for this, the *abject*, a concept that designates the object from the point of view of the subject's emotional response to it. For Kristeva, the abject describes what drives the child to the Symbolic order, the emotional relation, that is, which causes it to reject the mother. This shows a similarity to – and may have been inspired by – Freud's idea in *Totem and Taboo* (Freud, 1913) which I mentioned earlier, according to which the transition from quadruped to biped was attended by vision taking over as the predominant sense modality through a forceful repression of the senses of taste and smell. At moments of conflict, this repression tends to manifest itself in a feeling of disgust. Exactly the same is true for the act of abjection. It is propelled by the repulsion that certain perceptual stimuli arouse in us and this includes stimuli associated with early maternal functions, especially breast feeding. The abject, as an adjective, comes to denote a certain range of textures that represent decay, sickness and vegetative processes, as well as some types of viscosity, loss of contour, etc. The notion of the abject has been very useful in the conceptualization of certain reactions to art as well as of forms of art that intentionally engage this sensation.

The triangular, specular model, unlike the previous approaches, allows for the Third's activity by way of the Second's mediation. This is only the case, however, for the specular workings of the Third, whereas its principal medium is language. Language, of course, is also a mediating construct, but here the mediation is achieved by signs, letters and symbols, not by the other, not by an embodied agency (as is the case in specular dynamics). It seems to me, however that, in the family, the three-way processes of triangulation always remain specular to some extent, because the subject always understands and interprets the Third through the latter's reflections in the Second or while taking into account how the Third is perceived by the Second. The precise forms this takes have been abundantly illustrated by family therapists, but let me give and develop an example here as well.

The case I describe here appeared in the question and answer section of an internet site which is dedicated – among other things – to psychological counselling:

> I am a divorced mother of three daughters. I am having major relationship problems with my eldest who is 16. Her father and I have a very strained relationship and whenever circumstances require re-arrangement of the usual visiting times he refuses to discuss them with me and will only pass messages through my daughter. She then has to discuss them with me and make the arrangements. I feel that this is putting huge pressure on my relationship with my daughter as it puts an extra burden and responsibilities on her. I have tried to explain to her that she should not be in this position: she is still a young person who needs guidance and shouldn't be having to deal with all these problems and decisions. Am I being unreasonable? I am at my wits end. There are continual arguments at home and she is always defending her father's actions with me being portrayed as the 'baddie'. Please help. I really want a good, healthy relationship with my daughter.

The paradigmatic systemic interpretation of the situation the mother describes (let's call her Suzy for the sake of our discussion here; I return to her elsewhere in next chapter) will relate to the 'pathological' lack of communication between the mother and the father, will appoint it as the core of the triangulation and will identify with the mother's complaint. In my perception, some other things must be considered. Of course it is always better when communication is in good working order and things as they are described here are clearly problematic, but taken from the previously presented view on triangulation, other issues seem to require more urgent attention in the analysis of this situation.

First, Suzy herself must be at the focus of our analysis because she is the one who is talking (or writing) in the first person. It is she whose subject position we should examine. Initially, the interpretive act will be directed towards her rather than immediately focusing on the daughter. In analytic terms, there is a problem with the manner in which Suzy shifts the focus of the discussion onto her daughter. In so doing, she undermines her own subject position and this makes it impossible to deal directly with her own situation. I would say that Suzy's distress does not seem secondary to that of her daughter; rather, it is the direct result of the fact that her communication with the father is mediated by the daughter. In the normative situation, most communication regarding the daily life between parents and children will run directly between the parents and only part of it will pass to and through the child. This is not usually a problem. On the contrary, it is regarded as appropriate and fitting. But in the conditions that Suzy describes, this setup has changed. While communication between father and daughter flows, the connection with the mother has to be negotiated. Situations of this kind are not really so rare when girls grow up, even in families that are not separated, but the mother's discomfort concerns her felt exclusion from the position of the adult (subject). Suzy needs the father – her ex-husband – to maintain and confirm the set of identifications that allows her to feel she is occupying the right place, the place that suits her self-image as a grown up person. For Suzy, the father embodies the dissimilar other and this pushes the daughter to the role of the other who resembles her, the other who takes her place at Suzy's side, shoulder to shoulder. This constellation reverses the good, normative pattern of identifications. We can clearly see in this situation how the Second is constituted by being perceived as similar to the subject, while the Third is constituted by being perceived as different. From this point on, according to all analytic approaches (that I am aware of), further development – both therapeutic and ontogenetic – is afforded by the symmetrisation of the other's agencies. The positioning of the Second will avoid a dynamic of abandonment (or betrayal) only to the extent that it will be able to assimilate elements of difference, while the establishment of the Third will overcome a dynamic of alienation (and persecution) only through the assimilation of similarity. This is the triangular essence of positive Oedipal development. Of course, Suzy describes a much more disturbing situation than the usual triangulation, a situation in which the lack of direct communication with the father puts him so firmly in the position of the different, vexing other that Suzy has no way of mentally symmetrising his position. In a complementary manner, the fact that she must constantly negotiate the father's positioning locks the daughter into a role in which she resembles Suzy to the point of subverting the mother-child relationship. This puts the ethical development of both mother and daughter under pressure. By inference, the logic of triangulation implies that a satisfactory facilitation of being a subject affects not only the daughter, but also the mother, and most probably the father as well, though he – it would seem – has decided to address this need elsewhere.

The Otherness of the other

Just now, discussing Suzy's complaint, I wrote that 'the lack of direct communication with the father puts him so firmly in the position of the different, vexing other that Suzy has no way of mentally symmetrising his position'. In this context, 'symmetrising' means the perception of the other as someone more similar to the subject (for more on this, see the following section and Chapter 5). In my view, which in this case derives from Levinas (2000), symmetrisation has certain ineradicable boundaries: always, the other has aspects that are not amenable to symmetrising, that is to say, sides that elude the subject's attempts to understand them through empathy. I call these aspects 'the otherness of the other'. Experientially spoken, the encounter with the other's otherness is always unpleasant, always includes an element of discontent that casts its shadow over the relations with the other. This, I think, is what Sartre (1944/1989) meant when he wrote 'hell is other people'. The issue of the *vexing elusiveness of the Other* is among the most important in the psychoanalytic understanding of the subject's relations with the other – any other, regardless of the quality of the relationship with him. Though the preceding formulation attributes elusiveness to the Third (the Other rather than the other), elusiveness also occurs with the (small) other, of course. This is exactly why the ethical depletion of the dyadic setting becomes so destructive as to require the institution of the Third. If the triangular setting tolerates the otherness of the other and may even serve to leverage the subject, in the dyadic setting, this Otherness of the other is utterly insufferable because it leads to a defensive dynamic and to violence. Still, one of the main gains from the notion of the otherness of the other occurs because it is extendable towards people and groups with whom the subject may not be intimately acquainted and is not limited to the domain of object relations proper.

In the case of Suzy's complaint, for instance, with regard to the father, the other's otherness is clear and obviously tied up with his concrete behaviours and conduct: he is alienated and maintains his distance from Suzy in a way that is both aggressive and offensive. Suzy has a painful history with him and he cruelly sabotages her ability to function as a mother for her daughter. But what about the daughter? We have no information about how she functions in the world and how she feels in her role as mediator between her mother and father. Let us try and draw a fuller picture about her person and life, and let us now also assume that Suzy is in analytic psychotherapy with us and that in this context she gave the quoted account of the situation with her ex-partner. What I offer in the following paragraph is based on therapies I conducted. The resulting picture seems fairly realistic to me.

As it turns out, Suzy actually voiced her worries to her daughter Dana, who answered that it did not worry *her* and that it would be much easier to continue things as they are, rather than try and persuade her father to talk to her mother. Let us also assume that Dana is coping well with life. She is a good student in school and has good friends, but she is stubborn and she loses her patience when Suzy comments on the way she handles things between her mother and her father. When Suzy says to Dana, 'I don't want to go via you when I have to deal with your father, why won't you tell him to talk to me, rather than pass on his messages', this can drive Dana crazy and an explosive argument may ensue. Suzy in fact, on the whole, identifies strongly with Dana and thinks she resembles her, but it annoys her that Dana dutifully passes on her father's wishes and whims. She tells Dana, 'Just say that you won't talk about that with me. That if he wants to arrange things with me, he should talk to me himself'. For Suzy this seems so simple, why should Dana make a big deal out of it? Well, it is exactly here, at this point – and with Dana more than with her father – that the otherness of the other rears its head. This is where Suzy just cannot figure what is the point of all this stubbornness, however reasonable Dana's answer to Suzy may seem to the observer. For Dana it makes no sense to refuse passing on her father's messages when it is not at all obvious that this will lead to the hoped for results. The observer might also note that Dana could be trying to protect her father from Suzy's anger, and this too seems legitimate.

The otherness of the other always exists. Living with it cannot depend on understanding. By definition, otherness is exactly what I cannot understand in the other, even if in certain respects I do understand and accept his otherness. What is required for being together, what enables the formation of enduring partnership – whether this be of an intimate or more remote nature – is acceptance without understanding. Acceptance means designating space for the other without recourse to empathy or identification. For Levinas (2000) this is the fundamental stipulation on the basis of which the other is constituted qua Other. Wherever I understand the other, he is not at all other, for Levinas. This only occurs where the accepting attitude of the subject does not rely on identification, understanding, or empathy. The totality of Levinas's approach, in my opinion, does not allow for psychological subtleties regarding the different forms of acceptance or rejection of the other. That is why I prefer to consider this dimension as liminal, as the *otherness* of the other, rather than the other as such, in his very existence for the subject.

Let us then return to the father in Suzy's story. Let's call him Paul. As I have said, his otherness as an other for Suzy is relatively easy to grasp, as it is informed by a long history of antagonism and alienation. Paul's rejection, however, unlike Suzy's, is total. He is not prepared either to see her or to talk to her. Suzy's otherness, as far as he's concerned, is not just something that confronts him each time he tries to communicate with her, but something he is actively building and enhancing by means of his refusal to communicate. He builds and enhances an image of Suzy as someone with whom it is impossible to talk, someone he cannot even look at because she repels him so badly. When we consider the performative character of Paul's refusal, the manner in which his refusal to talk to her situates Suzy in terms of her agency, then it would appear an attempt to erase her as a subject. Remember that in the triangular perspective, being different is inherent in becoming a subject. Suzy's otherness can always be perceived as a specific way of constituting her as a subject, not a negation of Paul's positioning as such, but this is not the way Paul chooses it to be. Instead, he inexorably, totally undermines her subjectivity and thus erases it, or tries to erase it. Generally speaking, in terms of interpersonal tolerance, what we have here is an axis with two poles: the first is formed by the attack on the subjectivity of the other, while the second consists of the acceptance (or its lack) of the otherness of the other. These two are not the same. If the latter is the essence of *tolerance* then the former is the essence of *fanaticism*. Fanaticism, in fact, can be defined as the attempt to erase the subjectivity of the other. Here the consistency or pervasiveness of the definition is crucial. Each and every one of us carries aggression within her or him. In the wake of Freud, we really should not make such a big fuss about this. All of us will at times – at moments of anger, tiredness, or spite – find ourselves busy denying or erasing the otherness of the other, refusing any identification whatsoever and totally denying him as an other. But when a person is consistently doing this and, especially, if one has a reasoned explanation for it, then, I believe, he is a fanatic in relation to this other. Obviously, this does not prevent anyone from being tolerant and loving toward another person. Toward Dana, for instance, in Paul's case.

5
The Injury

The injury

Many people have wondered what it was that caused Freud to abandon his initial stance, according to which at the very base of neurosis there is trauma – trauma whose origins are not in a natural disaster of some kind, but in an offense from some person who, possibly not by choice, has an exceptional power in relation to the subject. To begin with, Freud believed that this offense was sexual and that the offender was one of the child's parents. Much water has passed under the bridge of child abuse since then. As opposed to Freud's stated reason for withdrawing his early theory, namely, that sexual exploitation in the family cannot reasonably be as widespread as are the neuroses – it was revealed that the phenomenon was more common than bourgeois hypocrisy was ready to admit in the first half of the twentieth century. It is quite possible that abuse was statistically not less widespread than the severe neuroses, even if there is no causal relation between them. Most probably, not all abuses led to neurosis and vice versa, not all neuroses were caused by sexual abuse. Many severely neurotic people have never experienced sexual abuse and vice versa. A question that must be raised, however, is why Freud formulated the hypothesis in the first place? To assume that he formed this idea on the basis of his experience with female hysterical patients does not seem logical to me. At the time when he came up with the idea, he had such a small sample of analytic patients at his disposal that any statistical validity would be unfeasible. Relying on this limited clinical experience also does not particularly suit Freud's scientific temperament in this period (the 1890s). Instead, I believe, the traumatic aetiology of the neuroses derived from Freud's fundamental understanding of the logic of the psyche and his consequent assumptions about what could have caused damage of such a profound kind as to result in long-term dysfunctions. People who grow up in diverse ordinary conditions are usually able to *know* what they want, as well as have reasonable ideas about ways of realizing their wishes. With this in mind, Freud sought to find out how neurotic persons can become so confounded about their most basic wishes and so unable to realize them even when they are able to express them. This was the sphinx's riddle facing Freud as he made his first analytic steps.

I do not know exactly how Freud's thinking evolved up to the point when he formulated the concept of trauma but, as I understand Freud's logic, the libido constitutes the part of psychic life that is directed towards the other (or the 'object', in Freud's language). In order to develop, this part requires to be nurtured by the other, be responded to, recognized and encouraged. If such nurture is forthcoming, if the parents are good enough, if the human environment is a source of joy (or, in Winnicott's terms, 'facilitating'), then the individual's will and awareness are bound to unfold. The individual will experience herself as a subject and she will be able to adopt attitudes and undertake actions which she will experience as hers, as an expression of her self. If, however, the others to which she turns consistently invade the space in which she can realize subject positions, when her parents engage with her in a way that she experiences as alien, strange, aggressive, and in violation of her desires, then injury becomes *traumatic*: the injury subverts the subject's will and threatens her self whenever she ventures to want something. The injury caused by the other's offense (in the libidinal domain, the domain of Freud's object drives) is what damages the individual's ability to be a subject. This is also true for the group experience of those whose wishes are ignored and whose ability to realize their subject positions, the only positions with which they can identify, is thwarted. This is the experience of those who are exploited in general (or the subalterns, in post-colonial discourse), and that of those living under foreign occupation in particular. In the latter case, the offense to the ability to take subject positions is very direct due to characteristic curbs on the occupied people's freedom of movement and absence of civil rights. Offenses against groups can be of a more subtle nature too like, for instance, in the case of the effects of Israeli militarism on Israeli women's ability to imagine themselves in positions of political power.

I believe that the insight that drove Freud to abandon the idea of sexual abuse as the source of the neuroses might have been of crucial importance because it shifted our understanding of the subject from the exterior to the interior, that is, from the conditions of life to the emotional make-up or the subtle balances of the personality. This insight should not be taken lightly. It provides analytic psychotherapy with its most fundamental interpretive tools. But it does not remove the utility and epistemological need for the notion of the injury, that is to say, the idea that what underlies the problems that are amenable to therapy is some form of offense to the individual's subject position. This injury may be grave and ongoing, but it may also be light and of a temporary nature – such matters determine the intensity of the injury – but what stays constant is that injury is always the issue with which therapy must grapple. By allowing the notion of injury to inform our theory of psychotherapy, we gain a number of important tools. First, it preserves the formative status of the trauma in understanding human dysfunction, but it allows trauma to act in symbolic – rather than concrete – ways. Second, it offers an explanatory principle that is inter- and intra- subjective, both at the same time. Third, it allows us to set aside medical language together with the notion that analytic psychotherapy comes to heal a sickness. As I have already argued in some detail, the medical model was very advanced in its time but its potential to take the therapeutic agenda further has been exhausted (Hadar, 2001). The concept of injury offers a suggestive alternative to that of illness because it takes stock of the basic negativity of the therapeutic enterprise. Finally, it locates psychotherapy in an ethical coordinate system and renders it as one force in the striving to better society. I will now formulate this in the language of therapeutic principles – principles without which, in the absence of a medical model, the analytic discourse cannot be understood as a therapeutic discourse.

1. Analytic psychotherapy is built around incidents of injury. An incident of injury is an interpersonal incident in which one side inflicts the injury while the other is its victim. Injury can originate in a singular incident or be an ongoing occurrence of a repetitive nature. This distinction is not crucial from the structural point of view, although it affects the severity of the subject's experience, its traumatic load, as well as the difficulty of the treatment. All in all, protractedness makes injury more severe in terms of its psychological effects. For analytic psychotherapy, all injury is injury to the patient's subjecthood. In this sense, the injury is always ethical in nature. It is part of the paradox of subjectivity (see Chapter 1) that the worst injuries to being a subject often are the result of physical injury.

2. While not everything that goes on in the analytic encounter consists of the treatment of injuries, the latter nevertheless is what constitutes the therapeutic core. It is not always easy to discern how some episode that comes to be narrated in the course of the therapy actually is an injury incident, but it is always a priority to clarify this possibility when therapy confronts new materials. One could say that therapeutic contents are new exactly in so far as they relate to injuries that have not yet been dealt with in the therapy. Perceiving a therapeutic event as new is, as we shall see, of considerable importance because there is a fundamental difference between the initial response to an event and subsequent phases in the therapy. As I showed in Chapter 2, by and large, bringing up a new event or incident in the therapy has the nature of an enactment and requires attention as such.

3. The subject of the injury is always the subject of the therapy, the patient. This is also the case when speech revolves around incidents in which the patient was the one who inflicted injury and not the one who was at the receiving end. In such a situation, the basic assumption of therapy is that the patient would not have brought the incident to therapy had she not been injured as well in one way or another. This is always a possibility because of the dialectic between subject and other as it is rendered in identification and in triangulation (see Chapter 4, in the section 'Triangulation and identification'). If, for some reason, the therapist is unable to consider the patient as the one who has suffered injury – i.e., is unable to be empathic in this narrow sense – and if this wholly shapes the therapist's perceptions, then analytic psychotherapy is in trouble and, in extreme cases, cannot take place. I present some cases in which I had a very hard time generating a position of empathy, including one in which I decided to terminate therapy against the patient's wishes.

4. When treating injury, one can suggest four phases. In the first phase, the nature of the incident as injurious should be clarified along with the identification of the perpetrator and the victim of the injury (the latter, in the present conception, is always the patient). Next, the patient's injury must be acknowledged, and this acknowledgement is essentially performative, because it situates the participants – mainly the therapist – in relation to their positions relative to the subject and the injury. The third phase is interpretive; it aims to mobilize a mental movement out of the victim position. This always takes critically longer than the first two phases and it constitutes the classic

core of analytic psychotherapy. I shall regard this process as *symmetri-sation* with regard to victim-perpetrator; in symmetrising, the patient moves away from the victim position (in relation to the one who injured her).

5. To the extent that the therapeutic relationship is a laboratory for life, reproducing subject positions of the patient in her most formative relations, the therapist will always assume, to a greater or a lesser measure, the perpetrator's role (vis-à-vis the patient). Only as a result of a successful symmetrisation will the therapist be able to properly remove herself from this symbolic role. This is why there is a nega-tive core in any transference and the primary task of the analysis of the transference is, indeed, to identify this element. Freud called this *resistance* – erroneously, I would like to argue, if resistance is conceived of as a by-product of therapy. Here, the negative core of the transference encapsulates the therapeutic nature of the analytic process. The recognition of this reflects recognition of the crucial role of injury in analytic psychotherapy. Melanie Klein should prob-ably be credited for being the one who first pointed this out and elaborated upon it.

I expand on these characteristics in the remainder of this chapter and illustrate them by looking at some clinical materials.

The analytic identification of the injury

Let us for a moment revert to the last clinical vignette I mentioned here, the episode in which Suzy complained that her daughter Dana was acting as the messenger for Paul, Suzy's ex-husband and Dana's father, in contacting Suzy and thus was operating as a go-between. In Suzy's complaint, Dana features as the victim of the injury because, according to her mother, having to do this negotiating puts her under undue strain. In her analytic therapy, however, Suzy is the one who matters and not Dana. The first therapeutic act, then, is to recognize Suzy's injury. This is not as simple as it might seem. Suzy had very good reasons to present the situation in a way that marked Dana as the victim. First of all, it is likely, though not necessarily the case, that Dana too is hurt by this state of affairs. The absence of communication between her parents may well emotionally trouble her and burden her more than is necessary. Second, and perhaps more crucially from the analytic perspective, Suzy has a serious investment in not considering herself as the victim of the lack of communication with Paul. As I already described, given Paul's systematic ignoring of Suzy's position as a subject, she has ample reason to feel hurt by him, but given their long history of hostility it is also rather embarrassing to continue being so hurt by him. It adds insult to injury because, even though he puts her off, Paul is still able to continue hurting her. It is mainly a narcissistic injury, one may argue, involving power games. But this is not necessarily so. First, such an absolute exclusion might well have hurt her coming from anyone with whom she had practical issues to settle, not just when it comes from Paul. This is to her credit in terms of interpersonal sensitivity. Second, by my own construction of being a subject, after years of partnership with someone, that someone becomes part of our existence qua subject. His removal from that place is never total and complete and the process will always be long drawn out and difficult, no matter what one feels for the other. All of these are important considerations for future reference in Suzy's therapy (see below), but here they merely serve to illustrate how hard it often is to identify the injury. It may in fact not always be possible.

Let us assume that I somehow say to Suzy that I understand Dana's problem in the situation as she describes it, but Dana is not in therapy here and I suggest Suzy describe her distress in a more direct manner, one which does not go via Dana. And let us also assume that Suzy insists that what bothers her is Dana, not she herself, and that if it is only about herself, then she doesn't care if Paul doesn't talk to her. She long stopped needing him if it were not for the children. Nevertheless, this way that Paul has of communicating with her via Dana causes Suzy a lot of discomfort, time and time again. The therapy, in so far as it concerns this theme, can be said to be stuck. Other themes can be discussed and Suzy's life can be considered in greater depth, her relationship with Paul and their triangular communication with Dana. This can all be valuable in its own right, and it may allow dealing with other incidents of injury from Suzy's past, in her life with Paul as well as in her life with Dana. The initial story, however, will remain untreated because the injury has not been recognized. I would like to stress that a therapy can successfully continue over a course of time without identification of the injury described in the opening story, the ostensible reason for therapy. But let us assume that at some point or another Suzy sees the personal injury involved in Paul's refusal to speak with her and understands that the injury, for her, originates in Paul but also in Dana. Now, we shall identify that Suzy refuses to accept the casualness – perhaps even pleasure – with which Dana cooperates with

Paul's boycott of her, Suzy. Another phase of the therapy sets in, the recognition of the injury.

While identification of the injury may demand and occasion analytic steps that bring out the injurious aspects of the patient's narrative, ethically speaking it does not form an interpretive step. Crudely speaking, the analytic moves aim to clarify the picture, but not to re-position the subject in relation to this picture. Where there is no problem of identification, where the injury is obvious, all that occurs is a description of the event, the narrating of a biographical episode. For understanding this first act, I wish to revert to a notion borrowed from the theatre, namely, that of raising the curtain, or lifting the screen: the background and the protagonists are introduced but the therapeutic drama has not yet started to evolve. Of course, there are plays which use no curtain or screen, and sometimes they do not have a circumscribed stage. This happens in therapy as well. Nevertheless, as a guiding image, lifting the initial screen works well enough. This act of stage setting and injury identification is formative in situating the patient as regards both the narrated event and the therapist. *Designating the patient as the victim of the injury also marks her, simultaneously, as the patient of the therapy.* This is not necessarily so in types of therapy that are not analytic, but it forms the most basic outline of the coordinates of the transference. Always, even if by the merest suggestion, the transference is characterized by the victim position of the patient (see below).

When I wrote that, following identification, another phase in the therapy of the event starts, this should not necessarily imply a sharp division into stages. It is not as though we were doing one thing until that very point and from then onwards, we do something else. In therapy, processes generally unfold in parallel and it happens frequently that the identification of the injury already involves recognition and a degree of symmetrisation (the third stage of treating injury in my approach). These stages mainly refer to the (psycho-) logical relations between the various aspects of therapy. The fact that a certain stage comes before another is therefore more a matter of logical than temporal precedence. And yet, from a bird's-eye view, on the macro level, these stages tend to mark typical phases in the therapeutic process. Identifying the injury is likely to be central at the start, and the therapist's recognition will probably require more therapy time afterwards, while symmetrisation may well dominate for a relatively lengthy period which will take the treatment of the incident to its conclusion. Themes of identification and recognition will similarly re-occur during stages following their initial achievement, when attention is already devoted to symmetrization. Though my writing distinguishes rather sharply between these stages, in reality they are less patent.

I would like to return to what critically installs identification of the injury as the beginning of therapy. In my view, the notion of the patient as ill is indefensible, so the question arises as to what constitutes the patient as patient. The minimal condition here may refer simply to the structure of the analytic discourse. The patient is its prime (and maybe only) protagonist. But with the idea of the injury, the patient-hood of the patient is posited more strongly. In analysis, the patient is the injured party. Only when she is recognized as the injured party in the drama of analysis does she fully occupy her position as a patient, as the one whose therapy it is. I use the word 'only' in its analytic meaning. It is the patient, obviously, who pays; it is she who decides to go to therapy and who in due time decides to stop going. There is a whole cluster of social actions, hence, that also situate the patient as a patient – exactly to the extent that being in therapy is a social enterprise. But only identification of the patient as the victim in a situation of (inter-personal) injury positions her as an *analytic* patient.

The analyst's recognition of the injury

I just wrote in the preceding section that, 'This act of stage setting and injury identification is formative in situating the patient as regards both the narrated event and the therapist'. It is not autonomous, this act, it does not stand in its own right, and it invites a similar act-in-response from the therapist. I use the word 'invite' to leave room for a temporary failure of the therapist in this act of identification, but the challenge identification poses for the therapist is far more demanding than 'invite' suggests. If the invitation is left without response, without recognition of the injury, then it will constitute a kind of therapeutic failure and may manifest in the variety of ways in which therapy may be stuck. While the therapist's recognition is an act in its own right – I even count it here as a 'phase' – it may be given without awareness, usually in the form of empathic communications.

The notion of empathy as it features in diverse analytic approaches – even where it does not play a central role – goes a long way in the direction of the therapist's recognition of the injury. And yet, there are some crucial differences between the recognition of injury and empathy. The most salient of these is related to the performative nature of recognition or, more precisely, its symbolic nature as an ethical act. Empathy is offered by one person – a significant other, a selfobject – to another. It is an emotional, interpersonal gesture whose main impact is in the positivity of the experience of sharing. Recognition of injury is offered by *a side or party* – Lacan's Other, for example – by way of recognizing the moral status of what happened to the patient, the injury she has suffered. It is more like receiving a verdict than it is like receiving a gift. This has diverse therapeutic implications.

The main clinical difference between empathy and the recognition of injury concerns the place from which the recognition of injury is offered, or rather, the authority with which it is given. In analytic psychotherapy, it seems to me, recognition is ethically constituted because it comes from the position of the third, from a position which relies on the therapist's *social* authority as a therapist. If recognition were to come from the position of friendship or from a parental place, then it would not be the same thing, and it may perhaps not be effective, that is, it might not give the patient the freedom to engage in interpretive moves, in the symmetrisation of her position as victim. Due to his symbolic status, the therapist's recognition is morally meaningful, that is to say, it is meaningful beyond the specific point in time and the place in which it is offered, as well as beyond the therapist's own personality and his emotional attitude to the patient. Empathy, by contrast, has the almost opposite significance. In its Kohutian formulation, empathy comes to compensate for a lack of parental amenability to selfobject functioning. The problem is that the selfobject is ethically situated between the subject and her projections and/or introjections, which is to say, in the language of triadic positionings, between the First and the Second. Empathy, therefore, emphasizes the specular dynamics of therapy, with its aforementioned dead-ends and shackles. Especially, as I argue in 'Transference and its injuries', the final section of this chapter, it obscures the negative core of the transference and might involve its denial. Moreover, because Kohutian empathy comes from an imaginary voice that is insufficiently distinct from the patient's own voice, it may allow the patient to identify with her position as victim, but it does not necessarily encourage her to challenge that position. On the contrary, perhaps.

I would like to illustrate this by returning to the film 'Waltz with Bashir', which models here as a kind of 'case history'. As I mentioned earlier, the discussion of this film during a relational psychoanalytic conference held in Tel Aviv in 2009 had an eye-opening effect on me in terms of the formation of my notion of injury in therapy. This was well captured in a felicitous phrase introduced by Rina Lazar, 'reflectiveness as ethical failure'. In the following lines, I develop an illustration that is based on 'Waltz with Bashir', but moves on to speculations that are entirely absent from the film. This illustration is, of course, wholly my own invention and does not rely on any information that I have about the film, its protagonist or its director. No such information has ever been available to me. Moreover, the illustration bears no relation to the intentions of the film's director, even if I am referring to events and a background that appear in the film. Let's assume, then, that a patient, Arieh, has been in therapy with me for a few years. In the background, not always explicitly, there is an experience of severe injury which is related to the first Lebanon War, in which Arieh participated as a soldier, and more specifically to the massacre in the Sabra and Shatila refugee camps. Arieh speaks of the personal guilt that he experiences with regard to the massacre. He feels terrible about it and finds it difficult to talk about this subject. Something about Arieh's guilt is unclear to me. First, he himself was not involved in what happened in Sabra and Shatila specifically, even though he was in Lebanon when the massacre occurred. The circumstances of this event, together with the obscure way in which he talks about it, cause me to look for the meaning of his injury in something other than Arieh's direct involvement in the massacre. Here the situation is unlike that of Suzy's in that Arieh does, from the start, refer to himself as the victim of the event, but the nature of the injury eludes me, thus preventing me from offering the recognition that would do the therapeutic job, or recognition that relates specifically to the injury. I might offer empathy for Arieh's suffering – I have no doubt that he suffers – and I actually do offer him empathy, yet while this facilitates trust between us, it does not reduce the anguish he experiences regarding the massacre. The issue remains a thorn in the flesh of the analytic work.

Now, I knew that Arieh was second generation to the Holocaust and I asked myself whether his guilt may be related to some identifications which put Arieh in the role of the victimizer of his parents. That seemed logical to me. Arieh was living a good life, he was very gifted and had many friends. He loved to go out, while – it was reasonable to assume – his unconscious identifications were always reminding him that his parents had lost the ability to be happy with simple things such as food, love, art. It was hard not to form the impression that what we had here was an emotional economy according to which what he gained was what they lost. Perhaps they could have enjoyed more if Arieh had suffered more, perhaps that might have removed some of the burden of the trauma. It was as though, unconsciously, his insistence on living a good life was tied up with their anhedonia and thus turned his parents into victims. I managed to communicate these insights to Arieh, not in the concentrated form in which I have just presented them here, but bit by bit. At some point, Arieh himself started talking from this type of position. He described the guilt that would creep into him on returning from a family dinner on Friday night; the effort he would make to enliven the atmosphere round the dinner table, his attempts to joke, to stir up laughter. The idea worked quite well with me too, in terms of my ability to offer recognition of Arieh's injury – that of a person whose ability to enjoy life would seem always to come at his parents' expense – it really was terrible, and I could feel a lot of empathy for him and considerable personal identification. Recognition of this injury occurred in a manner that was both extremely detailed and rich in contents. Arieh recounted episodes from his parents' Holocaust experience by way of a background for understanding his own experience with them; he told of moments when their traumatic memories interfered with their ability to generate a shared sense of well-being, let alone shared pleasure. This therapeutic theme was clearly effective. Things were getting unblocked inside Arieh. He wrote his newspaper features more fluently and felt that his writing improved. Still, Sabra and Shatila did not leave him in peace and after some time they took over again. Not as much as earlier, not in such an inscrutable and inexpressible way, yet now it was not only confined to his dreams. Yes, he was having nightmares about war from time to time, but he was also trying to write about it. He was writing a diary, a screenplay, a newspaper feature, a short play. But it wasn't working well, something there didn't fit in. In the attempt to understand, I was reminded of Arieh's war stories. Rereading my notes from the first year of Arieh's therapy I realized why something about the Sabra and Shatila trauma sounded as if his agony was misplaced. I felt that his injury may have been different from what Arieh was able to point out. Arieh always spoke from a distinctly anti-war point of view. Whenever he talked about injuries sustained by friends or by Lebanese soldiers, he always stressed how everything about this war seemed bizarre and superfluous. He thought that this was a war that we, Israelis, should never have embarked on in the first place, and once it started, it should have been brought to the speediest possible conclusion. Instead it just dragged on, and it did not end after this terrible massacre either, even after it the Israeli army lingered in South Lebanon. At the same time, however, there was something about his intonation. Arieh often narrated war experiences as if they were the tall tales of military heroism. The stories always came with some of the excitement of adventure, as if to say 'Look what places I have seen and what things were going on around me'. I thought that Arieh derived pleasure from the war stories which unconsciously clashed with his anti-war stance; that the latter might even contradict his fighters' adventures more explicitly as absolutely inappropriate. I was also put in mind of how I myself sometimes felt when I had the opportunity to tell about the time I served in Israeli army strongholds on the Suez Canal during the War of Attrition. I felt that we should have withdrawn from that place immediately after the 1967 war. It was Egyptian territory – why should we invest so much in it and at such a terrible price, both with regard to ourselves and to the Egyptians? Yet, whenever I recounted my experience in the stronghold, which was, altogether, an extremely traumatic one, I also felt proud about having such adventures to tell about my own life. Telling these war stories was always tied up with *jouissance*. In Arieh's case, there was something more. Palestinians, for him, formed an abstract category. While he always expressed his sadness about their suffering, it was never for a particular, flesh and blood person, a Palestinian whose suffering he had directly encountered, whose suffering directly saddened Arieh. It occurred to me that in the case of Sabra and Shatila, too, Arieh had not actually witnessed any concrete suffering. He had after all not been there. There was no specific image that had lodged itself in his memory. Palestinian suffering was always morally mediated, leaving its mark via an accusatory superego. It then occurred to me that Arieh's injury may be related to the clash between his concrete pleasure in war stories and his abstract identification with Palestinian suffering and its injustice. This story-telling pleasure is a deep and integral part of Israeliness generally and of ex-soldiers particularly, especially of those who have done combat service. It is hard to dissociate oneself from this. I thought that it was possible that the injustice committed against Palestinians associated in Arieh's mind with the injustice suffered by the Jews of Europe, like his parents. In that sense, the two versions of Arieh's injury addressed by therapy – the one related to holocaust heritage and the one related to military heroism- could be related to each other. Nevertheless, the dimension of the pleasure that the two versions involve seem different from each other; only the latter clashed head on with Arieh's moral position, as well as his implicit identification between the Palestinians and the Jews of Europe. As is always the case with injuries, here too, Arieh's injury subverted his agency and his ability to experience himself as a subject.

Non-recognition of the injury is part of what causes the constant return of the repressed. Thus, it may be that only by managing to reconstruct the manner in which Arieh fell victim to the conflict between his conscience and the Israeli ethos of heroism, he might be released more adequately from the Sabra and Shatila trauma. My experience with liberal Israelis leads me to believe that this injury, or one resembling it, is widespread and takes a variety of forms. Enlightened Israelis feel uncomfortable with the Occupation and with being an occupying nation that relies too much on military force. At times, they may even be conscious of this discomfort which, however, does not necessarily reach a state of poignancy that causes them to resist or act against our military culture. Often, the upshot is guilt of a type that is very hard to alleviate because it is so unspecific (Even-Tsur, 2011). Albert Memmi (1974) described similar phenomena with regard to the enlightened Frenchman in Algeria before independence.

My previous formulation of Arieh's injury leaves unclear the agent of the injury. On the face of it, there is no external agency but rather an unusually exacting superego which is tormenting Arieh for his pleasure in recounting war experiences and for his lack of familiarity with Palestinians as persons. My way of seeing things, however, does not easily tally with a construction in which the victimizer is a wholly internal agency. Something sounds wrong to me in assuming that 'I' can be a victim of my superego. An epistemologically more acceptable version of the injurious agency is therefore that of someone who approaches the Lacanian notion of the Other, which consists of a cluster of linguistically anchored cultural themes that have undergone unconscious personification.[1] The Other is not an internalized figure, but rather forms itself as a both internal and external agency from the very beginning. I would say that the Other is the one who inflicted the injury. It is important, though, to further specify the nature of the injurious Other in Arieh's case because, generally speaking, the Other is not one thing. For Arieh and the Israeli liberals, the Other who inflicts injuries of conscience is often the one who embodies Israeli culture's incorporation of militarism and war tales. As I understand it, this Other prevents Arieh from assuming the subject position that suits his moral views about the Lebanon War. In this way, the Other generates pleasures – or rather, *jouissances* – that subvert the liberal's subject positions.

---

[1] Judith Butler (2005) describes a process of self representation which resembles the present one by always including social elements that subvert our ability to know ourselves or, in her language, our ability to give account of ourselves.

Because of its moral nature, the recognition of the patient's injury offered by the therapist must be authentic. It makes no sense for the latter to come up with an act of recognition of something which she does not really perceive as injury. This is reminiscent of what Freud said about transferential love, namely, that all manipulative use of it is likely to be counter-therapeutic (and probably unethical). The recognition of injury, on the same lines, cannot be manipulative. To my mind, this is not always the case with empathy. Of course, the demand for authenticity (non-manipulativeness) may limit the therapeutic effect of dealing with events in which the therapist fails to see the injury, but this local loss goes hand in hand with more global gains of credibility and, with it, the trust of the patient. It happened to me on occasions that patients responded with lack of trust to empathy which I offered either too fast or without inner conviction. Part of the process leading to recognition, therefore, may well involve a re-definition of the injury in a way that will make it recognizable to the therapist. I do not disavow my contribution to the definition of Arieh's injury, but I justify this because this definition was what allowed me to offer authentic recognition of his injury.

In the course of the years, I have treated Jewish settlers whose difficulties with local Palestinians I did not recognize as constituting an injury and I refrained from offering recognition of events when such patients experienced distress related to actions by Palestinians. The patients sensed that therapy was conducted under these constraints and, I feel, did not expect identification from me, but I am sure that part of the usual therapeutic potential was not exploited in these cases. To the extent that they were effective, their vitality was probably derived from the fact that even when I ignored the encounter with Palestinians, there were plenty of other, ordinary injury events of the type I have been illustrating here. For these I could offer authentic recognition. From the ethical point of view, it would be quite reasonable for a therapist to refuse treating people whose injury she has no way of recognizing like, say, ex-Nazis or serious criminals. As for myself, I was able to treat settlers from the Occupied Territories because I separated between the aspects of their lives that were the result of their ideological principles and those that came about against a general, human background. It is, obviously, my personality as a therapist that allowed me to do this kind of splitting with some degree of success, but I am not advocating it as the proper, ideal professional stance. In recent years, I have actually become more hesitant about taking on settlers for psychotherapy and, when I have done so, I have tended to prefer to be explicitly critical about their positioning vis-à-vis Palestinians, rather than withhold my recognition of their experienced injury. There is a certain gap, when it comes to this, between analytic activism[2] – the principled readiness to treat any person who turns to psychotherapy – and psychopolitical activism, that is to say, working with the assumption that the political context has and should have an influence on psychotherapy (Samuels, 1993). The ability to recognize the patient's injury, in this sense, may put certain constraints on analytic activism. I can imagine refusing or stopping a therapy on grounds of being unable to offer authentic recognition of injury. I think that this is also an aspect of therapy as an ethical process.

The symmetrisation of the injury

To the extent that classic analytic interpretation allows the patient to be aware of things of which she was previously unaware, interpretation enables her to stand behind her words and her life circumstances. This is the central theme of Chapter 2, but how does this idea translate into the treatment of injury as I present it in this chapter? To me, it seems that the patient's position vis-à-vis the one who inflicts the injury and vis-à-vis the injury itself is similar to her position regarding the unconscious: both undermine her being a subject. In the case of Arieh, one could say that the unconscious functions like the Other, like a discursive field, that is, that imposes itself on the patient, not leaving him free to occupy a place with which he can feel reconciled, with which he can live in peace. This line of reasoning led Lacan to conceive of the unconscious as the 'discourse of the Other', namely, the part of the cultural discourse that underwent 'interpellation', to use Althusser's (1984) term or, in other words, the part of culture that evolved into an unconscious mental field. On this approach, the unconscious embodies, in certain cases, the Other's assault on the subject's subjectivity. Through the unconscious, a certain discursive field acts on the subject, and in some cases – like that of Arieh – the effect is repressive, perhaps even coercive (Butler, 2005). In these cases, the unconscious itself acts as a type of injury. Classical interpretation (of the unconscious) is supposed to enable the patient to assume her place at the site of the injury, to move, that is, from being in the position of the victim to taking participation in the situation. Even if the situation is one of injury, it is eventually

---

[2] I gratefully acknowledge Rivka Warshavsky who communicated the idea of psychoanalytic activism to me.

healthier, in terms of the psyche, to be able to adopt the position of someone who *chose* to be there, in some sense, or – in an earlier formulation, which I presented in Chapter 5 – the mentally healthier part is that of one who is ready to assimilate the injury conditions as part of her life. Interpretation is supposed to help the patient make this move. I call it 'symmetrisation', which comes to underline that the shift it denotes does not take place in a void, but always in relation to the position of the agency that inflicted the injury. As long as the patient's position in relation to the perpetrator has not been restructured, the therapeutic event remains untreated.

The reader, by this point, I imagine, will gauge the critical status of the recognition of injury. In the absence of the latter, the interpretive manoeuvre of symmetrisation is likely to completely blot out the ethical basis which regulates the patient's positioning in her social environment. If no recognition is forthcoming from the therapist, between therapist and patient, interpretive symmetrisation will evolve into a statement that resembles accusing the victim of being a victim, which is ethically unacceptable. The therapist's recognition of the injury comes to provide an ethical anchoring for the interpretive act, for symmetrisation. I would say that the source of 'reflexivity as ethical failure' is located exactly in the absence of such recognition, however, still, the point of interpretation is that it allows the patient to abandon the victim position. This is the very heart of therapy: the transforming of 'it' into 'I'.

Let us take a look at the possibilities for symmetrisation in Suzy's therapy. As mentioned, at the point where I recognized Suzy's injury, it was related to the fact that Paul, her former husband, was not willing to talk to her. This was a severe injury in itself, but the particular family setting also made it impossible for Suzy to fully occupy her position as the mother of Dana, because it was Dana who relayed family communications. This was an additional injury which we came to recognize in the course of therapy. For the sake of this discussion, let us now assume that Paul cannot be made to budge from his position. Suzy irritates him so much that he just has to hear her voice to become aggressive and verbally abusive, to know most definitely that he is no longer willing to be in this position, which has made their shared lives impossible for too many years. What kind of symmetrisation can there be between Suzy and the man who refuses to be in touch with her? What part might Suzy play in the formation and maintenance of the injury? A possible analysis will reconstruct Suzy and Paul's life together and will attempt to pinpoint her contribution to the decline of their relationship. This analytic process could aspire to allow Suzy to see the various ways in which her initial infatuation with Paul may not have been totally blind to his incompatibility with her own temperament. It may not have been a simple mistake for her to have chosen this partner. Rather, it could have concealed her general and perhaps deeply ingrained lack of faith in man-woman relations, a lack that could originate in experiencing the tormented nature of her parents' relationships. Perhaps, initially, choosing Paul seemed to have been the right thing to do. Even though she was impressively gifted as a jeweller, Suzy was so lacking in self-confidence, so restless and in need of stability. Living with Paul worked out reasonably well for a number of years, in spite of Suzy's growing doubts. She would complain and appease, but felt that her dissatisfaction was related to her own endless emotional needs – as Paul tended to understand it. But what became more and more obvious with time – Paul's emotional remoteness – was not so easy to deny or to relate to Suzy's own problems. She had Dana because she wished and believed that it would improve her relationship with Paul, but her second daughter was already conceived as a friend to Dana, Paul no longer was part of it, and the third daughter was a mistake, though Suzy did not regret it and she loved mothering the baby. She had also somewhat hoped for a son, though not too seriously, she was not really disappointed when she was told it was another daughter ('Imagine it had been sons, rather than daughters – then I would truly have gone crazy'). As the daughters grew up, Paul became more remote and spent less and less time at home. Suzy was at home most of the time, especially after Dana's birth, when she opened her studio in one of the apartment's rooms. Why did Suzy stay with Paul for so many years? True, it's hard to separate, and there are many fears to overcome, fears of loneliness and of economic vulnerability but, given how difficult living with him made her own life, one cannot avoid asking why she stuck to it. It seems to me that symmetrisation is not possible without the realization that Paul served Suzy in positioning herself as a subject, even when he drove her mad and desperate. Deep in her heart – or in her unconscious (it makes little difference in the present context) – Suzy may not have had – and still may not have – faith in men, no faith in masculinity, having had a basic experience of masculinity as oppressive towards women. I suppose it could have been better to divorce at an earlier stage, but what Suzy gained was the ongoing confirmation of her basic assumption concerning men's limitations and the relations between men and women. There is, of course, the secondary gain of being the victim, the way it releases one from responsibility. And there is the power one can gather from the sense that one has suffered injustice, even if this also leads to a sense of weakness and emptiness.

In spite of the fact that, for most therapists, symmetrisation, relying as it does on familiar analytic strategies, should be the easy component of the perspective I offer in this book, I would like to introduce another episode to illustrate symmetrisation at work in a more classical interpretive act than what I have previously presented with regard to Suzy. Let us have another look at the therapy I presented in Chapter 1, an episode in which the patient dreamt the following dream, 'I walk in an unknown, desolate city, when suddenly there appears an old, white-bearded man in a carriage pulled by two brown horses. The old man stops and offers the dreamer a ride, and when the dreamer asks 'Where to?' the old man replies, 'You know where'. The dreamer has no idea what place the old man has in mind. He takes fright, begins to sweat and refuses to climb onto the carriage'. In my earlier discussion of the dream I wondered how it could be processed in a manner that advances and sustains being a subject and in what way would this differ from a mode of processing that is aimed to self-discovery. Now I ask how can the dream be interpreted from the perspective of the injury, as an injury event? To pick up the argument regarding being the subject as it appeared earlier, the injury here is the patient's discontent at not knowing what he wants in life, at not taking responsibility, at not keeping his existential obligations. The perpetrator is clearly the Other, as it tends to be in most cases of generalized discontent (guilt, fear, and so on). However, in this dream, the Other features as a rather discernible, even if nameless, figure – an old man steering a horse wagon. Now, in this case, so long as the existential obligations of a more active attitude to life remain unexpressed and are experienced as an external agency, the patient will be unable to leave the position of the victim, the position of the one who is unable to make the fundamental choices of living. Here, clarification of the manner in which the old man represents an aspect of the patient's person may involve an examination of the patient's moral understanding of life. Such examination could build on classical notions of transference, indicating the affinities between the old man and the patient's father and then, again, the old man and the analyst. It could bring out the sense of obligation that the patient may have had in facing these figures. Analytic work that keeps the patient in his victim position, according to which society or the lack of paternal protection prevented him from getting ahead with his life and making something of himself – such work would perpetuate the ethical failure. This is especially felt where guilt – as opposed to fear – is the main expression of the injury by the Other, as we saw in the case of Arieh, but it also occurs where guilt is more subtle, for instance, in the case of the present dreamer. This is, I think, a very important point, partly because it illustrates how the injury perspective questions the very notion of interpretive purity of classical analysis. The therapeutic effect originates, to a great extent, in the power to give due respect to action, as part of the analytic framework. No interpretation of the previous dream will close the cycle of treatment of the injury if there is no change in the dreamer's basic positioning regarding a whole cluster of issues in his life, since the dream, to begin with, expresses how the dreamer has sunk into relative passivity with regard to these issues.

Transference and its injuries

If therapy consists of the analysis of injury events and if therapy is a labora-tory which makes it possible to process difficult contents with relative safety, then the core of the transference is always negative, always situating the therapist in the position of the perpetrator. Thus, it is one of the main skills of the analytic therapist to accept her position as perpetrator and to make the gradual and balanced shift to a more positive position as symmetrisation progresses. Obviously, as soon as a certain event has been treated with some degree of symmetrisation, the therapist will occupy a slightly different position, because there will now be a corner in the patient's mind in which transference has stopped being nega-tive and may even have become properly positive, i.e., not by way of masking negative transference. Here one can trust the positive transfer-ence because it builds on experiences of working through the effect of injury, experiences of relief with the victim position, experiences of transforming the positioning of injurious others. I also wish to remind us here that when transference acts on a symbolic level, inspired by the personification of the Other, it affects the therapeutic dynamics differently than when it acts on the Imaginary level, where the analyst is experienced directly as the perpetrator. In the symbolic case, transfer-ence positions the therapist as the representative of the social order, thus affording special therapeutic endorsement to the therapist's inter-pretations in general and to the therapist's recognition of the injury in particular. Still, as long as the therapy is vital and touches upon experi-ences of injury, there will always remain areas of negative transference.

Therapy evolves from zones of negative transference to the extent that it evolves from zones in which being a subject is problematic. This does not imply that positive transference does not have its uses, only that positivity should not be taken at face value and that one should pay particular attention to negativity and its manifestations. Here, too, I believe there is a problem with the Kohutian approach, whose practices present negative transference as part of a narcissistic pathology, while sidestepping negativity as an integral part of the therapeutic situation. This understanding has Freudian roots, especially if one considers resistance as the dynamic that underlies therapy generally, as I mentioned in the Introduction and as I further elaborate in the next chapter. Freud, of course, conceived of the transference as a type of resistance.

If therapy always has to cope with diverse amounts of negative transference then, in its initial steps, there is a limit to the intensity of injuries that therapy can process. Therapy may collapse under the weight of the negative transference. As it progresses, therapy is meant to spread the seeds of positive transference in order to enable the treatment of increasingly deeper injuries – although if the patient does not carry very grave injuries the transference can become essentially positive. On this view, the positive elements of the transference – or rather, the positively directed shifts in the transference – are a measure of the progress of the therapy, of the extent to which it has allowed the patient to position herself symmetrically in regard to the injury events that came up in therapy. It is somewhat oppressive, especially for new therapists, when one feels intuitively – and understandably – that successful treatment of a certain event tends to be reflected in the positive nature of the transference. This may weigh on the therapy as a subversive pressure to succeed. Let me illustrate these matters.

In Chapter 2, I mentioned Merav, an analytic psychotherapist herself, and the pattern that emerged during a certain phase in the therapy when we conducted discussions concerning diverse concepts in therapeutic theory. In the earlier passage, I explained the notion of subject position and regarded our arguments mainly as a type of discourse and the particular position in it occupied by the patient (and the therapist) qua subject. Now I would like to go back to Merav in order to examine the negativity of the transference as it emerged already in these argumentative practices. This negativity did not vanish when the arguments stopped. Merav usually perceived me in a positive way. Initially this concerned primarily my qualities as Other, i.e., my professional position and the books I had published, but later it also extended to the trust she had that she would leave our meetings feeling stronger, better in herself. She could trust that the thing that troubled her and which she had brought to the session would seem different from what she had thought beforehand. I would say that we were working well, but I was worried by the absence of explicit negative transference. When the therapy was in its third year, an especially tough phase set in between Merav and her daughter, who had started junior high school. Merav had been raising Sigal, her only child, by herself all along, from when the girl was three years old, when Merav divorced the girl's father. The father soon moved abroad and his relationship with the child grew weaker rapidly. Relieved to get out of a shared life that did not suit her, Merav felt all right about divorcing Sigal's father. She had had a number of men friends since then but was not tempted to try living with them; her current relationship too did not involve sharing a home. Merav asked herself, on occasion, whether this really was the way she wanted to live, but living together with a partner just never held enough attraction in order to risk the home life she had built and become used to since the divorce.

When Sigal started junior high school, a new pattern in their relationship emerged. Sigal felt Merav's presence as increasingly authoritarian and invasive, while Merav perceived Sigal's behaviour as narcissistic and self-righteous. The summer between seventh and eighth grade was a nightmare, riddled with endless rows and deep insults – on both sides – and with brief episodes of total disconnection during which Sigal would lock herself into her room and refuse any contact other than the most functional. It is hard to exaggerate how her relationship with Sigal troubled Merav. Her whole mental equilibrium drew on the life she had with Sigal, and it could drive her crazy that an innocent remark would quickly turn into a shouting match. It affected their home life, to which she was so attached, as well as her self-respect as a psychologist. She couldn't talk about anything else in her therapy – in marked contrast with previous issues, which had often been about work and her family history. Her current romantic relationship, too, suffered from these tensions in Merav's home life, and though her friend was a patient man, things between them became cooler. About a year into this situation, a new mode of talking between Merav and me evolved. In my usual way, I believed that therapy should address itself to the question of how the fights with Sigal were reflecting Merav's side. Though I have no doubt that she really suffered from them, she also had a need for these conflicts; if only there was a way to make them less fierce, they would definitely give her something, maybe some training in facing hostility, perhaps getting rid of the destructive threat of her own aggressiveness.

Merav argued that I was clinging to theoretical abstractions instead of digging into the real mess; this, she argued, was what made it impossible for me to come up with meaningful insights which would help her cope with Sigal. This was not a very dominant strain in our conversations. We spent most of the time with the description of Merav and Sigal's interactions, or alternatively, those between Merav and her man friend. Merav still went on leaving our session with a sense of relief, feeling that Sigal would somehow get through this difficult phase and home life would return to what it had been, perhaps even to something better. When we had an opportunity to discuss her work, Merav was happy that she had managed to let go of the business with Sigal, even if it was only for one short hour. But at times, especially following vacations or weekends, Merav would express profound frustration with therapy, how could it be that none of all these explanations and interpretations were helping her even one little bit. They only created an illusion of control.

I do not like it when people are angry with me, even if I take it as a formative factor in close relations, including analytic psychotherapy. But in Merav's case I felt that being able to be angry with me offered us an opportunity to work through contents related to a denied injury. In fact, I believed I knew what that injury was. It was something that had been mentioned and associated with Merav's relations with her mother. She knew this, of course, she was aware of it already from age four. The injury, however, took a more subtle shape than recurrent quarrels. Merav's mother, a very original and dominant character, was a successful academic. The family's cultural arena was always under her influence and served as a stage for her brilliant conversation. Merav never thought of herself as someone with qualities that might be similar to those of her mother, and she submissively accepted her place as an admirer, like the other members of the family. True, it was hard for Merav to be an individual in her own right in the presence of her mother, it was hard to make an impression or gain a place that was not somehow derivative of that of her mother's. But, first, it was quite a privilege to grow up with someone like her mother, and second, it was obvious how her own academic ability had profited from her mother's tutoring. The mother, however, did not really appreciate Merav's intellectual competence, and this was reflected in the latter's insecurity and in her abilities, even if she received unambiguous feedback, either in the shape of high grades or her teachers' positive evaluations. Maybe her mother's critical attitude had caused Merav to achieve less, academically, than she might have done with more confidence in her abilities, but everything comes at a price, and being a psychologist suited Merav better than being an academic. Our conversations about her arguments with Sigal allowed Merav to consider her mother's dominance regardless of the latter's brilliance, as pure aggressiveness, as a symbolic erasure of Merav's (symbolic) subjectivity. As a result, the injury the mother had caused no longer appeared in its attenuated form but, on the contrary, in a decidedly blunt manner, as an aggressiveness that Merav had internalized and adopted herself, something which was expressed in her relationship with the most important person in her life, Sigal. To some extent, her quarrels with Sigal reversed the symbolic lack of power that Merav had experienced with her own mother and, as such, was a step towards symmetrisation. Of course, the agony it aroused in Merav did not allow her the full benefit of symmetrisation, which could be enhanced by the recognition of her injury, rather than role reversal.

What I want to emphasize in my interpretation of the patterns I previously described is that, in spite of Merav's anger and my own discomfort, I held the image of the one who was not enough attuned to the details of Merav and Sigal's interactions and who instead was clinging to the therapeutic principle according to which Sigal was not the issue in this therapy, that it was Merav and the manner in which the rows with Sigal were embodying an important dynamics in her own life, that is to say, her ability or inability to take a subject position (intellectually speaking) in her mother's presence. In this narrative, on which I did not unduly insist, but which I mentioned here and there, Merav's unconscious identification was actually with Sigal, while her speaking (first) person was identified with her mother. Sigal's struggle effectively enacted Merav's denied need to fight for her subject position against her mother. I believe that by staying with the core of negative identification, when both I and she herself took the role of the mother (I with regard to Merav and she with regard to Sigal) it became possible for these issues to be worked through and allowed us at a later stage to reposition ourselves more positively in the transference. This shift enabled an attenuation of Merav's conflicts with Sigal.

The idea that there is always a negative core of the transference is tied up with the distinction between two ways in which the patient positions himself vis-à-vis the image of the therapist as the one who inflicts the injury. One way is concrete and attaches to specific patterns in the therapist's conduct and the other is more abstract and attaches to the (structural) role of the therapist, her function as Other, as the meta-personal other. This distinction between two types of presence of the therapist in the analytic dynamic forms the basis of my approach to the transference in general, as I have explained in a recently published paper (Hadar, 2010a). There I argue that we might understand the transference as an ongoing movement in the patient's situating of the therapist – now as the other, and now again as the Other; or as I formulated it in the paper, at times as the 'second' and at other times as the 'third' (see Chapter 3, 'From the personal other to Other'). In this respect, the crucial thing about the transference is that even when the therapist qua other is experienced in a very negative way, qua Other she may be subject to positive transference. In such a case, it is the concreteness in the therapist's approach that gets associated with negativity, while the Other's abstractness allows for the positive aspect of the transference, contrary to what may happen in other cases, for example, in Arieh's case which was previously discussed. Thus the patient's oscillations between positing the therapist as other and as Other will be reflected in her fluctuations between positive and negative transference.

In the story of Merav's therapy, the transference, in its first years, was dominated by my image as a third and it was extremely positive. From time to time, however, my image as a second would slip across my image as a third. Then, I was someone whose theoretical competencies were a threat for Merav, and then she would fight my conceptualizations from a threatened position. This was, experientially speaking, the hardest phase in the therapy because of the denied and split off nature of the negative core of the transference and due to the dissociative character of the therapeutic conversation. Later on, when discussing Merav's fights with Sigal, it was my image as a second – my conversational presence, my ability to perceive things from an unusual point of view, the quality of my speaking voice – that became positively coloured, while on the macro-level, as a therapist who is supposed to know, as a third, my image took on a rather dark hue. What occurred here was a very complex interaction between my position as an agent – now from the place of a second, then from that of a third – and the emotional nature of the transference – which at times was positive and at other times negative.

The injury perspective and the formulation of the negative core of the transference enable us to take therapeutic concepts further into other situations in which the need arises to offer reparation in the face of protracted injury to the ability of either an individual or a group to take their subject position. A better understanding of conditions that corrode an other's or Other's (in the case of a group) subjectivity may lead us to therapeutic insights which would not be possible without this broader perspective. As I have already mentioned at a number of points, flashes of the injury perspective as well as its extension from the individual to the group level have often been manifest in the past – in Freud's work more than in that of many others, but especially in the writings of thinkers like Frantz Fanon and Jessica Benjamin. This is why the present attempt to methodically develop the injury perspective looks at these thinkers and others like them for the sake of constructing a historical context. This is the point of departure in the next chapter, in which I present two concepts that articulate the semiotic extension of the perspective of the injury, the colonial condition and the condition of occupation. The first of these is the broader concept, which originated in the subjugation by technological cultures – 'the West', 'the North', to put it in geographical terms – of pre-technological cultures in Africa, Asia and America. The notion of colonialism, however, has undergone an extension in the course of the past half-century and it has become predicated on any social-political setting in which one group of people, defined by some commonality or another, uses the resources of another group of people by depriving it of some critical cluster of its subject rights. Exploitation, in this sense, is not absolute. The dominant group usually extends limited subject rights to the dominated group, rights that allow them to benefit from certain types of wealth belonging to the dominated group in the first place. At the same time, other subject rights are simultaneously being denied in such a way that the expropriation of some local wealth – in the form of both commodities and working force – is made possible. This situation, when exploitative strategies are complex but still rely on direct forms of domination is captured by the notion of 'occupation'. 'Occupation', then, refers to practices of partial oppression whereby certain subject rights of the dominated group are denied by the exercising of force, while other rights are granted in a manner that allows the long-term exploitation of the dominated group by the dominant group.

6

From the Analytic to the Post-Colonial

The (post-)colonial

One could say Frantz Fanon (1952) started a revolution in the intellectual effort to understand and conceptualize the colonial condition. He introduced psychoanalysis into this field by discussing the psychic dynamics that the colonial condition creates, a dynamics which always re-produces the identities of oppressor/oppressed. Over and beyond the expressive power of his writing, what impresses me in Fanon's work is the depth of his understanding of the dialectic of identification and the way taking a certain social position – that of either oppressor or oppressed – issues in an identificatory constellation from which the individual cannot extricate her or himself without an ongoing conscious effort – a determined effort, we may say. As part of this enterprise, Fanon succeeded – better, I believe, than the empirical research – to show the black person's identification with the white person, and, by extension, the implicit identification of the oppressed with the oppressing outgroup (Duckitt, 2006). Fanon also described the role of *visibility* in the perception of a person as Other. Here, external difference does not remain external only and becomes an incessant reminder of the other's alterity. In that sense, the visual presence of the mark of alterity obliterates the difference between other and Other. But more than any of his other contributions, what is especially relevant to this book is the similarity between the processes that are formative of the oppressed person's identity and those that go into the making of the neurotic personality, which Fanon described so pointedly. In both cases, disorder is the result of a protracted attack on the individual's or the group's ability to situate themselves as subjects. For someone like me, who is sceptical about the validity of the medical model of the psyche, the notion of neurosis can be profitably replaced by the notion of injury, and this allows me to reformulate Fanon's ideas as follows. The personal and the collective reactions to protracted injury can be described and conceptualized with recourse to the same terms. We may even say that there is a parallel between the colonial condition and the therapeutic condition. Both concern an ethics of injury, the mutuality between aggressor and victim, and the attempt to repair the damage caused by the injury. Psychoanalytic thinking, in this sense, is relevant to both.

Fanon had many adherents and this is not the place to enumerate them, but I would like here to briefly present the ideas of four of his followers (while some others will make their appearance in the next chapter of this book). Edward Said, the first of these, may well be the leading figure in the post-colonial thinking of the late twentieth century and relates especially intimately to the Mideastern issues with which this book is concerned. Said's work– while including the late essay on 'Freud and the Non-European' (2003) – touches less directly on my book's psychoanalytic preoccupation, but more directly on my Mideastern concerns. Despite sharing many sensibilities with Fanon, Said nevertheless subverts the notion of ethnic identity – a notion whose problematic was at the centre of Fanon's work. In his *Orientalism* (1978), Said analyses the West's attitude to the East, starting from the ancient Greeks until the present, including the West's willingness to condone the denial by Israel of Palestinian human rights in the Occupied Territories. Said presents this history as the gradually consolidating construal by Western culture of the oriental and Muslim as the threatening Other. The alterity of the Orient stops short of being absolute, perhaps, but it still defines an Other whose existence casts a threat on Western culture. Said shows how this construal failed to generate coherent concepts for the understanding of what it is to be Eastern or oriental, but was extremely successful in promoting the oppression of the Arab peoples in the Middle East and their exploitation by the West. In *Orientalism*, Said fatefully anticipates the rise of the anti-Islamic strain in the post 9/11 Western world. In his book on Freud (2003), Said analyses Freud's late monograph, *Moses and Monotheism* (1939). Here Said completes his lifelong construal of ethnic identity as an instrument of discipline rather than a means for transcending individuality. In his essay, Said applies this idea in order to understand the role of Jewishness in the establishment of a modern European identity. Said argues that Freud's conception of a Jewish identity – as expressed in *Moses and Monotheism* – is an example of the fundamental interdependence between subject and Other, inasmuch as it inserts Egyptian monotheism into the heart of

Judaism. Thus, Freud regarded it as essential to Jewish monotheism that the person who inaugurated it – Moses – was an Egyptian who created Judaism as a new version of an Akhnaten-type of monotheism. As such, the otherness of Akhnaten/Moses is situated at the heart of Jewishness. Said extends a similar logic to the emergence of European identity in the twentieth century when, this time, it was the Jew who functioned as an Other for the European. Said construed Freud himself by analogy to Freud's Moses, as the Jew who alerted Europe to its emerging identity. By playing this logic again, Said too, in his turn, could be seen in the role of the formative, oriental Other who acts at the generative heart of an even wider, Western identity (as it pits itself against the 'Islamic', oriental identity).

Another key figure in the project of the subversion of notions of group identity in general, and of ethnicity in particular, is Homi Bhabha (1994), who sees himself as a successor of Fanon and Said, but holds a psychologically more radical view, whose core notion is that of the negation of the subject as a self, the negation of the internal unity of identity on both the individual and the group levels. Bhaba's point of departure is rooted in a consistent a-ontological tradition which does not conceive of the subject as an existing entity, as Heidegger or Sartre would have it. The subject, instead, is the sum of choices which do not, in principle, constrain each other in terms of the cultural context from which they derive, even if they are semiotically interrelated, that is, even if their thematic connection can be traced. Referring to a diversity of texts – including biographical testimony, literary works, poetry and theoretical writings – Bhabha argues for the *hybrid* character of the subject of oppression and describes the manner in which different elements of other identities, and especially those related to the oppressor's culture, take their part in the oppressed person's self-consciousness. The (occupied) subject can, at any given moment in time, determine his position with reference to another cultural source. While this is, as Fanon argued, exactly what represents the occupied person's condition of being oppressed, it equally and simultaneously represents the possible sources of change. Thus, it is the hybrid nature of the identity of the oppressed that acts as a leverage for their liberation. Motives of oppression may not, on their own, best act as the ground for the development of a new, free culture. In fact, change cannot base itself on absolute negation (the absolute negation of the oppressor's culture), because it is exactly such absolute negation that is wholly hostage to the forms it comes to reject. The very absoluteness of the negation already produces its own lack of meaning, being a form emptied of substance, because here substance is the exclusive product of what has been negated. Negation must be partial if it is to avoid being voided by the very act of negation.

This idea is taken up by another scholar, Gayatri Spivak, a colleague of Said's at Columbia University and a major advocate of the deconstructive agenda in the English speaking community. Spivak (1999) agrees with the notion of the death of the subject and of the absence of a personal essence (or self) constitutive of either the individual's or the group's identity, but she underlines the action-political context of her theory. Here, the individual's hybrid action is meaningless. Instead, there is a need for group action on the one hand and for activist consistency on the other hand, needs that are still best served by identity-like definitions. In fact, action is not possible without the umbrella assumption of an ideological group identity. Methodologically speaking, then, we must act from within a 'feminist' or an 'anti-colonial' agenda, or with reference to any other socio-political identity mark. In doing so, we make informed and supportive use of the degrees of freedom between theory and practice. This can be captured under the statement, 'Think freely and act with commitment', with 'free' referring mainly to freedom from categories of group identity and 'commitment' relating to the ability to make a sustained effort. Spivak's work highlights the significant changes in post-colonial theory's definition of the subject that have occurred since Fanon. While Fanon talked about distinct and marked ethnic groups, dominated and oppressed by a ruling Western group – usually a state – Spivak is concerned with many different groups which live in different conditions of exploitation that impair their ability to exercise a full subjectivity (or an optimal one, in the relevant historical conditions). In order to conceptualize the status of a group which is being exploited in terms of its being-a-subject, Spivak adopted a notion from Gramsci, the historical leader of the Italian communists before and after World War II, the *subaltern*. This concept comes exactly to reflect that post-colonial theory aims to conceptualize the subject injury of *any* group – the *subalterns* – and not just that of the victims of classical colonial oppression.

Finally, in my short review of post-colonial thinkers, I want to consider Judith Butler, despite the fact that she is usually considered a theorist of gender or queer studies. Yet, even her earlier work may be grasped as post-colonial inasmuch as it concerned itself with the subversion of group identity. Thus, her work may be seen as devoted to the idea that any approach that assumes gender identities, no matter what position it takes within the field of identities, falls into the error of objectification on one hand, and the reproduction of gendered power relations on the other (Butler, 1990). Definitions and categories as such operate within the dynamics of power. Butler comes to question the fixed nature and rigidity of gender categories on the one hand, and the resulting identities, on the other. In the course of her work Butler, like Spivak, concluded that oppressive relations act in similar ways over a wide spectrum of group relations, creating different kinds of domination ('subalternity' in Spivak's terminology). Especially, one needs to be weary of naïve use of identity concepts on either side of the domination equations because these tend to enact and preserve the whole range of identity categories within their semantic extensions. By using identity categories, one may find oneself trapped in the ideas they come to unsettle. Butler (2004) turned her attention to a range of oppressive relations – both at an advanced level of abstraction (in her work on the relations between body and mind, for instance) and through very concrete forms of expression (with reference, for example, to the Israeli occupation of Palestinian territories). The lesson I learned from Butler concerns the paradoxical locus of the body in relation to subjectivity and the constitution of the body as a social site. On the one hand, various categories which were traditionally grounded in the body, like for instance gender, are not fundamentally corporeal but rather social. Culture here utilizes the body by way of promoting and preserving agendas that are essentially social. On the other hand, our emotional attachment to the other, which tends to be considered as an abstract category of psyche or spirit, is actually tethered to the body in an irremovable way, whether this is through bodily contact with the other or through our dependency during infancy, old age, or illness. In this sense, Butler offers the most radical conceptualization of the body as subject, as the site of subjectivity, because in her work the body features as predominantly the medium of being-a-subject, of social connectedness. Approaching the body as thing-ness, as deterministic physicality, turns it into an object for the imposition of other's will, the Other's will, and thus puts the body in a state of oppression. This approach produces the mind-body relation as a colonial relation. Butler's work, from this point of view, I would say, deals with the formation of the body as a subject-site, or in other words, with the liberation of the body from subjugating categorizations. Through this prism, Butler has also examined more usual sites of colonial oppression, among them, between Jews and Palestinians in the Middle East.

From what has been said so far in this chapter, it should be clear that the notions of subject, injury, and identity form the pillars on which the interface between therapeutic theory and post-colonial theory rests. However, I believe these are not the only relevant concepts. I already wrote in the Introduction about the concept of *resistance* in its two-fold reference to therapy and politics. In this current chapter, I expand on this idea, in addition to the notions of trauma and memory, because they seem pivotal to my ethical agenda. Also, I consider some more tangential concepts which allow further cross-fertilization between therapeutic theory and post-colonial thinking.

Jessica Benjamin

Psychoanalytic theory has considered a plethora of social issues ever since Freud's articles about how social and cultural situations can be understood in terms of unconscious processes. One of the most systematic undertakings of this type was by the Frankfurt School, where sociologists (Adorno, Horkheimer), philosophers (Marcuse) and psychoanalysts (Fromm) joined in the effort to approach social and cultural processes from a psychoanalytic perspective. Most prominently and famously, members of the School investigated the socio-psycho-political dynamics that allowed the rise and protracted activity of the Nazis and the question of how an open society can protect itself by gaining better insight into the interrelations between the social, the political and the psychological. In the project of extending the analytic perspective to social processes, the work of Jessica Benjamin is singular thanks to the persistent and comprehensive theoretical effort she has made to advance our understanding of therapy as a process of negotiating the subjectivities of patient and therapist, alongside the understanding of colonial oppression in terms of therapeutic processes. From the very outset of her theoretical work, Benjamin apprehended clinical psychoanalysis as an investigation of a particular social arena, in which the subjecthood of the individual is always in interaction and mutually formative relations with the subjecthood of other individuals, both in daily life and in the transference. Indeed, following the conclusion of her undergraduate studies in intellectual history, Benjamin studied social theory in Frankfurt, where she also began to work with psychoanalysis in the field of social pedagogy. While her theoretical writings initially dealt mainly with the interaction between psychoanalytic theories of development and gender domination (Benjamin, 1988), in recent years she has written extensively on the relations of doer and done-to that arise in the analytic process, while she has also been exploring the clinical process of negotiating inter-subjective power relations. These dynamisms operate on both individual and group levels (Benjamin, 2009a, 2009b). In this chapter, I present the gist of Benjamin's thinking on this issue.

The individual's basic injury, according to Benjamin, originates in the dyadic setting but it is not the result of intentional practices of any of the subjects in this setting: rather, it follows from the fundamental configuration of the relationship between them, from its asymmetric nature, its 'split complementarity', as Benjamin (2004) calls it, a split which always appears on the active-passive axis; the axis of the one who does and the one who is done-to, the perpetrator and the victim. This basic pattern of splitting is what – under the diverse social conditions that allow it to emerge – generates the full panoply of subaltern injuries, stretching from gender-related injuries to those associated with class, with colonial oppression, or with therapy. Progress, much as it is also the point of therapy, originates in the ability to transcend the logic of splitting and establish in its place a logic of symmetry, where the two participants – individuals or groups – act on the same plane of subject-hood and are able to recognize each other's subjectivity. This symmetri-sation, in and of itself, can lead to coordinated actions and enactments that allow the otherness of the other, not just because otherness cannot be avoided, under duress, as it were, but in mutual acknowledgement and with an awareness of the beneficial potential of such acknowledge-ment. What seriously undermines symmetrisation in a split reality is what causes me to relate to the *logic* – and not just to the praxis – of split relations. When two subjects have been in a split situation for a period of time, a more abstract plane comes into being which moulds any perception of each subject's action into the same conceptual frame, the frame of split complementarity. Whatever is said or done is experi-enced in keeping with the basic split, regardless, at times, of the concrete or intended nature of the words or action in question. Once the frame is established, it becomes difficult to communicate messages that are outside of the split logic, no matter how eagerly both sides would like to achieve exactly that. The split setting incorporates all acts into its meaning system by ignoring either the intentions or the concrete char-acter of the actions of the other side. Moreover, the meaning system is mediated by an identity, that is, a set of images whose maintenance protects the subject from guilt as well as the threat of annihilation. The more extreme the split, the heavier is the weight of threat from the other and the need to circumscribe him in his identity domain. Each action – no matter what its objective or its reality – only deepens the split even further. In such a situation, what can be done other than to keep apart (which is not always possible)?

In Benjamin's approach, the road forward involves the introduction of a third position into the dyadic setting. Without defining its concrete features, Benjamin calls this position 'the third'. Most notably, the third does not need to have a body of its own in order to operate and/or express itself. The third emerges as a result of each of the subjects' turning toward the other in the dyadic setting. If each succeeds in creating a place within himself that is designated as the place of the other (or, even more so, the other's otherness), a place in which the other's otherness is represented without constituting a threat to the subject, then these othernesses may evolve a dynamics of their own. More specifically, the newly created internal othernesses of each subject can make direct contact with the internal otherness of the other, a contact that constitutes a different logic, the logic of alterity. The third, hence, is the unity that arises between two dynamisms of otherness that evolve between two subjects when they truly turn toward each other. 'Truly' here designates primarily a tolerance to otherness.

That the third requires a directedness toward the other does not imply that it is some elevated intellectual product which can only develop among subjects with an especially cultivated self-consciousness. Benjamin (2009b) stresses that other-directedness is an utterly basic function, which comes into existence soon after birth and manifests itself initially in the matching of sensory-motor rhythms between infant and mother. For adult people, however, there is added importance – therapeutic as well as post-colonial – to the conscious recognition a subject gives the otherness of the other, a recognition that allows the internal place of the other, and along with it that of the third, to develop. This form, which comes about through recognition and awareness, Benjamin calls the 'moral third'. For adult people, the third constitutes the principal egress from the dynamics of split complementarity.

The inner representation of the other or of otherness is the closest Benjamin comes to defining the unconscious, which is exactly the sense in which her approach is inter-subjective. In this, her ideas resemble the Lacanian unconscious – which is defined as the discourse of the other – but in Benjamin's case, the unconscious is the product of an activity whose aim is exactly this, creating a space for the other and his otherness. It is worth taking note of the point at which Lacan and Benjamin diverge. For both the unconscious emerges as the by-product of an intentional activity – but the activity is different for each of them. For Lacan it is speech as such, whereas for Benjamin it is the recognition of the other in his otherness. While for Lacan the unconscious emerges as a result of the logical gap between the content of speech and its conditions of existence, for Benjamin it comes about in the subject's directedness toward the other. Benjamin's unconscious is the inner space that the subject has reserved for another person, for something that the subject is ready not to understand, but without rejecting it as such, without rejecting his own bafflement, in that respect. Benjamin, hence, and as opposed to Lacan, refrains from calling the internal other 'unconscious', not so much because she thinks it is, indeed, conscious, but in order to avoid the reification of that which is not conscious.

If, nevertheless (and unlike Benjamin), one does relate to the internal other as of an unconscious essence, then the third may be conceived as the product of mutual projective identifications. In each of the subjects, an inner otherness comes into being with which each respective subject identifies, or perhaps better, an inner domain of identification appears from which the subject differs. The emerging dynamic between these two produces a third entity, a third form of intentionality, which is essentially unlike the modes of intentionality (both conscious and unconscious) of each of the subjects. This, indeed, is how Ogden (2004) defines the third. Benjamin differs from Ogden in a manner that resembles her difference from Lacan, namely in her refusal to engage in an analytic discussion in the reified terms of unconscious mechanics. Wherever there is an other, there is a subject, and the other way around. Wherever there is a subject, there is an other – and this is what makes the third possible. Possible, but in its moral form, not necessary. What happens, moreover, between two sides that are trapped in ongoing hostile relations is exactly that a moral third cannot evolve between them. The fact that the moral third is absent from the relations between one subject and another does not, obviously, mean that it cannot come into existence between that subject and yet another person. The absence of thirdness in one dialogic context does not imply the inability to create thirdness. This is the ground from which reparation can be made.

Though the third is not necessarily an external entity, separate from the two subjects who constitute the core setting, in extreme cases a concrete third may be inevitable. In a sense, the need for the third forms the very foundation of dynamic psychotherapy. The main sphere of injury is always located between the patient and a significant other in his life, but the therapist represents, from the outset, the possibility of joint (moral) otherness. This is something that therapy can enact, to begin with in the realm of the past, and later in the realm of the transference. But the need for an external third becomes especially palpable in the group dynamics of colonial oppression, where mutual destructiveness prevents the organic emergence of a moral third. Nevertheless, here too, there are many examples of the emergence of a third as a result of the inner dynamic of the two entities that are struggling over subject positions (Chapter 9 of this book offers a number of such examples). Where there is an external third, it is relatively easy to understand how the split dynamic is transcended – even where it may be hard to achieve in practice. Here, the third acts as a negotiator, mediator, arbitrator or other legal decision maker and we are all familiar with how these instances operate. Yet, even where the external intervention of the third is successful, and assuming that the subjects continue to be engaged in dyadic functions, an internal dynamic must develop so as to allow continued interaction that will not regress to splitting. This is true for both the individual case (psychotherapy) and the collective case (conflict resolution).

I wish to illustrate the issues of splitting by means of an episode which Benjamin (2008) presented in a lecture she gave in Vienna, commemorating Freud's 150th birthday. This episode describes something that happened during a supervision master-class, so to speak; supervision in front of a professional audience. As such, the event that evolved was on both the personal and the group levels and therefore demonstrates processes that are particularly pertinent to deep reconciliation of the kind that took place in the Acknowledgement project (see Chapter 9). The supervision class took place a few years earlier in Germany and aimed to demonstrate the inter-subjective analysis of, presumably, a fairly regular analytic episode. On the eve of the event, the supervisee – a candidate psychoanalyst in training – brought Benjamin a transcript of the two sessions on which the supervision was due to focus. In these sessions, the patient – a young man aged about thirty – recounted two extremely violent dreams. In the first, his family killed someone they loathed, but for unknown reasons, while in the second, he himself cruelly killed some small animals, after which he tried to hide the blood that was left at the site. During the supervision, Benjamin asked about the associations the patient had come up with after telling the dreams, a rather routine move but, surprisingly, the therapist could not offer any material – neither by way of associations, nor as background themes or in terms of articulating her own feelings in the sessions or thereafter. Puzzled by this neglect, which was out of keeping with the supervisee's professional experience, Benjamin felt a rising panic about possibly causing the supervisee embarrassment. When she raised the possibility that the dream involved guilt related to the Nazi past, the therapist was sceptical in view of the patient's young age, but when Benjamin asked about others in his family, the supervisee revealed that the patient's father had served in the Nazi Stormtroopers (SA). This service had been the occasion of the father's deep crisis after the end of the war – a crisis that included a short spell of hospitalization. Moreover, it turned out that the patient's uncle was executed by the Nazis because he suffered from mental illness. All this information, the therapist conveyed without particular emotion and making no connection with the dreams that featured so centrally in the supervision. This caused Benjamin to fear even worse, sensing that powerful defences on the part of the supervisee, related to the Nazi past, were making impossible any joint work on the episode. In an attempt to somehow address this, Benjamin commented that, possibly, analysis brought out the powerful guilt feelings the patient felt about his father's Nazi past. Yet, this tentative, general comment did not unblock the supervision, but rather involved the entire audience in the denial of allusion to Nazi past. A disconcerted silence set in, slowly giving way to audience discussion that moved completely away from the specific themes of the case and focused on theory instead. Throughout, Benjamin continued to feel intense, if manageable, anxiety. Hours later, in a different setting, in the course of a designated discussion about Jews and Nazis, Benjamin became aware of the total split in which she had found herself during the supervision, the split between Nazis and Jews, between victimizer and victim. Her position as a supervisor had, against the background of the Nazi past, been completely erased and become that of a Jewish woman's *j'accuse* towards her hosts. It was clear as well, though, that the team that prepared the supervision had helped this situation to come about by choosing the specific case for presentation. In the ensuing supervisory event, a situation developed in which each side shifted between the poles of victimization and victimhood. Sadly, it was only hours later that Benjamin acquired an understanding of the episode which could be used to develop the position of the third in the actual situation of the supervision. In its absence, the supervision went deeper and deeper into split complementarity.

Trauma and memory, Shoah and Nakba

If psychoanalytic *personality theory* classically constitutes itself on the basis of concepts of sexuality and the unconscious, then the psychoanalytic *clinic* emerges from the concepts of trauma and memory. As I argued in Chapters 1 and 5, Freud believed, in his early work (Breuer & Freud, 1895/1955), that trauma was the origin of all neuroses, of all psychic disturbance other than absolute madness. The concept of trauma is narrower than that of injury. Not every injury results in trauma in the sense of the word Freud had in mind, or in that which mental health workers use. Trauma refers to a particularly grave event during which the subject experiences as real the possibility of dying. In its intentional form – which is crucial to my construal – the possibility of dying has a subject of its own, it forms a threat. The fear of death is an experience that is extremely difficult to digest, and this experience maintains its vivacity (sic!) for a long time to come. Sometimes, indeed, and unlike other forms of injury, it persists over years. In the case of more regular injury, one may say that time heals, even if, as we have seen, scars remain. Trauma, however, often neutralizes the effects of time. It does not subside, it is not subject to entropy.

Another difference between trauma and injury is that the former is not necessarily the result of interpersonal harassment. Trauma may follow a situation which involves no personal factor at all, say, an avalanche. Someone who got caught up in an avalanche may develop a traumatic response even though there is no 'injury' here, because the terror in question was not produced through an intentional assault. Still, and quite overarchingly, most trauma is actually occasioned by someone's concerted action against the victim. It is as though the fear of death as such is not so devastating for mental life as the intended destruction of subjectivity. I think that this emerges quite straightforwardly from the present ethical thinking, in which the subject is constituted by the Other. Nothing is more harmful to subjectivity than the determination to assault it. This logic suggests the possibility that trauma arises from a paranoid groundwork. The damage results from the experience that someone – someone who may even be crucial to our being-a-subject – could have wished so blatantly to hurt us, to the point of threatening us with violence or even death.

In the classical Freudian approach, trauma is traumatic because it cuts the continuity of time: the self before it is not the same as the self after it. The obliteration of the temporal continuity of the self positions the experience of trauma outside of time. It can appear at any moment in which it is triggered and it can appear with the same intensity, the same vividness. In cases of trauma, this is why the therapeutic strategy is often to reinstate the temporality of the traumatic event, to reattach it to time's coordinates, to embed it in a more densely reconstructed memory line. For this purpose, the patient must produce a detailed biographical narrative which reconstructs – both concretely and symbolically – the traumatic experience. This is conventionally done through speech, but other media – say, art – can also enable reproductions that are sufficiently rich to rehabilitate the continuity of self, of being-a-subject. The cognitive capacity that makes this rehabilitation possible is, of course, memory. It is through detailed recollection that the patient produces a biographical narrative, on the one hand, and forges links between the trauma and the rest of his mental life on the other. The biographical story emanates from the overt part of the memory, whilst the covert part makes the connections between the traumatic event and other memories. This alone may suffice to extricate the traumatic experience from its imperious isolation and to neutralize its destructiveness. Hence, the psychoanalytic treatment of trauma goes via recollection (Laplanche, 1992).

What is striking about trauma is that in those cases that involve a determined assault, it is not just the victim who experiences trauma but also the victimizer. On the part of the victimizer, as well, the assault may detach itself from the rest of psychic life (a process that produces the experience of trauma) and may repeat itself in an imaginary way (the phenomenon of post-trauma). Especially famous are the responses of US soldiers who participated in the military action in the Vietnamese village of My Lai in 1968. There they killed unarmed inhabitants, including women, old people and children. Twenty years later, the soldiers still suffered from repeats of the images of the massacre, at an intensity and with a clarity that had diminished very little over the years. Some of these ex-soldiers spent the rest of their lives wandering, day and night, in their hometowns, sweating and trembling. They never returned to a reasonably functional life (Hagopian, 2009).

Though its origins are controversial, the trauma of the victimizer, many researchers believe, is related to identification with the victim. The victimizer imagines himself in the place of the victim and experiences in his imagination the latter's suffering and terror of annihilation (Grand, 2009). As is the case with trauma generally, not all victimizers experience trauma and its occurrence seems related to factors of conscience, that is, to cognitive factors. However this may be, clearly, the emotional relations between victims and victimizers are complex and the resulting identifications go in both directions – the victims identify with their victimizers and the other way around. Offenses that lead to traumatization underline the mutual dependency between subject and other, as each side displays signs of identification with the other side. Maybe this is the most dramatic example of the master-slave dialectic as Hegel first conceptualized it and which has since been developed – by both philosophers and psychoanalysts – as the most general conceptual frame through which we may consider the reciprocities between subject and other.

A very similar way of thinking also serves us in reflecting on collective trauma. Here too, there is a formative traumatic event which involves the loss of life, usually on a large scale. And here too, trauma is especially grave when the loss of life was caused by an agent who intended to have this effect. Usually the traumatic event is not only about the loss of life but also brings about massive displacement and homelessness. In this context, as in others, the home represents the spatial anchoring of subjectivity. If the body represents the private and autonomous subject, we may say that the home represents that subject as a cultural entity and, more specifically, as a family member. As with the individual case, on the group and social levels too, trauma isolates the traumatic episode within the continuity of history. It disrupts the narrative order with which the collective identifies itself and introduces a cut in historical time. This alters the collective's fate. As such, in spite of the destruction involved, the collective trauma always also institutes the new history of the group. Much like in the case of the individual, here too, there is a need for practices of recollection in order to link between the narratives that preceded the traumatic event and those that follow it. We see all these factors in action whenever there is collective trauma. Thus, for example, in the Holocaust we can identify all of the previously mentioned features, and that any Jewish sense of continuity was so deeply disrupted that historical narratives required a total retelling in order to rehabilitate Jewish history writing. The rehabilitation of the subject of the Jewish collective became inextricably tied up with the recollection, inscription and creation of symbolic representations (of the Holocaust and what came before it).

Not only does recollection allow the rehabilitation of the subject's identity – it also helps to prevent repetition of the trauma. Here I restate the basic principle of analytic psychotherapy which I dealt with at length in Chapters 1 through 3. The trauma is bound to be reproduced by various means and symbolic reproduction, by virtue of its structural richness, is more facilitative of mental function than concrete reproduction. The victim who does not remember with adequate resolution is bound to repeat in a more limiting and damaging fashion. It seems to me this lesson was understood by those in Israel and in Zionist circles elsewhere in the world who took it upon themselves to maintain and develop a Holocaust-related discourse. Yet, in this case, the machinery of recollection and restructuring was tied up with ideological and political interests in a way that limited their rehabilitative value. Especially, the rejection of the victim-position, which constitutes a considerable portion of the Holocaust rhetoric in Israeli and Zionist circles, is constrained by the need to justify various political and military acts by reference to Holocaust victimhood. This has brought the symbolic construction of Holocaust narratives in Israeli and Zionist culture to a total deadlock between upholding the victim position and breaking free from it.

In a rather critical sense, collective trauma differs from its individual counterpart. While the latter arises only in those who have direct experience of the traumatic event, the former occurs also – and perhaps even predominantly – to those who have not experienced it at first hand. I would like to stress this: trauma does not become collective trauma if it is only registered by those who have had direct experience of the event. This only happens where it also registers among those who have no such immediate experience; indeed, with time, most of the carriers of the trauma are secondary experiencers. Collective trauma, therefore, has no overt signs which manifest themselves as post-traumatic symptoms. Those who share the trauma are not likely to wake up at night in a cold sweat, yelling, 'No, no, no!' Collective trauma's main effect is on the manner in which those who participate in it understand reality. It operates as a point of view and a way of seeing events, it functions like a filter through which those who share it perceive reality on the macro-level. Or, to use Lacanian terminology, collective trauma is a formative principle of the Symbolic order. But from the fact that it operates in the Symbolic order, it must not be concluded that collective trauma is all conscious and transparent. On the contrary, its conscious parts only mask the parts that are unconscious and this is done by means of a steady and irremovable slanting of the grasp on reality. If the traumatized collective's understanding of reality is not distorted, then the 'trauma' is not a trauma.

It is fascinating that the traumatized sense of reality always undergoes the same type of distortion and amazing that blindness can be so stubborn, so persistent. The traumatized view of reality always produces an imaginary threat that is attributed to some other collective and it does so always in a disproportionate manner. The other collective will never be perceived by third parties as being so dangerous as it is by the traumatized party. In order to maintain its bias, the traumatized perception of the Other ignores all evidence to the effect that the threat is not as big as it seems, not so total and includes diverse nuances, cracks even, which significantly diminish the Other's threatening potential. To maintain its traumatized understanding, the collective evolves a paranoid-schizoid world view in which the wall that separates between the traumatized identity group and the imaginary-threat group is impermeable and total. Yet, we should not forget that, because of its collective nature, trauma here acts as a statistical tendency and individuals always have the ability to exit the traumatic perception of reality.

It is clear from the preceding that in collective trauma, memory heals and preserves the trauma both at the same time. It allows, on the one hand, the enrichment of the narrative textures around the traumatic period – both before and after it – and, through this, it restores the thematic continuity of group identity. It also, on the other hand, recycles the trauma itself inasmuch as it repeatedly structures the historical narrative as traumatic. Here memory always marks itself as 'traumatic', even where, in and of itself, it invokes no sense of threat for the individual. While memory allows the rehabilitation of the collective identity of the group of people that underwent the trauma, this rehabilitation has the effect of inscribing the trauma inside its own well-being. This inscription takes the form of a slanted reality perception on the historical level. It is not that the traumatic event loses its objectivity – on the contrary, the collective nature of the event's construction settles it more firmly within external coordinates. However, the trauma's continuity depends more critically on the memory-negotiated-structuring of the event. There is no other modality in which the collective trauma can be processed, the way it can be in the individual case. At the same time, the individual's ability to construct herself qua subject in conditions of collective trauma, to experience the trauma as belonging or relevant to her, depends crucially on her ability to identify with the collective, to experience herself as belonging to it, and to perceive social reality as one that prescribes a commonality of fate between her and others.

Of course, the Holocaust illustrates all of the previous factors, but it presents a complex picture because it occupies a point at which various collectives experience trauma. First, the Holocaust is traumatic for the Jewish people, for those, that is, who identify with the collective that underwent the Holocaust. The acts of symbolic construction that allow Jews from extremely diverse cultures to experience the Holocaust as theirs are extensive. Some of them were not aware of the Holocaust when it occurred and only learned about it in recent decades; what brought it to their consciousness is also what altered their own history and redefined their identity. In addition, the Holocaust is also the Germans' collective trauma, as Jessica Benjamin's story in the previous section illustrates powerfully. That story also shows the main workings of collective trauma, that is, the way it creates zones of blindness regarding the distressed Other which, in this case, is the national identity group of those who were present in the traumatic encounter (the Germans). Furthermore, the Holocaust constitutes the trauma of Christian Europe, for though the Germans were the main agents and executioners of violent anti-Semitism, Christian Europe as a collective was, to a certain extent, a historical partner in this (though not in quite the same way, of course). Then there is also the trauma of other groups who were involved in the Holocaust, like the Roma (gypsies), gay and lesbian men and women, mentally ill people, and others. The exclusive appropriation of the Holocaust – or Shoah – by some dominant groups in the Jewish people is the result of a basic blindness to the disaster that also struck other communities in Europe. From the present point of view, the significant impact of this blindness lies not in diverging from the historical truth, but in putting a Holocaust-marked reality perception at the base of paranoid constructions. The formation of Israeli Jewish collective identity by reference to the trauma of the Holocaust has, from the start, been associated with statements such as 'the whole world is against us' or, less of a slogan, with the conviction that those who criticize Israel are its anti-semitic enemies. Israeli national rhetoric, with its deep Holocaust awareness, is unable literally to see the critic who has the country's good at heart.

Unfortunately, the Holocaust is closely bound up with another form of blindness, whose long-term consequences have been tragic. Talila Kosh (2009) describes how the Jewish Holocaust survivors who immigrated to Palestine were confronted with the local Jews' lack of empathy. The ability to maintain the combative identity of the new Jew in Eretz Israel ('greater Israel') depended on a lack of compassion with victims of any kind – even if they were fellow Jews. What the survivors met, rather than compassion, were ideological structures and constructions that were painful to the point of cruel, 'Like lambs to the slaughter' was often the way Israeli Jews described the non-resistance of European Jews. Israeli Jews often refused to listen to the stories of Holocaust survivors or treated them impatiently, as stories of a submissiveness typical of Diaspora Jewry. As a native Israeli, I have very powerful childhood memories of our refusal to hear or listen to the stories of the Holocaust survivors (Hadar, 2009). I suppose this memory left such an impression on me because of the clash between our impatience with their stories and the sense of almost religious awe with which the survivors were, nevertheless, surrounded. In my understanding, this lack of compassion, occurring as it did in an ideological context of Holocaust victimhood, became associated with an identification with the aggressor. In the paranoid post-war world view, where Germans or Jews are the prime protagonists, the determination to be strong – to be able to resist – led to identifications with German prowess. Israeli rhetoric, then as now, became cluttered with traces of this identification.

The previous interpellation (Althusser, 1984; Dimen, 2011) of the ideology of confrontational strength intensified dramatically in the 1948 war, when Israel was established. During this war, thousands of Palestinians were driven away from their homes, either by direct force or as they were escaping in fear of the war. The Nakba – 'catas-trophe' in Arabic – emerged as a collective Palestinian trauma. For Israelis, the Nakba became the trauma of the Other, the Other trauma. Other, that is, to the Shoah. The dialectic of Shoah and Nakba was such, that the blindness to the Palestinian travail of this period thick-ened the collective Jewish trauma as well, but in a totally dissociated fashion. This dissociation deepened by the positive framing of the war period as the liberation of the Jews from their historical victim posi-tion, so terribly taken to its extreme in the Shoah (Hadar, 2009). The result was a massive denial of both the Palestinian catastrophe and the Israeli identifications with the (German) aggressor. This reinforced the cultural entrenchment of the Holocaust as a justification of aggres-sion towards Palestinians.

In contemporary Israel, the Holocaust is embedded in complex and prodigious memorial formations – something which, on the face of it, should have facilitated the processing of the trauma and the dimin-ishing of paranoid perceptions among Israeli Jews. Indeed, within some Jewish circles, it led to a gradual shift away from the combative slogans that characterized the post-war era ('Never again like lambs to the slaughter', for example) towards a more compassionate tone towards the survivors. But memory formations had the contradictory results that are characteristic of collective trauma: memory, to a large extent, exactly *is* trauma. No shift from paranoid structurings to compassion could become central to Israeli culture without conscious actions that balance the identifications with the aggressor, on one hand, and the denial of the victim trauma of the Palestinians (the Nakba), on the other. These two interpellative dynamics, which directly reinforce one another due to the historical adjacency of Holocaust and Nakba (and their respective roles in the construction of the new Israeli identity), create other blindnesses to the traumas of other groups. These blind-nesses lead to the isolation of the Jewish-Israeli ethos, which in turn may bring about another collective catastrophe. In the interpellative economics installed between the various catastrophes and identifications of the Holocaust and the Nakba, it seems to me that it is only through a comprehensive recognition of the Palestinian Nakba that the paranoid intensities dominating the Jewish-Israeli ethos can be modified so as to avoid the next disaster.

7
Occupation and Analytic Psychotherapy

Resistance

The notion of resistance defines practices which, on the face of it, polarize between psychoanalytic and post-colonial approaches to the rehabilitation of subject positioning. This is so even though both examine the relevant issues from a similar perspective, namely, that of being-a-subject. While in psychoanalysis, of course, being-a-subject relates to the individual, post-colonial theory addresses the subject qua group. But while post-colonial practices are directed at the oppressor and the state of oppression, psychoanalytic practices are directed at repression, namely, the mental processes that ensure that certain ideas – memories, fantasies and so on – are kept out of the patient's consciousness. This difference between manifest action (resistance to occupation) and wholly internal dynamics (overcoming repression) would seem to erase the possibility that the notion of resistance refers to similar processes (the rehabilitation of being a subject). Freud, however, already spoke about resistance not only as an internal state but also – and perhaps even mainly – as actions aimed at the therapist and the therapeutic process in so far as they function as the stage on which the relations between consciousness and unconsciousness are played out. For instance, in the radical approach to interpretation that Freud proposed as part of the topographical model, it is only the resistance that the therapist interprets. In this approach, the unconscious material does not take a passive role vis a vis the subject, but is in constant activity, in an attempt to connect with reality. The unconscious, one might say, rumbles and bubbles, and the reason it does not reach consciousness is the same as the one due to which the material becomes unconscious to begin with, namely, its offense to the self's imaginary unity. In this Freudian approach, what the therapist needs to do for analysis to move ahead is to interpret the resistance and thus help remove everything that gets in the way of the unconscious material's rise to consciousness. In Freud's own words (1914, p. 147):

> Finally, there has evolved the consistent technique used today, in which the analyst gives up the attempt to bring a particular moment or problem into focus. He contents himself with studying whatever is for the time being on the surface of the patient's mind, and he employs the art of interpretation mainly for the purpose of recognizing the resistances which appear there, and making them conscious to the patient. From this there results a new sort of division of labour: the doctor uncovers the resistances which are unknown to the patient; when these have been got the better of, the patient often relates the forgotten situations and connections without any difficulty. The aim of these different techniques has, of course, remained the same. Descriptively speaking, it is to fill in gaps in memory; dynamically speaking, it is to overcome resistances due to repression.

This interventive minimalism is very elegant and, more crucial in the present context, it presents an approach in which resistance is the therapist's main accomplice. Resistance is what the therapist is after, and without it therapy is impossible. This is why Freud believed psychotics cannot be treated by means of this method. The psychotic collapse of self results in an absence of resistance, and when this is the case the therapist's main accomplice is missing.

Where it came to the transference, Michal could have been Merav's (p. 58) mirror-sister. Both were therapists themselves, for both their professional interest was part of the therapeutic process and both undertook impressive steps to change their lives in the course of analysis and were influenced by their analysis, but while Merav developed a positive transference that deepened as the therapy went on, Michal developed a negative transference, and any attempt to change it, even just to achieve a degree of comfortableness during our sessions, crashed spectacularly. What evolved was a tense discourse which very frequently brought up serious complaints about a lack of empathy on my behalf, and with occasional real insult. Though this was not the only thing going on between us – on another level, Michal rather put me on a pedestal – it painted our communications in the sombre colours of negativity.

When she started her therapy, Michal was in the early stages of her specialization as a clinical psychologist. At the conclusion, she also ended her specialization which, I think, went well for her, even if not always smoothly. On the whole, she was liked and professionally appreciated. Michal captivated me, during our initial meetings, with her combination of lightness and seriousness, her self-absorption and her attentiveness to me. My first reaction, when she asked how I was as she sat down in the patients' chair, was that she really wanted to know. I was pleased that she had come and I thought it would be nice to work with her, so I was quite astonished when I understood, sometime between our fifth and sixth meeting, that it was going to be difficult. She insisted to discuss anything that came up from the point of view of her rows with her partner. She said that that's why she was here, to help her shift her friend out of his stuckness, his inability to commit to anything. Not a more or less planned schedule for the week, no living together, let alone even the slightest mention of marriage – at least not if she does not want to risk him disappearing without trace for a few days. And when he would vanish like this, he also had an annoying way of turning off his mobile phone – no message would be possible, there was no way of reaching him. She could be in an accident and he would not know. On the micro level, on the level of just being together, he was the best. He had great considerateness for her, the way in which he touched her, the huge satisfaction he felt when she liked the food he prepared – all this caused Michal to feel extraordinarily attached to him. What was she going to do about this big gap in him between presence and absence, what could she do about the fact that when he was there he was totally present, which did not prevent him from then disconnecting again, always marking this option for disconnection in direct and indirect ways. At times, when Michal would erupt into one of her rages, his disconnection would be total and take several days. Her frustration was about the impossibility to make the critical decision that would make her feel that they were together, that their relationship would not vanish without a trace. I was amazed at Michal's insistence that what therapy should achieve was to get her boyfriend out of this shifty place and that nothing else was relevant. She just had to help him with this defect which prevented him from moving ahead in their relationship. At the age of 35 – she said – she thought she actually was his last chance of making a family.

As of about ten meetings into the therapy, it became clear to Michal that I was going to repeat with her a certain mode of non-commitment to her agenda. I was interpreting everything as though it was about her, as though she was the problem here. Maybe it was not absolutely total. Here and there I came up with an interesting insight about her friend and this, apparently, justified our continued enterprise, but on the whole, this was my approach. It was with great reluctance on my part that she managed to extract from me the insights about her friend. That's why I was so angry with her, she would say. Because she insisted on the way she thought and on her needs and because she wasn't wild about my original interpretations. Our meetings moved between talk about her arguments with her friend and discussion concerning her resistance, my resistance, she knows I could help her, but I am locked in my therapeutic abstractions, in interpretations which – though they are unusual, in a deeper sense – are always eventually orthodox. When for some reason or another I could unburden myself of the antagonism that marked our meetings, when, for instance, we would not meet for a few sessions, a couple of weeks, I was able to enjoy Michal's perceptiveness. I remembered many things she said about me.

About two years after we started our meetings, Michal moved in with her friend. But he still refused to get married. Sometimes she felt they had become even more stuck, that they were just enacting the possibility of living-together-without-making-commitments, that this way of being which really drove her mad was only getting more and more deeply entrenched, but she understood that she was not going to be able to get anything more out of me, and so it might be a better idea to talk about her own work with patients. I was really at my best, where it came to her patients. It seemed, she said, that the lack of commitment that marked our conversations about her patients – she was receiving quite a lot of supervision other than talking with me – allowed me to be more flexible and even more generous, in terms of my communications. When Michal completed her specialization as a psychotherapist she also stopped her therapy with me. Many thanks, she really made great headway, especially in professional terms, but also because she was having less fights with her friend, though here she was not sure and perhaps she was even more desperately stuck in a relationship that held no future. A woman who had half of what she wanted.

I am not sure to what extent I have managed to convey a picture of a therapy which was entirely marked – from beginning to end, at each moment almost – by the trap of an inexhaustible resistance. I often felt bad in this therapy, I put a great deal of thought in it, sometimes I couldn't quite believe it was really happening. What did Michal gain from being so stubbornly invested in the agenda of changing her friend? From where I am today I would say that she profited by confirming the position she was able to hold in the fullest manner, at the time, and hence constituted her being a subject. In this position, the best relationship in which she was, was also the most frustrating one. If she could be in such a deep and intense relationship without losing her mind, her self, maintaining her sense of subjecthood, then she had a basic existential security. It was, at the same time, perhaps due to her separation anxiety, that a true sense of safety for Michal could only come about from within the sphere of dissatisfaction, of protest, even. This is where she encountered herself in a radical manner, by fate and by choice simultaneously. Her resistance regarding me illustrated this very well. And her leaving the therapy – something about which she did not feel wholly convinced – was an expression of the degree of freedom that resistance gave her. I don't know whether Michal became happier as a result of this therapy. I believe she became less antagonized. But to the extent that she enacted subjecthood in the resistance – to the extent that resistance embodied her subject position – her quitting the therapy seems appropriate, therapeutically speaking. It's not pleasant, considering that I felt she should continue, but that's life.

By stressing the constructive qualities of resistance I am, of course, not trying to say that the negative definition of resistance is lacking in interest. Not at all. Resistance is always defined through the negation of the entity at which it directs itself. Resistance forms itself by way of negation with reference to (the abusing) authority. This negative core means that resistance cannot be total, because it is always defined by its object. Destroy the object, and you have destroyed the resisting subject as well. By avoiding totality, like in analytic practice (and some theories), resistance constitutes, from the outset, the very grounding for therapeutic progress, exactly that progress that allows the subject to escape from abuse and injury. The logic of the negativity of resistance as it features in therapy resembles the logic of negativity in the various philosophical approaches that originate in Hegel. In all of these, negativity marks the sites that possess a potential for development, sites where the subject's relative weakness suggests a potential for growth. Wherever the subject is positive and full, wherever she is comfortable, there is a certain degree of subjective density, a kind of developmental satiation which leaves neither room nor motivation for movement, for changes of position. There where the subject feels defined by the other (an experience which always carries a sense of injury), there one finds room and motivation for development. This is the place that resistance marks in the subject's field, together with the subject's wish to change and her ability to, perhaps, do so (ability and wish may resemble each other to begin with, in fact). It is in the context of this logic that Freud's view of analysis in psychosis needs to be understood. Where there is no resistance, like in psychosis, the field of the subject is homogenous, undifferentiated, flat, so that it is impossible to establish a potential zone of development in the patient's life, one which presents itself as injured on the one hand but as enabling on the other. In the case of psychosis, either everything is equally injured or the realm of injury is so devastated that it offers no hold for potential restoration or rehabilitation.

Now if the negativity that resistance marks forms the foundation for development in functional individuals as well, then there is no reason to perceive the injurious, offending other as total negativity. This is the basic truth about the not-too-good mother or the bad enough mother.[1] Where parental injuries are not catastrophic and do not destroy the subject's ability to rehabilitate (a level of destruction which psychiatric language calls 'psychosis'), injuries, from the analytic point of view, are not simply bad. Parental 'failures' stake out the areas of possible development of children's subjectivity. This is a fundamentally analytic statement. Morally speaking, injury is injury and therapy – as I have argued in the previous chapter – must recognize it as such if it is not to err into the trap of an arid reflectiveness. But analytic theory is essentially committed to symmetrisation in situations marked by injury; it is committed to the possibility of escaping the irreconcilable split that injury defines on each of its sides (victim and perpetrator). The dialectic of resistance and the way it constitutes the offending Other as relative (or relatively negative), as an anchor for rehabilitation, has always been and remains the cornerstone of the analytic clinic. Relational approaches in general, and inter-subjective ones more specifically, clearly and firmly put symmetrisation at the centre of the therapeutic act, but they tend not to acknowledge the role that resistance takes in delineating areas of interest for therapy.

For the general understanding of groups, and of post-colonial theory more specifically, my construal of resistance has far-reaching implications where it comes to understanding the role of the aggressor or of the oppressor. This is not to say that the oppressor inaugurates the progress of the oppressed – as colonial rhetoric would have it, starting with D'Israeli through to Golda Meir – but resistance defines the possibilities of progress and thus turns evil into relative evil, into the object of symmetrisation. This has some major consequences for resistance in the (post-)colonial field. The first thing it implies is that any rhetoric that presents the oppressor as the object of absolute negation always offends against the truth, while also blocking certain options

---

[1] This is a pun, of course, on the Winnicottian notion of the 'good enough mother'.

for resistance. Construal of the oppressor as absolute negativity first causes a reduction in the purview of resistance. A second implication is – as Dr Eyad Sarraj (to whom I will return in the chapter dedicated to the mutual acknowledgement project) has often stressed – that the work of resistance will have to be carried out with the cooperation of significant circles within the oppressor's society. The very possibility of resistance inaugurates the oppressor as not entirely negative and hence as a potential partner in the praxes of liberation (see also, Frosh, 2010). This is a recurrent phenomenon in all anti-colonial struggles, though it is not sufficiently reflected, for a variety of reasons, on the level of the political manifesto.[2] By implication, in order to sustain itself over long time frames, resistance should have modest aims in anti-colonial struggles. Defining the aim of resistance as the destruction of the offender is socio-logically erroneous, for instance. This has been recognized in analytic theory from the outset, through the very recognition that therapy is possible, but (post-)colonial theory is still undecided on this issue. I deal with this in the chapter on 'Violence'. This has its consequences for the understanding of the dynamics of boycott, namely, of the effort by the oppressed to establish the absolute exclusion of the oppressor. I will discuss this at some length with regard to the Israeli-Palestinian issue, in Chapter 9.

Violence

The inner logic of violence is always the total negation of the Other's subjectivity. This is true even when it is directed to political change and does not aim at collective murder, even when the point is educational – its logic is destructive and undermines the other's subjectivity more totally that other acts. This is one of modernism's major insights, though progress along the relentless logic of this discovery has been accompanied by apparent moral qualms. While the other – in both the colonial and the therapeutic fields – may be able to survive violence, its manifest logic remains destructive. From its inception, psychoanalysis has been trying to confront the issue of violence – eventually along the lines drawn by Freud (1920), when he argued that the human psyche, in motivational terms, is divided into two

---

[2] Usually the manifesto is the text that connects between the theoretical-philosophical and the practical-political. This is why it is very influential, but I cannot here deal with this aspect of the (post-)colonial discourse.

parts: one is moved by the principle of the other, whose main impulse is sexuality, while the other refers to the principle of self-preservation, whose main impulse is violence. Freud's early linking between motivational categories in the individual's behaviour and action, on the one hand, and the inner construal of self and other, on the other, is more fully elaborated in the work of Melanie Klein, especially in the insights that went under the heading of the paranoid-schizoid position or process. The source of the absolute nature of violence's negativity, in these readings, is structural. Violence fixates the separation between the field of the self and that of the other and any representational traffic between these comes with extreme repressions and denials. All of the subject's practices that come to ensure the water-tightness of the separation between self and other- in both their internal and external manifestations- are violent to a certain extent. Although violence aims to impinge upon the subjectivity of the other, it need not be total, it need not aim at homicide, but it always involves physical coercion. Even when it is not homicidal, its main import is still to attenuate or suppress subjectivity in the field of the other and to sustain and support it in the field of the self.

Conversely, acts that aim to impinge upon the subjectivity of the other will tend to be acts of domination which, in turn, will tend to be violent. One can start off from being merely manipulative – affect the subjectivity equation in subtle ways – but these dynamics too, which may not be fundamentally destructive, eventually issue in violence. When mental material does not move between representations of self and of other, where there is no mental flexibility, any other subjectivity will form a threat to the self, who will become increasingly destructive and violent with the other-as-threat. This is why Lacan believed that the specular dynamic ends in violence. In the Kleinian paranoid-schizoid dynamic too, there is always an unconscious blockage of the transfer of material between self and other and hence the destruction of the other's subjectivity is doomed to repeat itself with ever-increasing intensity. Clearly the psychoanalytic logic of this dynamic leads to self destruction – for the subject feeds on representations of the other – and this forces the individual to adopt another dynamics, one which Klein calls 'depressive'.

These Kleinian features of the paranoid-schizoid dynamics are so obviously present in the attitude of Israel and Israelis towards Palestinians (and probably vice versa) that one is hardly surprised at the remarkable violence towards them, which Israel maintains by way of routine. In some sense, violence is the only-to-be-expected outcome of the paranoid-schizoid dynamics, so well incarnated in the so-called 'disengagement' from Gaza in August 2005. The demonization of Gaza and its inhabitants has a long history. Gaza has for long been described by military-political spokesmen in Israel as 'the vipers' den' or 'the wasps' nest'. But with the disengagement, tendencies, currents and motifs became entrenched in the paranoid-schizoid structure of forces which enabled the imaginary transformation of Gazans into Israel's absolute Other, an Other whose every expression of subjectivity (e.g., self determination) forms an immediate threat to Israeli subjectivity (e.g., security). Once, with help from Israel and the US, Hamas was removed from their democratic rule of the West Bank – and was almost ousted from governing Gaza as well – Hamas came to embody evil. It became the representative of a kind of otherness whose subject positions, as such, are a menace to democratic cultures. With the completion of Bush and Olmert's rhetorical manoeuvre, Gaza and the people of Gaza had become constituted as devoid of subject rights on all levels – from the physical to the symbolical. Israel's military attack on Gaza, in the winter of 2008 to 2009, fully and tragically bore this out, while the almost total support for the action among Israeli Jews illustrated how deep rooted have the paranoid-schizoid positions become in Israeli culture. What it also showed was the degree to which this dynamics is tied up with increasing levels of violence.

The absolute nature of the paranoid-schizoid dynamics locks the cycle of violence and prevents the creation of a Third from within this dyadic setting. Many analytical insights in this context have been constructed by reference to the notion of 'identification with the aggressor'. Violence produces itself as a formative structure in its victim. Those who have been tainted by violence are dragged, helplessly, into its sphere, as a replacement for the very subjectivity which the violence aimed to eliminate, as a form of death. This is the secret of violence: even when its victim survives it, the violence perpetuates itself inside him in the form of a traumatic region, a region which will always cast a threat on being-a-subject. Though the traumatic region is not the only thing that survives – survival always includes elements that are not dominated by the logic of violence – it always maintains activated the threat to being-a-subject. This hermetic sealing of cycles of violence and the helplessness to resist it call out to us from the souls of the victims, sometimes across generations, as can be witnessed in Israeli Jews and in the heritage of many of the Holocaust survivors (Hadar, 2009).

As I see things, the light beam of hope for reducing the level of violence in civilized life originates in the change of attitude, following the Second World War, towards violence to children. In Western society (as well as in some non-Western societies), violence against children has stopped being acceptable in the public sphere, in the symbolic order. Corporal punishment has effectively vanished from the school system. Consequently, one of the most damaging scenes of violence in daily life – and one that probably perpetuated violence in social conduct generally – has been formally stigmatized and practically reduced. Of course, other manifestations of violence – military violence, violent crime and so on – continue to threaten the field of subjectivity on the whole, and human culture in zones of violence more specifically, but if we take seriously the idea of identification with the aggressor, then the stigmatizing of violence towards children is a major step forward.

In contrast with psychotherapeutic discourse, which rejects violence outright, (post-)colonial discourse is less definite about this issue, in spite of over 70 years of Gandhi-inspired doctrines. As a signpost, one may recall Marx's dictum, whereby 'violence is the midwife of history'. His idea was that the dominant forces will always be conservative, so that anything new requires violence in order to overcome oppression. Nevertheless, social thinking has become weary of the kind of child that violence is capable of helping into the world. It seems to be a child that perpetuates violence. Still, as a descendent of, among other things, Marxist thought, (post-)colonial thinking is especially challenged to explain how it is possible to escape severe and systematic injury – applied under conditions of domination and clearly biased power-relations – without counter-violence, without violent resistance. Ever since Fanon (1961) and Sartre, writing at the end of French domination of Algeria, it has been a fundamental principle of all liberatory activism that there is neither a moral nor a pragmatic way of denying the right of the violently oppressed to bring about their liberation by violent means. Violence by the oppressed against the oppressor instantiates their right to self-defence. The oppressed, of course, are in the position to decide on the acceptability of violence, they may decide against it, as non-violent liberation groups have been doing throughout, and increasingly so in the Palestinian-Israeli context. Do psychological considerations favour non-violent strategies in a principled fashion, as my dynamic discussion on the individual level seems to suggest?

The crucial step in the individual understanding of violence was the understanding and acknowledgement of the fact that violence goes on with its destructive effects even after- sometimes *long* after – its more obvious and transparent expressions have come to an end. We see this on group level just as much as on individual level: violence continues to be practiced across generations, as is evident in all struggles for liberation in the (post-)modern era – from India and China, on one side of the globe, to Ireland and South Africa on their respective sides. In all countries which have seen protracted, violent conflict, the achievement of political agreement and the discontinuation of the harshest forms of violence, did not put a stop to its damaging effects to the new cultural institutions. This damage may have appeared in new forms of violence – but the new forms also became deeply ingrained and structural. This psychological tyranny of violence, the manner in which it infects and corrupts anyone and anything it touches – victim and victimizer alike (Grand, 2009) – disqualifies its use as a tool in the struggles for liberation in the fields of conflict that I am familiar with, even if I accept the victim's right to self-defence. Let me put it like this. Setting aside categorical statements (e.g., 'violence is evil'), the reduction of violence in the social domain is always of moral and practical value. This value implies that one should be willing to discuss violence reduction with anyone who shows a readiness for such a discussion, regardless of their political views or social vision. A violent reality demands that we should be creative in our modes of resistance, find unconventional ways to struggle against oppression and oppressors. More violence destroys such creativity.

Before I move on to other issues, I would like to comment briefly on the question of symbolic violence in its various forms. In the public discourse, this notion – which may originate in Bourdieu's (1991) elaborations – is often cited as equivalent to real violence, and this is something Bourdieu certainly did not intend. There are of course many and different ways of effectively and painfully interfering with the subjectivity of the other, and some of these are patently symbolic. This is the basis for the present book's definition of injury, and I am aware that there's no end to humans' inventiveness where it comes to direct and camouflaged modes of such harassment. In this sense exactly, the therapeutic domain is boundless because of the symbolic nature of human existence. But physical violence, in my opinion, has a status all its own. It is in relation to the body that the subject's dependency on the other emerges in its most undeniable forms, so that when the body is injured the need for the other is most extreme (Butler, 2004). Here, the status of physical violence as the epitome of the anti-cultural is singular and does not carry over to symbolic violence. As I moreover argue with regard to activism, symbolic violence has some important functions in the development of various forms of resistance to states of oppression, and it often acts as both engine and litmus test of 'post-type' activism. In contrast with physical violence, symbolic violence offers a legitimate and sometimes effective tool for resistance.

Reconciliation

If the notion of resistance produces a contrast by its positive function in (post-)colonial theory and its negative function in classical psychoanalytic theory, then the notion of reconciliation creates the inverse of this contrast. While it will frequently be unacceptable as an element in post-colonial struggles (as long as oppression persists), it is central in setting free the patient in psychoanalysis (though under a different nomenclature, which I discuss in the next chapter). The objection to reconciliation in the colonial condition is the combined result of political as well as psychological reasons. As long as there are no agreements on the macro level – agreements that aim at political liberation from the most direct and harshest forms of oppression- there is, it would seem, no room for reconciliation on the micro level. On this approach, it is wrong to entertain welcoming human relations on the individual and community levels if oppression persists on the overarching, 'state' level (a level which, even today, more than 150 years after the European Spring of Nations, is still defined with reference to ethnic identity).

Is it possible to formulate a notion of reconciliation that can be equally translated to the field of psychoanalysis and the field of (post-)colonialism. In accordance with the general approach of this book, an initial – though in itself insufficient – condition is the recognition of the Other's subjectivity, even where we are unable to identify with it, where it is incomprehensible to us. This, actually, was my definition of *tolerance* (see Chapter 4), but *reconciliation* is more constructive than tolerance, because it involves closer and more active forms of *living together* rather than the *co-existing side by side* (evoked by tolerance). This wish to engage in an active relationship is well represented in the name of one of the most interesting groups in the Palestinian-Jewish sphere, *Ta'ayush*, an Arabic word that means 'living together' or even 'living reciprocally', as against 'co-existence'. Reconciliation does not merely signify the removal of violence in order to settle the relations between the antagonistic groups, but also implies the fostering of a joint sphere of activity, of collaborative relations: in a way, the level of living together, of collaborative activity, offers a measure of reconciliation. Where there is reconciliation the Other's subjectivity is not just tolerable but becomes the positive foundation for shared ways of living, the foundation for creating a concrete as well as symbolic living environment which promotes the being-of-a-subject among all its constituents.[3] In its advanced stages, reconciliation adumbrates tolerance of exactly those practices that traditionally divide between the subject definitions of both sides – symbolical and ethical practices, that is. Hence, mutual participation in functions that are related to the difference between the sides, e.g., religious ceremonies is considered exemplary of reconciliation.

As I present it here, reconciliation is basically a source and expression of well-being, of enrichment. Those who are partners to reconciliation live under fuller, richer circumstances than they would without it. Given this positivity, it is not clear why reconciliation should wait for the emergence of political agreements that undo repressive, or more specifically, violent practices. This gives state level a social supremacy that it does not deserve in terms of the ability to live a valuable life. Instead, reconciliation could and should evolve on various levels of existence that affect life in regions of conflict. It will not be comprehensive or involve all the members of the groups who are part of the conflict, but it will enrich the lives of those who participate in it, of those who take it upon themselves to live with the Other, rather than at her or his side. Why is this so seldom advocated in conflict zones?

The first and foremost argument against steps towards reconciliation prior to political settlement of the conflict is that it creates an illusion of normalcy, disburdening the oppressor of the moral and political pressure to end their oppressive activities and reach agreements that recognize the subject rights of the oppressed. This is, in fact, the Palestinian argument against any Palestinian-Jewish collaboration which is not dedicated to the ending of the occupation and the institution of due human and civil rights for the Palestinian people. The most active pole of this position is formed by those who call for a more or less total boycott on any form of contact with the oppressor (i.e., Israel) or with anything that is labelled as Israeli, anything, that is, which in some way represents Israeliness.

In so far as arguments against reconciliation are motivated by this idea of *political effectiveness*, of leverage on the Israelis with the aim of ending the occupation and achieving recognition of the human and civil rights of the Palestinians, I do not know what to say; it has not

---

[3] Though my discussion is mainly limited to dyadic dynamics, reconciliation can also be thought of as taking place among a larger number of groups.

been terribly effective so far. But in so far as the argument is about the ethical-psychological consequences of reconciliation, or its absence, I am not sure that it operates in the way that its critics present it. If one were to translate the political argument against reconciliation into this book's psychological language, one might put it that reconciliation undermines resistance. The logic behind this is that resistance is practiced by the incessant marking of the oppressor's moral failures, especially where non-violent practices are espoused. Reconciliation prior to political settlement would blur this marking.

However, in terms of my current analysis, the previous arguments form 'manifesto' positions which are built on paranoid-schizoid considerations, inasmuch as they underwrite the total and categorical separation between oppressor and oppressed and the figuring of one side (that of the oppressor) as the incarnation of evil. According to the ethics that this book is trying to promote, this reasoning has something essentially unacceptable. Of course, the construal of one side as evil implies that its subjectivity deserves no recognition and no reconciliation. Nevertheless, on the present views, the subjectivity of the oppressed is tied up with that of the oppressor. The effort to eliminate either will weaken the subjectivity of the other. This is a logic that has been recognized by post-colonial thinkers for some time now. Resistance to reconciliation that is motivated by the branding of the oppressor's subjectivity as unworthy of recognition, in this sense, proposes positions which, psychologically considered, weaken the resistance of the oppressed rather than strengthening it. As I explained in the previous chapter, paranoid-schizoid logic – which envisions the total rejection of the Other's subjectivity – promotes dynamisms of self-destruction, since being-a-subject incorporates the recognition of the Other. Without it, psychological growth is undermined and the subject loses its inner resources, impoverishes. The extreme of this impoverishment is that no action seems possible other than suicide. Here, the Other comes to occupy a paradoxical position: On one hand, by being regarded as totally evil, the subjectivity of the Other deserves no recognition at all. On the other hand, the Other has such a crucial function in establishing the subjecthood of the subject that his elimination implies the elimination of the subject as well. Suicide incarnates this logic. Annihilating the Other implies annihilating oneself; a paranoid-schizoid logic working on the side of the oppressed. The dual truth of recognizing the pathological nature of paranoid-schizoid modes of action is that reconciliation – locally and constrained as it may be – reinforces resistance by subverting self-destruction.

The resistance aspect of reconciliation can be observed at work, positively and directly, in the Israeli-Palestinian domain. There is considerable exhaustion among Israelis who oppose their country's occupation of Palestinian land – exhaustion that is due to their social isolation, the huge pressure from their surroundings, their fellow Jews' willingness to operate and witness an ever increasing degree of violence towards Palestinians, and also due to the ongoing erosion of democratic rights in their country. Under such conditions, when recognition is forthcoming from the Palestinians, recognition whose main tool is joint activity, it limits Israeli activists' burn out and offers a source of inspiration. It seems to me that the greatest moral uplift among the Israeli radical left I have witnessed has often been the outcome of some joint Jewish-Palestinian action. To the 100 or so Jews who were present in Ramallah early in 2005 and conducting a two-day meeting of Jewish and Palestinian activists to discuss and assess joint projects and their possible objectives, this meeting was an extraordinary source of encouragement. By contrast, the ideological postponement of joint work until after the signing of political agreements is one of the greatest causes of the loss of heart among the Israeli left.

As for the Palestinians, I have already indicated how the negative side of paranoid-schizoid dynamic leads to self-destruction – but there is no dearth of positive illustrations, where crossing the paranoid divide promoted Palestinian resistance. Zakaria Zubeidi, I think, is an exemplary figure here. Of the armed gangs that were active in the Jenin area following Israel's 2002 'Operation Defensive Shield', his was the only group that managed to sustain ongoing activities against the Israeli army and to survive. The remarkable thing about this is that his attitude to Israelis was not one of total rejection. Zubeidi always distinguished between Israelis who support and promote the colonization of the Palestinian territories and those who oppose and resist it. He recognized the value of sustaining his connections with the latter at the same time as he fought the former. This attitude probably eroded his position within the Palestinian community in recent years, when growing circles within Palestinian society are embracing paranoid-schizoid strategies, but it allowed him to sustain a remarkable record of the most active resistance over many years.

More examples of how the subversion of schizoid logic enhances resistance can be observed in the activities of joint Palestinian-Jewish organizations such as the Parents Circle Families Forum, Combatants for Peace and others. The longevity of these groups is due to a large extent to the fact that they are collaborative ventures. Indeed, often, in different locations in the occupied territories, those who lead the direct resistance in protests and in bringing legal actions, even in raising support for various forms of boycott, are Palestinian people who are in regular touch with Israelis and the main part of whose activities are joint ones. The best known sites of resistance in this respect are located along the separation wall, in Bilin and Na'alin, for instance. But this is also valid in Tel Rumeida (in Hebron), with the activities of Youths Against Settlements (jointly with B'tselem and Ta'ayush) or at the outskirts of Nablus and Tul Karem (jointly with Combatants for Peace). Often, moreover – and this is possibly the most enlightening example – both resistance and joint activity is led by Palestinian ex-prisoners who have spent extensive time in Israeli jails. Because their time in jail opened channels of communication with Israelis – by which I mean, psychological channels of communication, not concrete ones – their resistance developed along those lines as well, i.e., through differential relations with Israelis.

A lot of what I say here about the value of reconciliation and the need to evolve frames for joint Jewish-Palestinian activity is the result of a fear that the occupation is with us for a long time to come. I don't see signs of the social dynamic that could bring it to a relatively speedy end, even if some political headway may be made. Resistance, in such a case, must derive from long-term processes, and one of the best ways of ensuring this is by having a strong element of joint Palestinian and Jewish activities.

Psychoanalytic reconciliation

In the theory of analytic psychotherapy there is no explicit reference to reconciliation – either to the notion or to the diverse practices that it may engender. This absence, which has consequences that border on theoretical negligence, has two main reasons: One is that, except for some intersubjective approaches, analytic approaches define therapy only in terms of the patient's subjectivity, while reconciliation presupposes a mutuality that does not fit in with therapeutic asymmetry. The other reason is that the majority of analytic approaches – and the Kohutian foremost among them – do not acknowledge interpersonal conflict as a formative factor in the analytic situation. As was the case with injury (and its place in the dynamic that leads up to therapy), psychoanalysis transferred the analytic conflict from the interpersonal domain to the intra-personal one (until the reverse motion started with object relations theories and relational approaches). From that point onward, interpersonal conflict was seen as a secondary expression of intra-personal conflict and hence did not mark a therapeutic objective. But, as I have already shown, the interpersonal aspects of conflict cannot be thus taken as merely secondary. In fact, Freud (1912) argued from the start that transference designates a fundamentally conflictual field, so that resolution of the transference is inherently a process of reconciliation. We consider this now through the prism of Michal's therapy, which I already mentioned earlier in the chapter.

As mentioned, Michal was annoyed that I did not accept as a prime goal of therapy her agenda of helping her boyfriend, Gideon, to change and appreciate coupledom more gracefully as a way of living together. Despite her annoyance, in the course of her therapy, we dealt with other issues in her life, and often at rather great depth, but she ended the therapy, eventually, when she completed her own clinical training – to a great extent against my opinion. I do not think I ever made it sufficiently clear to Michal, but I actually really admired her for insisting on her way of seeing things, which was unlike mine. I was sorry, sometimes, that the therapy had come to an end before the transference was resolved, before we managed to reconcile, but it is not always possible to complete the analytic course within the confines of one analysis. Though we did not conclude with a reconciliation on the macro level, Michal's therapy had been full of makings up, and it is these that I would like to examine more closely now, as forms of analytic reconciliation.

Although Michal usually felt that I had not accommodated her wish to influence her friend, not all our talk about this had been marked by conflict. For my part, I made significant efforts to say meaningful things about the friend's motives in particular episodes or about his personality. And Michal sometimes mentioned how something I had said had served as a source of insight for her, an insight that even related to Gideon's ability to commit, or not commit, to their relationship. This was important in terms of Michal's ability to maintain the therapeutic alliance, as well as in terms of my ability to feel that I was good for her, that I was offering her something she could appreciate. Almost every time I tried to 'see' the friend, to understand what might be going on with him, especially where it came to a steady relationship, this had a conciliatory effect, one in which therapy would unfold in a more relaxed, amicable way. But my (repeated) stance on this matter resonated somewhere in the background. Sometimes I formulated it harshly, claiming that she deposited with Gideon her own resistance to a steady relationship, and that therapy should make a real effort to identify and articulate this resistance. My words sat stuck like a bone in her throat, but they also formed the background to our most dramatic reconciliation episode, which occurred in a therapy session in the beginning of the second year of therapy, when she told me how Gideon had 'disappeared' for a few days.

No sooner than she sat down, Michal announced that Gideon had fled home that night and that she was unable to contact him. She was upset, showing a mixture of fear and anger. I asked her whether she worried that something might have happened to him, but she said there was no chance, she knew him, he wasn't someone who took risks, and it was just like him to leave home after an argument. The argument had occurred at night. She started to talk about something that troubled her concerning their relationship, he said he was too tired and wanted to go to sleep. Michal insisted they should talk and Gideon left. Initially his mobile phone was busy, then he closed it and it became late. That is why she could not phone his close friend, but when she called him in the morning the friend said that Gideon had slept there and had left earlier. Michal spent about half the meeting describing what had happened, regularly inserting references to Gideon's distorted personality, his weakness as a human being, his inability to deal with feelings and his avoidance of intimacy. At some point, I took a deep breath and spoke at some length. I said that there were some serious problems with the way she was talking. First, if Gideon was so terrible, then what was she doing with him? Maybe, after all, there was something right about him as a partner – and if there was not, there ought to be if they meant to continue together. Second, he might really not be able to maintain a reasonable relationship, in which case surely his value inhered in the way he enabled her to deposit with him her own objection to couple relations. However it be, her way of thinking about this relationship was a recipe for disaster. It was, I think, this choice of words of mine, 'a recipe for disaster', that caused Michal to grow pale. She raised her voice and said, anguished as though a disaster, indeed, had happened, that she couldn't believe that she was hearing these words from her psychologist, after a year of meetings, I should know how she suffered in order to somehow maintain this relationship with Gideon. What? Had I turned into some second-rate agony aunt that I now suggested, no, demanded, that she separate from Gideon? How did I dare to say that everything in their relationship was a dead loss? And what kind of attitude was this to her? Why did she have to hear this kind of criticism? Without my noticing it, we were coming very close to the end of the session and it was very important for me to establish some containment by anticipating the end of the hour. I said to Michal that we had too little time left but that my failure as a therapist was very important and we should go back to it in our next meeting. I said that I was sorry if I hurt her, this was not my intention. Michal made an effort to collect herself, said she could really do, right now, without my hostility, and I mumbled that I did not feel hostile. I tried to appease her with the quality of my voice and had a moderate success. In fact, a very limited success.

Three days later, Michal arrived in a tense mood to our next meeting. She sat down and remained silent. I asked what was going on, and she said that she had considered not coming in. Our sessions gave her more trouble than she already had anyway. What use did she have for a psychologist who refused to understand what was hurting her, and how painful it was. I stayed silent. She said she did not understand how I could have said what I said, and that even if it was true that her relationship with Gideon was not worth much, she had been talking about it for a year, so why should this suddenly come out, exactly when she was so distressed anyway. I remained silent, and Michal said, 'Is there nothing you can say?' I noticed that she had actually passed the opportunity to say something more prickly like, 'So now, suddenly, you have nothing to say?' This gave me some space. I said that it did not seem to me that what I said was that the relationship between them was of no value, that I had not expressed an opinion about their relationship as such. Michal asked me to explain what it was that I actually had said. I answered, 'Even if we look at it with a view to promoting your relationship with Gideon, there is something not right in the way you position yourself vis a vis him, on the one hand, and vis a vis therapy on the other'. Michal said she really did not have the energy to philosophize about all this. I said that it might not be the right time but that it would be important to try and see things differently from her usual way. I apologized for talking in the name of the truth, some sort of truth, instead of giving her emotional support. I said I could see her distress, I could see – my eyes were closed by now – how the ground under her feet gave way when Gideon got up and left the room. I could imagine her trembling with a mixture of fear and anger. At this point, it seems to me, the atmosphere changed a bit. The session continued on a melancholy note and Michal talked differently for a number of meetings, in a minor key, less aggressively. We mourned together our helplessness in negotiating some of our close relationships.

Another conflict with Michal was about what she called my communicational stinginess. I write 'what she called' because that is what she did, not in order to invalidate her perception of me. Communicational stinginess, one could say, was crucial to the way in which I conducted myself. 'I want to hear *what you have to say*', she would say, 'this is not some fucking Freudian analysis'. Michal sometimes took pleasure in talking to me in rough language. She said that one could see how I squirmed when I was addressed in slang. When I responded with a somewhat embarrassed smile she'd say, 'Oh dear. Would you rather I said: "For godsake"?' And when I stayed silent she said, 'But of course you would prefer this. You, who always speak in his name'. 'Whose name?' 'God's name'. 'Ah, always?' 'Well, sort of'. My natural communicative stinginess may of course have been what led me to become an analytic psychotherapist. I admit that I tend to fall silent when I'm told to say something. But I have read and reflected a lot on this and I have many reasons in favour of communicative stinginess in analysis, and against treating my words as *what you have to say* (see Hadar, 2001). Certain cases excepted (see for instance below and also Chapter 8), I don't think that what I say in therapy is the same as my opinion. Rather, it is an attempt to bring in certain neglected possibilities, possibilities that escaped attention. In therapy, I believe, it is not my role to feature as a regular conversational partner. Still, with Michal, I made an occasional attempt to speak at greater length, to explain how I understood the matter at hand. From her side, Michal would then try to talk seriously, to avoid complaining or accusing me about my style of speaking. Occasionally, one of us felt clearly that the effort to talk differently was made especially for them. This had an appeasing effect, almost invariably.

The previous illustrations clearly show that what I call *analytical reconciliation* relates to motifs which, in the professional literature, go under the heading of *rapport*, or the *psychoanalytic alliance* or, as Greenson (1965) called it, *the psychoanalytic working alliance*. These notions refer to what allows the patient to take a containing position in the therapy and, where the need arises, to cope with negative transference by means of higher-order insights that allow the continuation of analysis. The analytic alliance enables the patient to work even in negative regressive conditions, even when they evoke strong resistances. The notion of reconciliation, however, differs from the psychoanalytic alliance in being part of the dynamics of analysis, part of a process of colliding and making up, stagnation and progress. In the psychoanalytic alliance, containment by the patient is always external to the transference and overcomes the negativity of the transference, whereas reconciliation builds itself on the basis of this negativity. Reconciliation is part of the transference and what makes the life of psychoanalysis bearable or even pleasant. There is no guarantee that therapy will actually be pleasant, but it is a possibility that is inherent in the logic of transference, part of its dialectics. As such, reconciliation in analytic psychotherapy, as in groups, has a life-giving value, a value of persistence and of potential joy.

8
Activism

Activism

In this book, I refer to *activism* as a collection of social and political phenomena. Though rather general – many things can go under 'activism' in my definition – activism cannot be just any social or political activity. I have no urgent claim to the objective validity of my definition of activism (see the following paragraph), and would only like to delimit or define as well as possible the field of phenomena this book, and this chapter, deals with. Here are some of the features that I have in mind when I think of activism.

In principle, activism is unpaid voluntary political or social activity, which does not function as a source of income. It is not by chance that I put this characteristic at the top of my list because it is this that defines social political involvement from the start as a subject positioning act, as an activity of choice, as self-expression, as a practice whose relation to being the subject is relatively direct and easy to identify. In this way, activism connects directly to the central theme of this book, the ethical theme of being a subject. There are, of course, non-governmental organizations whose main business is a strongly value-driven social involvement, and some of their workers do receive salaries, but these workers' identification with their organization's principles is crucial to their employment, as is the case, in Israel, with organizations like *Zochrot* or *Adallah*.[1] This is a very interesting issue, sociologically speaking.

---

[1] The examples in this book refer to leftist activism, but many of the characteristics I am relating to here also obtain for activism with a rightist political orientation. It is the former, however, with which I am enough familiar for the purpose of this discussion.

Many contemporary activists refuse to draw the distinction between salaried work and activism and they make a great effort to be employed in organizations and functions with which they can emotionally and morally identify. In such cases, my first characteristic is of no use, but it is not my intention to generate some tight sociological formalism, and this first characteristic affords a fundamental sense of direction. As such, there may be added value to its not being simply correct.

Second, activism is conducted by groups. Therefore, it is a group phenomenon, often an organizational phenomenon, including a structure and a hierarchy. This is a point of principle, as activism is a multidimensional expression of social solidarity. Often – though certainly not always – the relations within the group are an intrinsic part of the activism, something which is particularly prominent in what I call 'postist' activism (which I expand on in Chapter 9). Here the group attempts to conduct itself according to the very principles it is trying to advance more broadly in society at large. As in the previous case of voluntariness, I would again like to say that this is not an absolute principle. It is not that there cannot be a type of activist who works on her own, but in that case too, the activism will spawn certain, formative relations between that activist and the various groups at work in her thematic field.

Third, and in spite of what I have said so far, activism is not defined by group *membership*. Much, if not most, of the activism on the Israeli left is done by people who are not members of the organization that coordinates the activities in which they participate and who are, maybe, members of no organization at all. It may be best to consider activism as a redefinition of group or organizational membership relations as such, a definition which comes much closer to a notion of affiliation or 'friendship'. The affiliation relations afforded by activism are the opposite of classical membership relations like those, for instance, marking a political party. Again, I am aware that what I am saying does not stand up to a formalist scrutiny, and yet I think the attempt to clarify the nature of activism is extremely valuable: *If party membership is formally unambiguous and requires no specific activity, activism promotes friendship relations that lack a formal dimension but have a basic active element.* One cannot be an activist if one does not act, whereas it is not hard to be a party member without doing much at all.

Finally, activism promotes a critical stance. Of all the features I have presented, by way of an introduction, this is perhaps the most problematic one. It seems to me that participation in the activities of an establishment movement or organization cannot count as activism. Take for instance, an officially sponsored advertising campaign like 'Buy blue and white' (Israel's national colours). Though very many people would agree with this idea, even support it enthusiastically, and even though a lot of promotional activity is invested to boost national commerce, I find it hard to think of this as activism (and I doubt that anyone of the people involved in the campaign do so on a voluntary basis). Activism, like being a subject in general, requires resistance in order to be defined, requires negativity which it usually formulates in terms of a critique of some facet of social function. Thus, an establishment-oriented action group may include all the features I have mentioned so far, and yet I might still not consider it an 'activist' group because it is not defined by reference to its criticism of certain norms (Segal, 2008).

Postness

Contemporary leftist activism, including activism in the Jewish-Palestinian domain, brings something novel into the field of human solidarity practices. I would like to call this 'something' *postness*, by which I mean a particular kind of activism, one that is characterized by the loss of an absolute ideal. Postist activism is constituted around the loss of faith in the possibility of perfect or ideal social regulations. It seems to me that it is in this respect, more than in any other, that leftist activism takes its position opposite rightist activism, on the one hand, and religious tendencies, on the other (even if its own activists may be religious people themselves). This has far-reaching consequences for the fundamental relationship between means and objectives in the guiding principles of postist activism, as well as for the organizational dynamics of the postist group, consequences which I discuss in this chapter. The 'cases' that I discuss in the following paragraphs offer concrete examples, gleaned from activism in the Israeli-Palestinian arena, of the ideas I present here about postness in general. But before I turn to postist activism, I would like to address postness in more abstract terms, as a central current in contemporary thinking, such as in the humanities, the social scieces and the arts.

The basis for the wide use of the prefix 'post-', which I am trying here to apply to certain forms of activism, can be found in the context of the theoretical and political ideal of the Enlightenment. It is an ideal whose origins are relatively easily traced back to the social and the scientific-philosophical thinking that led to the French and the American revolutions. The critique of the Enlightenment ideal under the heading of 'postmodernism' took off as early as in the late nineteenth century, and from then on the term became increasingly widely used. Its current momentum, though, only derives from after World War II. The person who, it seems to me, influenced postist theory more than anyone else – and seems to have forged the lion's share of its analytic tools – is Michel Foucault, even though he himself did not use the term and even though it is difficult to forge his postness in formal terms. For the present purpose, I refer to two of his books, which are related to one another (the second being a kind of continuation or further elaboration of the first), *The Order of Things* (1966/1970) and *The Archeology of Knowledge* (1969/2002). In these books, Foucault presents a powerful critique of Franco-German theories of the humanities, especially Marxism and Existentialism, on one hand, and the Anglo-Saxon analytic methodologies that informed modern natural sciences on the other. Foucault showed that the attempt of economic, social, scientific and other types of modernism to generate fixed, objective and universal principles mainly came in the service of ever-increasingly sophisticated methods of control and discipline, and led to the replacement of direct and physical force by indirect symbolic force. Foucault showed comprehensively and methodically how various institutions, grounded in enlightened modernity, such as prisons, hospitals, legal courts, schools, universities, were used to wield control in order to preserve existing structures of power. Along with Foucault, a whole group of postist thinkers emerged in France, driven most probably, by their disillusion with communism, existentialism, and structuralism, which had given rise to the first wave of (European) continental thought following World War II. This first wave still believed that general principles of social progress can be formulated against the destructiveness of Nazi technologism, but the unveiling of the horrific practices of Stalin's communism gave this project a mortal blow. In this sense, postness reflects the internalization of the crisis of modernity which World War II brought in its wake and aftermath. Both Nazi and communist ideologies, as indeed contemporary US practices of global domination, had relied on some of modernity's greatest achievements. This has greatly shaken the belief in social progress as a guiding principle. To name a few of the main figures of postist thinking, I would refer to Lacan, Derrida, Lyotard, Deleuze, Bourdieu, Agamben (a very partial list indeed, just pointers, really).

In contemporary activism, postness marks itself in the absence of an imaginary ideal, of a to-be-wished-for or optimal social order. The point of departure of postist rhetoric resides instead in a critique of existing social conditions and procedures, as well as the attempt to identify a possibility for change that will locally improve the situation, with regard to the concrete issue at hand. A clear and typical example, which supplies the central axis for the present discussion, is furnished by Israel's military occupation in the Middle East.[2] In contrast with the political rhetoric and practices that are characteristic of most activity based in party politics, postist rhetoric does not offer comprehensive solutions to the existing state of oppression. It rather identifies specific oppressive practices (e.g., the lengthy detentions of underaged Palestinians), analyses their immorality and focuses on the need to change them.[3] The question which order should be installed instead of the oppressive practices does not need to be answered or agreed upon for activism to occur. In principle, and often implicitly, activism accepts any political order that does not resort to the oppressive practices. As a result, postists may conduct intense common activities despite considerable differences in their political visions. This does not imply that activists give no time and effort to think through and formulate possible political solutions, but the effort they put into this will be marginal in relation to their work on a certain issue, within a particular thematic domain. Within this domain, their prime time will go into critical analysis and practical effort to influence events, without making this dependent on a larger, political change. This, it seems, is why Israeli anti-occupation activism has spawned around interest groups which address one or a small set of issues, giving rise to many small groups. To name a few, Be'tselem engages with documenting human rights violations; New Profile struggles against the influence of the military on both daily life and policy making in Israel; The Committee Against House Demolitions objects to collective punishment of Palestinians; the Parents Circle Families Forum

---

[2] It is not my intention, here, to define the geographical boundaries of Israel's occupation, nor am I actually convinced such a thing is possible. In this book, the occupation is defined by reference to Israel's oppressive practices and the denial of human and civil rights with regard to those who are not Jewish, in general, and to the Palestinian people more specifically. This oppression is not the same everywhere. The oppressive practices directed against the inhabitants of Gaza are much more severe than those against the Druze citizens of Israel, but given the resolution of this book, which is neither a sociological nor a political treatise, these differences are not of the essence.

[3] There is an old, intense debate within activist circles about the value of any activity that envisions the *amelioration* of oppression (rather than its elimination). The concern is that amelioration only extends the life of the oppressive practices. The counter-argument is that postist activity should not be willing to tolerate conditions of existence that are worse than what would be possible in the name of a hypothetical good that is to arrive at a later stage.

works primarily with the educational system; Psychoactive engages with issues of mental health; MachsomWatch monitors the military conduct at checkpoints; Combatants for Peace organize various activities that equally involve Israelis and Palestinians and so on.

In modern approaches to socio-political activity, it was the belief in an ideal or an optimal order that enabled the distinction between means and ends and, along with it a willingness to defer ethical gratification for the sake of activist effectiveness. The postist attitude to violence contrasts with the kind of anti-colonial rhetoric that dominated modernist progressiveness of the post war era (late 1940s and 1950s), when violence was advocated by radical leftist organizations in Europe (like the Baader-Meinhof group or the Red Brigades), as well as by the more theoretical formulations of Fanon and Sartre. Postist activism, by contrast, does not allow for this kind of tension. The ethicalness of the end must be reflected in the ethicalness of the means. Postist activism, in this sense, is marked by an ethical impatience. It is not prepared to tolerate present injustice with a view to future reparation. This is perhaps the most consistent grounding of the objection to violence as a means toward liberation. A praxis as injurious as violence is unacceptable as a means to liberation because there is no ideal whose apparently absolute good justifies the suspension of ethicalness.

Postist ethical impatience is also related, I believe, to the insight that moral universalism as per Kant may issue in the abuse of power no less than a Nietzschean nihilism, or a practical nihilism like that of organized crime, or an elitist nihilism of the kind displayed in the attitude of the West vis-à-vis, say, South America or the Middle East. Moral universalism is behind some of the most execrable episodes of violence of known history, whether it originated in the monotheisms or in the great social revolutions. The tools of change proved themselves, no less – and perhaps even more – than the ideals that propelled the social revolutions to be deeply formative of the emerging social patterns following redemption. This is particularly striking in the case of communism, but it is also apparent with regard to the liberation from colonialism. This is why postist morality is always a relative morality.

On the level of the individual, ethical impatience is also reflected in activism's tendency to look for personal satisfaction. Postist activity does not wave the flags of suffering and sacrifice. On the contrary, it asks for inspiration and aesthetics, and it is joyous. The activist is no longer satisfied with the fact that his actions are righteous or justified. He no longer makes do with an abstract positiveness and strives for something more concrete, something that finds expression in an experience of gratification, or even of joy or pleasure (I use this term here in a sense that also allows for a degree of experiential negativity, of difficulty which, with hindsight, still incorporates pleasure). The activist needs to be able to say to herself something to the effect that the activity makes her feel good, that she is glad that she took part in the activity. Lacanian pleasure (*jouissance*) always exists in emotional experience, is always part of the motivational setting, but Postist pleasure is not always ensured. It cannot be only moral. It occurs when people can say to themselves, post hoc, that they are happy to have been there, to have been part of the activity, to have joined in the event. In a television interview, Ilana Hammerman put this with a manifesto-like succinctness, as she was talking about a project that takes Palestinian women and children to the Tel Aviv seaside, an activity which requires breaking the Israeli law and involves a degree of personal risk to those who conduct it.[4] 'Part of the point for me here is that the activity is done with real pleasure', she said. She then went on to describe the great pleasure with which the women, who never saw the sea before, slowly got into the water, laughing with excitement.

In formulating the idea of postist pleasure, I am also reminded of the Nietzschean challenge of modernist epistemological seriousness in The Gay Science (Nietzsche, 1974). Even scientific knowledge need not necessarily be tied up with somberness or suffering and may, instead, involve playfulness. For those who grew up with utilitarian morality, gayness also implies the subversion of the ideal of effectiveness ('the outcome test', as it is called in Israeli military rhetoric). The straight line may be the shortest between two points, but it is not an ideal of postist activism. The gender-related subversion of straightness, of course, fits well into this picture and often offers a model of postist activism.

Postist activism celebrates personal involvement in the sense that the individual is called upon to take an active role – as is the case in any activism – but there is something additional here. Activism itself often incorporates the personal issues of participants. This dimension has been most fully explored and described in the context of postist feminist activism, at least the feminism that is critical of the idealizations of femininity that informed earlier, modernist versions (Segal, 2008). Personal involvement of this kind also manifests in many forms and shapes in the Palestinian-Israeli field. In some groups – the Parents

---

[4] The Hebrew of the whole interview is accessible at the Channel 2 website: http://www.mako.co.il/news-military/politics/Article-3b184490dad8b21004. htm&sCh=31750a2610f26110&pId=786102762.

Circle Families Forum and Combatants for Peace, for instance – the activists' biography is the declared basis of their activism and forms the material which they use, to an important degree, to advance the group's aims (which always include an end to the occupation and Palestinian-Israeli reconciliation). Maybe it is through this dimension of personalized activism that feminism enters so prominently the struggle against the occupation; many of the groups in the field identify themselves as feminist. Of course, objection to militarism, in and of itself, also plays a role here, but feminism plays a much lesser role in the non-radical, non-postist struggles against the occupation (e.g., party political struggles). Of particular interest for the present book is that, because of its personal dimension, feminism is especially formative of the more psychological lines of action in the activist sphere. Therefore I return to this in the following chapter when discussing psychological routes of activism in the Palestinian-Israeli arena.

9

Psychological Activism in the Israeli-Palestinian Arena

The Parents Circle Families Forum

Activism as it is practiced in the Parents Circle Families Forum offers an especially instructive example of what I have been trying to explain here concerning the formative role of a sense of loss in the emergence of postist activism, the centrality of ethical impatience and the way in which the modes of activity make up a model, on the micro level, of the macro-level objective. Most conspicuous is the very concrete realization of negativity as the consolidating core or background for the activist agenda. Negativity, in fact, creates a two-fold psycho-ethical dynamic around bereavement. Once regarding the experience of loss, and another – no less important – regarding the decision to act against the forces that have caused the loss. The violence that is inherent in the occupation and enacted by practices that perpetuate the occupation. The second negativity does not, of course, derive from the former. It does not depend on it yet, in the absence of this first form of negativity, there is no postness – though activism would still be a possibility, like, for instance, of another organization of bereaved parents, one which struggles against the release of Palestinians from Israeli prisons (like, in prisoner exchange deals).[1] These two groups are both instances of ethical impatience in response to bereavement, but they differ in terms of the recognition of the subjectivity of the Other. The response that expresses itself in an attitude against the release of Palestinian prisoners perpetuates the primary bereavement and transforms it into a model for activist negativity through the negation of

---

[1] See for instance the following news item http://www.haaretz.co.il/hasite /spages/1069182.html.

the Other's subjectivity. The other type of negation, manifested in the Forum, is marked by a transcendence of the primary negativity, that of bereavement. This ultimately leads to postist pleasure – something that requires more discussion, because it runs counter to our basic intuitions regarding bereavement. But before doing so, I introduce the Forum's activities and objectives which, to my mind, offer an excellent example of ethical impatience in the postist sense which I am trying to describe here.

The Forum's main activity is public, with diverse forms of meetings during which activists explain the need for steps aimed to bring about an immediate reduction of the violence in a certain situation; for instance around the question of the renewal of negotiations between Israel and the Palestinian Authority in the spring of 2010, or a series of ongoing, regular encounters with influential public and media figures who may have an impact on the foreign policies of countries that could, in their turn, influence Israeli-Palestinian relations. Another ongoing project, which involves even more frequent encounters than the previously mentioned one, centres on Israel's education system, in the schools, community youth centres and youth organizations. Here Forum members engage in dialogue about fundamental aspects of reconciliation, the practical and moral need for reconciliation, and viable ways of realizing it. In all these activities, the Forum is always represented by both a Jewish/Israeli and a Palestinian member. The same is true for the Forum's organizational structure. There is a Palestinian functionary for every Jewish functionary and for every activity that addresses an external agent, there is a symmetrical representation of both sides. Various things may be said about this symmetry such as that it reinforces the differences between Jews and Palestinians; that it reflects an overly schematic interpretation of the notion of symmetry; that it reproduces identity politics, and so on. But what is true beyond doubt is that, in its organizational conduct, the Forum carries out its own principles (reconciliation and equality based on a shared existence).

As I said before, the Forum's activities offer a clear and simple illustration of how the principles of postist activity can be brought to bear. I take some time here, however, to reflect on postist pleasure because, intuitively, pleasure should be difficult to express in the Forum's activity, because of the central role of bereavement. As I also already mentioned, pleasure is part and parcel of the Forum's activity in the form of its negation of negativity, the determination not to surrender to a victim position and not to become worshippers of mourning – not to cultivate mourning for its own sake – but rather to grow from it and make things grow, to do something with it, something that connects with the forces of life. To quote Aziz Sa'ara:

> Every day that I am alive I refuse to become like those soldiers, fifteen years ago [who murdered his brother in jail, UH] and I choose to put aside the rage which I felt all through my adolescence. This choice will always be mine to make. It is a difficult decision to abandon revenge and the easy road of following one's emotions. But hatred brings along more hatred, and whatever it is you use in turning to the other, the other will use, in due time, in regard to you. As a result of my decision, I am obliged every day anew to choose to love and to forgive those who are around me.

Or, in the words of Robi Damelin:

> The years in the Forum have been an amazing experience for me. I have learned so much, and this has contributed to my inner growth, along with the work I do (which is perhaps the only reason why I get up in the mornings). I feel almost obliged to do this work. I am not doing anyone a favor, it is a kind of personal mission. I know reconciliation works. I believe that when one gets rid of the stigmas which exist on both sides and gets to know the person on the other side, then one can stop being afraid. It is also a way of understanding that the long-term process of reconciliation is possible. There's a connection, here, to my South African background, to the fact that I saw the miracle happening in South Africa, how it all happened, and that it is really possible.

To emphasize the issue of postist pleasure, I refer to some testimony from the forum's daily activity, not very typical, in this case, but still representative. My material is drawn from a broadcast of September 1, 2010 on 'Radio Kol Hashalom' (The All Peace Radio, but Kol ('all') is also homophonic with 'voice') which came to sum up a year of joint broadcasting by Bassam Aramin (from Combatants for Peace) and Rami Elhanan (from the Forum). The programme offered discussions, interviews and commentary related to various issues in the Jewish-Palestinian interface in the region. The following is part of a written report by a listener of the content of the verbal opening of the day's broadcast, offered by Rami and Bassam on transferring the broadcasting slot to other persons. [2]

> With much excitement and joy (mixed with the sadness of saying goodbye), Rami and Bassam told their faithful audience about Bassam and his family's long awaited travel to England, where Bassam would start his studies; therefore, this broadcast was their last. 'For a whole year we enjoyed each other tremendously, the lively conversation, our warm and shared feelings, as well as our listeners' heart-warming reactions. We are now starting on a new, fascinating and challenging road. We express our deep gratitude to the tens, if not hundreds, of good people who helped realizing this dream. Thank you again!

This citation offers a fairly straightforward expression of delight in doing the joint broadcast, but for me it is important that the joy is not anchored in external achievements but in the process of acting, of broadcasting in this case. Neither is joy subjected to the big ideal, that of peacemaking which, of course, lies in the background. Still, the joy of broadcasting stands on its own right and is not directly conditioned by either real-world achievements or moral purity.

The Mutual Acknowledgement Project

The Mutual Acknowledgement Project (the Project, as I call it henceforth) was motivated by a radical concept regarding the analogy between colonial oppression and psychotherapy. The project was an attempt to combine the two processes of resistance that inform both personal and communal liberation from repressive forces, and it attempted to stretch these processes to their limit, theoretically as well as in regard to the practices it aimed to implement. The project involved a fusion of therapy and activism occurring at different levels of social engagement evident, for instance, in both the formal procedures of the workshop and the constituency of its participants. From this completeness of conception, however, it should not follow that the project was without its flaws. It was an experimental project and, if it is resumed, many things have to be pursued differently. Unfortunately, the project's funding grounded to an unexpected halt at a point when the interpersonal processes it was trying to advance were in an early evolutionary stage. Even so, the project was far reaching in the way it brought to bear the insights it

---

[2]   http://www.theparentscircle.com/hebrew/newsnMain.asp?id=529&sivug_id=

generated regarding (colonial) group oppression and therapy. Thus, some unique lessons can be learned from it.

The Project was initiated by Jessica Benjamin in January 2004, while she was visiting Israel to attend a conference of Faculty for Israeli and Palestinian Peace (FFIPP).[1] For some time, Benjamin had been considering how to bring to bear her ideas regarding various questions of the post-holocaust Jewish condition in general and, specifically, the fact that (Israeli) Jews have become an oppressive force in the Palestinian territories. She took the opportunity of the conference and the tour of the occupied Palestinian territories, organized by FFIPP, to get into touch with Eyad al-Sarraj, psychiatrist and president of the Gaza Community Mental Health Program, an organization which has led mental health services in the Gaza strip since its inception in 1990.[2] Sarraj too had been dealing for years with issues concerning the paranoid conditioning of both Palestinians and Jews in a reality marked by colonial oppression, and with the question of how to escape such conditioning and replace it with different patterns of communication that will allow them to cooperate in resisting the occupation. It was Sarraj's belief that such cooperation might act as the main lever towards ending the Israeli occupation and reaching a just political settlement. Being Benjamin's host during this visit, as well as an old acquaintance of Sarraj, I too was involved, though somewhat as a bystander, in these initial steps. Benjamin and al-Sarraj found they had much in common in the way they saw things and they prepared an outline for a series of workshops dedicated to an innovative way of processing the group traumas of both Israelis and Palestinians. This involved an open and sincere approach to mutual hostility and prejudice, as well as to difficult experiences of encounters with the other party, allowing also for the expression of desire for a different kind of co-existence, a more caring one. Given that the dynamic of this process was difficult to anticipate, though hard feelings were obviously going to be vented, the initial vision of the project also included persons from outside of the Middle East, Internationals, who could act as containing witnesses. For the same reason, it was also decided that the first learning experience would be with mental health professionals, who are well versed in dealing with complex emotions. A working group emerged which included, in addition to the three that I already named, Yitzhak Mendelson, an Israeli psychologist who had much experience with dialogue work between Palestinians and Israelis, as well as a good knowledge of Benjamin's ideas regarding this issue. Also included in the design of the project were psychotherapists working in the Israeli and Palestinian communities – the latter both within Israel and the occupied territories – who had experience in work with groups. This team wrote a project proposal which put together Benjamin's theories (see the previous chapter) and group dynamics as roughly practiced according to the Tavistock model (Miller and Rice, 1967). This model offers an opportunity for intensive work by creating various sub-group formations within the larger group of participants. The model requires that participants spend a few days together in an environment that allows group discussion in diverse formats, including accommodation and meals, which is a cost-intensive set up. The proposal was submitted to the Norwegian foreign ministry and its funding was approved in the summer of 2007.

Once funding was ensured, the coordinating team began to look for participants who might join the project. The participants from Gaza were drawn from professionals working at the Gaza Community Mental Health Center, whom Benjamin had met at the earlier stage, a group which was very coherent in terms both of its understanding of and identification with the project's objectives. To help lead the project, Judith Thompson joined in. She had done her Ph.D. research on recon- ciliation processes and had experience in dialogue groups in various areas of conflict, including Israel-Palestine. It was her task to recruit people who did not live in this region so as to create the function of 'the third' (see the following discussion); this group was meant to contain the anticipated emotional intensity between Palestinians and Israelis, as well as facilitate the small group discussions. Palestinian citizens of Israel were represented by Mustafa Qossoqsi, a clinical psychologist who was previously involved in dialogue-based Israeli-Palestinian activities. It was especially difficult to get mental health workers from the occu- pied West Bank to join the project because of their increasing unwilling- ness to collaborate with Israeli Jews in any project that was not directly political. Such collaboration tended to be perceived as another cover up for the colonial-oppressive presence in the West Bank. Eventually, Bassam Marshoud and Laila Atshan agreed to take the lead of the West Bank group of participants. The strong reservations of the West Bank participants caused us to decide that Israeli-Jewish participants would be people identified with peace activism. It was assumed the Israelis' activism would make it simpler for the Palestinians to engage in a joint project with them. I took it upon myself to find Israeli Jews who met the requirements. Hannah Knaz, a long-time activist with 'Physicians for Human Rights', was the logistics coordinator of the project.

In May 2008, the first workshop of the project was held in Aqaba, Jordan. The Gazans could not make it because the Israeli military authorities refused to give them travel permits. This was a serious blow for the project, both morally and structurally, and we had to make the necessary adaptations. Participants who did make it to Aqaba included five Palestinian residents of Israel; nine Palestinians from the occupied West Bank; twelve Israeli Jews, and ten so-called Internationals. The organizing committee, which included the leaders of each group, together with Yitzhak Mendelson and Jessica Benjamin, got together one day prior to the arrival of the other participants in order to draw up a detailed plan of the meetings, to select the group moderators, and to consider the type of moderation that would be best for the purpose. On the eve of the workshop, when all participants had arrived, there was an introductory meeting during which Benjamin and the group leaders spoke about their feelings regarding the upcoming workshop. We were excited, tense and worried, all at the same time. But the first plenary meeting on the following day allayed many of our concerns. In an email sent a couple of weeks earlier by Judith Thompson and Teresa von Sommaruga-Howard, who were the plenary moderators, the participants were asked to recount a significant personal story touching on the relations between ethnic groups or, if possible, Jews and Palestinians. They had also been asked to bring along an object which they felt was connected to their story. During the morning plenary, following a short introduction by Thompson, participants started, one after the other, to place the objects they had brought with them in the middle of the circle and to tell their stories, which were very moving and at times traumatic. The plenary discussion was followed by small groups, which were aimed to enable further processing of and reflection on the morning session. Some of these discussions were also held in ethnically homogenous groups (the Internationals functioned as another ethnic group), others in mixed groups. Following the midday break, there was another plenary meeting which was aimed for participants to reflect in the large forum on the day's experiences. In the evening, we watched a film brought in by a South African participant about the truth and reconciliation committees that were held in South Africa when the country's rule was handed over to the black majority. The viewing was followed by a short discussion. The coordinating committee then assembled to review the day and prepare the next day's program.

I cannot go into more depth in terms of the stories that were told on this day, or expand on the other participants' responses to them. Instead, I wish to make one observation and tell one short story about the afternoon's meetings. First, at the end of the day, some of both the Jewish and the Palestinian participants were left with a feeling that things were going too smoothly, too pleasantly, in a way that failed to reflect the antagonistic nature of the group traumas. They felt that the positive atmosphere concealed underlying hostilities that have not come to be voiced. This unrest largely informed the dynamics of the second day. Second, one of the afternoon's small group discussions was conducted on an ethnic basis via Jews, Palestinians and Internationals. As we began these sessions, two Palestinian citizens of Israel surprised the Israeli-Jewish group by joining them. When asked about their presence in the Jewish group, they reported that they had met during break time and decided to split up, with participants joining either the group of West Bank Palestinians or the Israeli Jews. They made this decision in order to express the constantly split identity with which they have to live. Once the Palestinians offered their initial explanation, the following exchange ensued (I recapture the discussion sketchily, as best as I can from memory):

Jew: 'Yes, but this is not a meeting of Israelis as such, but a meeting of Israeli Jews'.
Palestinian: 'Of course, I know. That's why I am here'.
Jew: 'But you're not Jewish'.
Palestinian: 'I am. I am not only Jewish, I am Palestinian too – but I am Jewish as well. That's why we split up and some of us went to the meeting of the West Bank people'.
Jew: 'So you are Jewish just because you say so? Does it seem such a subjective business to you'?
Palestinian: 'Do you want to check my grandmother's identity papers then? Or find out how many of the *mitsvot* I actually keep'?
Jew: 'No. I just want to understand in what sense you are Jewish'.
Palestinian: 'Hebrew is half my mother-tongue, I studied the Bible from when I was six and Bialik at seven. Sometimes I awake from a nightmare in which I am chased by a German soldier – is that not enough'?

It was, and the Palestinians stayed in the Jewish group and participated fully throughout that day. During the following two days, however, Israeli Palestinians acted as a separate ethnic group. This event, this action, symbolic and concrete at one and the same time, illustrates more than anything how substantial our work in this workshop was, inasmuch as it concerned the incessant undoing and constructing of group identities.

The second day of the workshop structurally resembled the first, but it started off with a meeting of the small groups. The plenary assembled in the afternoon, and it was here, at some point, that one of the Jewish participants – I refer to him as A' – expressed the earlier mentioned discomfort with things passing so smoothly, in spite of the often difficult subject matter that had been brought up during the previous day's plenary. A' added that he felt uncomfortable with the fact that some of the Palestinians, especially one West Bank participant, let me call her S', spoke about resisting the occupation without clarifying that they do not support violence. In his mind, A' said, this reflected the asymmetry in commitment between the Jews and Palestinians, and he believed it would be appropriate if the Palestinians asserted their opposition to violence. S' was very angry and responded pointedly, 'We've heard a lot, here, about Israeli violence', she said, 'but none of us demanded a statement from the Israelis about their opposition to violence. All of the Israeli participants served in the army and perhaps some of them still do reservist duty. If there's anyone who should worry about violence it's the Palestinians, not the Israelis. And still none of us approached the Jews with a demand for statements. Violence is not my way – on the contrary, my way is to practice medicine – but resisting the occupation is our human right and I shall not voice my reservations about the method that some of my compatriots have chosen, even if it is not what I opt for'. A' too responded with intensity, saying that he was not ready to talk with someone who, by remaining silent, supports violence directed against Israelis. Another Jewish participant commented that doing military service does not automatically make all Israelis active participants in violence directed against Palestinians. Most workshop participants, though former soldiers, devoted much of their time to the struggle for Palestinian rights. The debate became heated as a deep rift began to emerge. Many of the Israeli Jews responded by supporting the Palestinian woman's words, or more precisely, they supported her desperate stance facing the (male) Jews. There was no prearranged activity for the rest of the evening, but most conversations, in pairs or small groups, seemed to relate to that afternoon's clash. The coordinating committee discussed the incident at length. We wondered whether just one day – the last day of the workshop – would suffice to prevent the collapse of participants' readiness to join together in-group processes, but Mustafa Qossoqsi, the one with most dialogue experience amongst us, assured us that in each encounter he had so far attended this type of crisis of confidence had occurred and that it had usually allowed the group to continue talking at a more profound level. This is how it turned out to be on the third day.

Thompson opened the morning plenary by saying that she had heard that A' had felt very bad after the previous day's plenary and had even considered not to continue attending the workshop. Thompson asked him to tell us how he felt, and he said that he had never yet felt so lonely in his life, so abandoned by his friends. All the empathy during the previous plenary, he said, had gone toward S', and he felt he had been labelled the bad Israeli while all he was trying to do was to be a sincere Israeli. He felt that his Israeli friends had completely let go of their human and group identity. His mood was distinctly bitter. There was a silence after which Thompson said how she appreciated what A' was doing, and that she thought his presence in the workshop was not just welcome but brave and crucial. Without it no sincere discussion would be possible, which was after all what those who were present wanted. She then invited others to respond to A' and some extended their support to him as well. At some point, S' said that the discussion was reproducing the colonial reality. The attack yesterday had been directed at herself and her fellow Palestinians, and it had come in the form of the demand to state their opposition to violence along with the justification of Israeli military service. We all know what Israeli soldiers do. If anyone was in need of support, then surely it was the Palestinians, but instead the Israelis screamed for help and the US coordinators rushed to their assistance. Some participants, including Jewish Israelis, agreed with S', and when it was time, in the afternoon, for the small groups, A' joined the Israeli-Jewish group in a bad mood.

While the discussions in the small groups continued being difficult, the final plenary was extremely positive, more than could be expected. Participants dwelled on the deep and intense process they had undergone and expressed their commitment to future workshops. All took their turn to speak. Some took the opportunity to sing or recite a poem. We left with the sense that we had survived the workshop and that this survival had enriched us. By evening, this feeling of relief had grown into a celebratory mood, and the final party was one of the most moving I ever attended with close and accepting mutual involvement. On the last day, most participants went on a sightseeing trip to Petra. A' and S' were among them and they talked with each other during the trip. They both returned with a very good spirit.

I described the Aqaba workshop in relative detail in order to try and convey something concrete about the personal, interpersonal and group processes that happened there. This should enable me to develop some theoretically and practically significant thoughts in Chapter 10. The second workshop, held this time in Larnaca, Cyprus, in November 2008, was basically similar to the Aqaba event, though it set out from a very different starting point and ended up with deeper connections as well as cracks, and with stronger connections built over the cracks. Though events and processes which we had not witnessed in Aqaba occurred in Larnaca, I shall not go into them here for considerations of space and balance. In addition to the Larnaca workshop, in the interval following Aqaba, the project members also had occasion to encounter power abuses brought about as a result of the Israeli occupation, and these had the effect of significantly and decisively enacting some of the themes of the workshop. For instance, two female Palestinian project members, on their way home from Aqaba, were detained for a body search at the Eilat airport. This search was conducted in an extremely coarse way which deeply insulted the two women. When news of the ongoing search came through from other members who were there with the Palestinian women, we became extremely upset and tried frantically to intervene through contacts, but to no avail. In the next few days, there was intense communication in the Project's electronic distribution list, exchanging information and consulting on possible courses of action. The project members' response to this incident was impressive, offering support on the one hand, and protest to the Israeli authorities on the other hand. Especially A' undertook to write and distribute among relevant individuals and authorities a sharp letter of protest. The response of the group to this incident, I think, is indicative of the extent of solidarity that has been created in Aqaba.

Sometime later on another occasion at the invitation by one of the Palestinian participants, a number of Israeli-Jewish participants joined the Palestinian olive harvest in Tel Rumeida, Hebron. Their presence turned out to be critical in a violent incident which then developed when the local Jewish settlers turned their aggression upon the harvesters. Again, members of the Project were actively involved in resisting the settlers' violence, negotiating with Israeli security (who decided to remove the harvesters) and writing a letter of protest.

There were also informal meetings which each ethnic group held among themselves as well as between the Israeli Jews and the Palestinian. But perhaps most noteworthy were the meetings that included Israeli Jews and West Bank participants in the absence of the internationals, which meetings took place in Beit Jallah, near Beitlehem. Two such meetings took place, one after Aqaba and again after Larnaca. An especially powerful meeting was the one after Larnaca, following Israel's military attack on Gaza at the end of 2008. Despite very hard feelings of all participants, everybody showed up and expressed their mind. A difficult discussion ensued expressing anger and despair on all parties, but the conversation nevertheless managed to maintain a listening environment. Another powerful meeting in Beit Jallah occurred a year later, effectively acting as the concluding meeting of the project, held once it had become clear that there would be no more funds for additional workshops. The extraordinary processes of both meetings related to the potential space which the workshops inaugurated. Again, I cannot expand on this here, but I hope a more extensive publication documenting the Mutual Acknowledgement Project will be published soon. For now, I would like to briefly comment on one issue that seems especially important to me.

It is not difficult to discern – both from the group dynamics during the Aqaba event, but also in the Beit Jallah meetings and in email exchanges – the usual coordinates that typically both regulate and trouble the relations between subject and other. This encompasses the need and, simultaneously, the difficulty to negotiate between the wish for the other's recognition (associated by Freud with erotics) and a confrontational stance toward the other, in defence of one's own subjecthood (associated by Freud with aggression). Although this is a somewhat reductive construal, the processes that occurred in the course of the project could be meaningfully described in terms of the oscillation between these poles – the erotic and the aggressive – each with its independent and indispensible value. *In the absence of one of these coordinates, no credible solidarity could evolve.* The insistence on the role of aggression in creating solidarity between Palestinians and Jewish Israelis probably established one of the unique aspects of the project. To quote Eyad al-Sarraj, during a meeting with the Israeli-Jewish group in the period between Aqaba and Larnaca, the point was not to obscure, hide or deny the weaknesses and pernicious sides of us all. Instead, the idea was to identify and look at them, on both the personal and the group levels and perhaps even to accept them. We all carry some viciousness in our luggage. What we were here to do was to prevent this viciousness from taking the upper hand in our relations. Whatever in the past we had been or had done, we had not lost our ability to see the other and to decide to live together in neighbourliness or friendship, depending on what we were able to achieve as subjects and or in accordance with what the conditions allowed.

Thus, the erotic and aggressive dynamisms equally contribute to mutual acknowledgement, but from this it does not follow that they function symmetrically. While erotic discourse develops gradually, aggressive discourse has the effect of instantaneously swallowing large emotional resources. This could be seen to occur in all forms of communication that we practiced as part of the project, and I noticed it was a dominant pattern in other settings of political activism as well. It is enough for one person to start talking in an angry and confrontational manner to turn the entire discussion towards the confrontational themes, no matter how secondary they could have been seen beforehand. Aggression always seems to have the effect of heating the debate and intensifying the pace of communication. Perhaps that is its contribution in activism – notching up intensity and pushing to action. Abandoning angry discourse and returning to a discourse that seeks the other's recognition – an erotic discourse – requires making an effort. I suppose that this effort could be described as one of the functions of the third, something I discuss in more depth because it bears relevance to all dialogic activity and perhaps to all group dynamics, certainly in the sphere of social-political activism. The erotic discourse, moreover, requires a great deal of caution and attention in order to attain its purpose. It was the achievement of the Mutual Acknowledgement Project to reveal clearly and in considerable detail how the third can function to help regulate these forces.

The Third in Jewish-Palestinian activism

The mutual acknowledgement project was designed to be a project of mental health workers not in order to steer clear, somehow, of an aggressive discourse, but so all participants would be able to contribute to the transition from an aggressive discourse to an erotic discourse. In other words, the functions of the third could be shared by all participants. This actually happened and justified the design of this experiment. Participants' function as a third was reflected in all the episodes I have described here such as in Palestinians' ability to adopt partial Jewishness and Jews' ability to accept Palestinians as good-enough Jews; in succeeding to have a reconciled final plenary in Aqaba even in the absence of comprehensive reconciliation processes in the wake of the conflict between A' and S'; and in the fact that all partners came to the impromptu joint meeting in Beit Jallah, following the Israeli army's attack on Gaza – an event that was particularly traumatic for all participants. I am convinced these processes occurred mainly thanks to the analytic dynamics I described in the previous section. It is these events to which I draw attention because they did not rely directly on the containing presence of Internationals – a presence that carried special significance during the longer workshops, both in Aqaba and in Larnaca. In order to bring this out, I must first explain the ways in which the Internationals acted as third, which was the rationale of their inclusion in the first place.

Much of the influence of the Internationals did not depend on them taking a very active role at all. Even in the absence of direct involvement (in the form of speaking and facilitating), their presence helped to contain and attenuate the feelings of threat which we all experienced at one time or another. I would argue the threat was all about the question whether each of us would be able to maintain her or his subject position in the face of imagined non-recognition. This was probably coupled by the fear that maintaining such a position was likely to pull us into aggressiveness. This was particularly threatening, given that our particular group was so centrally defined in terms of participants' aversion to aggression and violence. In and of itself, the expression of aggression could involve a loss in our sense of subjectivity, of being ourselves. The presence of Internationals mitigated these threats by being able to offer recognition – real or imaginary – to all parties. Moreover, an imaginary safeguard for subjectivity was afforded by the Internationals in suggesting and implying the possibility to survive as subjects even under conditions of the most intense real-world violence. Some of them had had extreme experiences, especially in South Africa and Northern Ireland. Their contribution relied on their occasional descriptions of how, in their communities, the transition had been made from violence and hostility to co-existence and reconciliation.

However, the most accessible interventions as third were offered by Internationals in their role as facilitators, when they acted toward the mitigation of the expressions of aggression and encouraged the establishment of an other-directed discourse. In many cases, of course, this had a bridging and conciliatory influence yet, with hindsight, I wonder whether this function of the Internationals did not get in the way of stimulating the evolvement of 'a third in the second' – to borrow on Benjamin's terminology. I ask myself whether this did not negatively affect the participants' ability to generate the functions of thirdness out of the group dynamics between Palestinians and Israelis? This idea has a number of implications for the understanding of some specific episodes that occurred during the workshops, as well as for the development of participants' ability to maintain working relations over and beyond the actual workshops. I discuss the second of these further because, of the two implications, it seems the more crucial, both in terms of theory making and in its projected influence on activism.

The Internationals' absence and the improvised nature of the Beit Jallah meetings made them fall outside the project's 'containing frame', so to speak. This could lead to the collapse of thirdness, but what we saw instead was actually an intensified action of thirdness. What was the source of these capacities? During the Beit Jallah meetings, in the absence of any Internationals, it was the steering committee that most markedly took over the functions of the third.[3] They were the ones who thought it important to have the meetings, they initiated and organized them and they contextualized the meetings by maintaining the sense of value of the project as a whole. Here, the difference between how they positioned themselves and the attitude other participants took was, at least to me, impressive. This was far from obvious. All participants were interested in having meetings and they were all extremely involved, emotionally speaking. For me the implication is that the constant shifting between participation and leadership significantly boosted the development of thirdness functioning among the steering committee members. At this stage of the project or, more generally, from the moment a considerable degree of recognition and solidarity among participants has evolved, the value of taking a leading position is crucial, probably because it affords a broader view of the activist effort. To translate this into organizational terms, I think that further progress in mutual recognition depends on all participants' ability and willingness to take leading roles, whether it is a logistical effort – initiating and coordinating meetings – or group facilitation, in the workshops or during the meetings that take place in between workshops. Progress in mutual acknowledgement seems to require that the separate status of the third's functions be mitigated as the process progresses. This does not necessarily mean letting go of International participation. Rather, it would seem that the Internationals' potential would be much more fully exploited if they shifted from facilitative leadership towards regular participation. Internationals need not be defined as professionals,[4] and should rather be thought of as people who, for a variety of reasons, have grown emotionally or activistically involved with the Israeli-Palestinian issue. Indeed, in the sphere of joint Palestinian-Israeli activism – in the Parents Circle Families Forum, for

---

[3] In a recent paper (Hadar, in press) I elaborate on a different agent of thirdness in the Bet Jallah meetings, namely, the one enacted by Israeli Palestinians.

[4] This obviously has its parallel in therapy which, in relational approaches, features centrally in the question of therapeutic neutrality. In the classic Freudian approach the therapist must be neutral – that is, emotionally uninvolved – with regard to the subject matter at hand. Relational approaches actually use the therapist's emotional involvement in order to advance the therapy. For these therapies, moreover, neutrality can be an obstacle as it may mask unconscious involvement while also dissociating synergistic forces (Mitchell & Black, 1995).

instance, or in Combatants for Peace – this is exactly how international activists feature, namely, as additional participants more than as negotiators or mediators. It seems to me this is the case for all bi-national activist groups. Here is a clear difference between international involvement on the political level – where they critically engage in negotiation and mediation – and the activist level, where thirdness emerges organically as a result of the dyadic dynamic and the internationals act in support of the dyadic synergy.

Although evolving the functions of the third from dyadic dynamics is fundamentally possible, it requires a concerted, and possibly even skilled, effort. Benjamin (2004, 2009a) has put much thought into the possibility to generate these functions in therapy, but her work, too, reveals how difficult it is to achieve this after a considerable period of negative transference (see the earlier section 'Psychoanalytic reconciliation'). This difficulty is only compounded in the activist situation, where emotional intensities are amplified by interpersonal resonances, while ideological pressures tend to cause the individual to become entrenched in rigid positions. Activist organizations, therefore, have evolved a sophisticated mechanism of consensual decision making. To the present purpose, decision making, however, is not the issue. What interests me here is the impetus and willingness to act. In this province, it seems to me, activism is vulnerable to great burnout. Organizations emerge and disband, people come and go. This may, on the one hand, be explained by the fact that grassroots activity has little visible impact on the political reality. In my postist view, on the other hand, political gain cannot play such a dominant motivational role, and there are organizations which have nevertheless managed to successfully and for considerable periods of time, reign in destructive forces for the sake of joint activity. What it takes is an organizational activity that aims to nurture thirdness. I illustrate this by describing an event which I helped to organize in January 2008, an event which centred on resistance to the Israeli army's siege on Gaza. The activity included a convoy of privately owned cars carrying banners, joined by more cars from towns along the way toward the army's Erez roadblock, at the entrance to Gaza. A demonstration then was held at the site of the roadblock.

The activity, which was coordinated by Israelis and Gazans, brought together many organizations, and disagreements arose around the content of banners and slogans, about the carrying of national flags, as well as about the official speakers to be included. Though the organizers reached agreements on all these issues, in real time, during the demonstration, flags were raised even so and ad hoc changes occurred in the list of speakers. There was a flurry of heated debate on the fringes of the demo. This event was one of the most impressive I attended, especially because it was entirely for the benefit of the Gazans and was not presented as if it (also) aimed for the good of Israelis – something which is often the case in leftist activity in Israel and is known to be especially effective in situations where victims on the side of Israel are, or may be, involved. Present were a number of convoys which had started out from Tel Aviv, Haifa, and Jerusalem, counting scores of cars covered in posters calling for an end to the siege on Gaza. They slowly advanced along some of Israel's major traffic arteries on a rainy winter's day. The demonstration itself was attended by about two thousand people who had come together at this remote and godforsaken place, the Erez roadblock, with the sole purpose of expressing their solidarity with the people of Gaza and to voice their protest against the siege. It was truly impressive. A few days later in Tel Aviv, there was a concluding discussion of the activity with representatives of most of the participating organizations. I was in a good mood, looking forward to a review of what, I believed, had been a very successful event. Because there were many people, the moderator asked for those who wanted to speak to keep it short, and the discussion took off immediately. I was amazed at what followed. For over an hour, representatives of all the participating organizations did their best to make clear why her or his group was not responsible for the failure of the event and why some other organization should take the blame. It took a while until I understood that the failure they were all talking about was to do with the list of speakers and the carrying of flags – issues which to me, in my blindness to the tensions between and within certain organizations, had seemed negligible. And at some point, this was exactly what I said. That I found it strange how people could not let go of their less important agendas and that I was sorry that they were unable to be pleased with a very successful event. I made a point of mentioning each and every success – as I previously did in this chapter – and I added that I couldn't figure out where all this had vanished, just because of some failure to maintain inter-organizational agreements. I believe that the people attending this meeting were grateful for my words, for the fact that I had insisted on taking the wider perspective, the point of view from which animosities counted for less, certainly not enough to taint our entire view of the demonstration. Such third functions should be inbuilt to activism to contain frustrations and disappointments and pass through them to a place that is not destructive. Of the activist organizations that I am familiar with, the one that most succeeds in doing this is Psychoactive – Mental Health Workers for Human Rights and this is why I now take a closer look at how it generates the third as an integral and ongoing part of its organizational routine.

Psychoactive

The roots of mental health workers' activism in the Jewish-Palestinian domain go back to the previous century, to a variety of activities aimed to implement psychological insights in the social context, in general, and in regard to Palestinians and the occupation more particularly. A highlight of this type of activity is marked by the group *Imut* (*validation*) – Mental Health Workers for Peace which, during the 1980s, initiated political-professional conferences, assisted in setting up mental health services in the territories occupied by the Israeli army and took part in a choice of activities on the Israeli left. Many of its former members found a place in Psychoactive, their experience contributing a great deal to the modes of work of the new organization. The beginnings of Psychoactive emerged around the 2004 imprisonment of Majed Kenaane, a clinical psychologist who was doing his internship at the Israeli Ministry of Health's mental health centre in Jaffa.[5] Majed's detention on grounds of assisting in terrorist activities, his trial and the ensuing, terrible sentence came as a shock to his colleagues at the centre, who knew him very well and were – and continue to be – convinced that even if Majed actually offended against one of the security rules, he did not consciously act towards any violent action; moreover, his subsequent ten year imprisonment does not agree with the principle of proportionality between punishment and actual harm done and is more appropriate to a Kafka narrative than to an enlightened trial.

During this period, a circle of psychologists in the Tel Aviv region started meeting regularly in order to investigate the possible applications for social and political involvement of concepts of mental health and of psychotherapy. Among the participants were some who worked in the Jaffa clinic and it was they who brought Majed's case to the circle in an attempt to understand the political-legal culture that had allowed it to happen. They hoped to initiate more public activity along psycho-political lines, with the aim of helping Majed. At the time, I was asked whether I wanted to join the group, but I refused claiming that these matters should be kept apart. Politics in the manner of politicians and psychology in the manner of psychologists. I felt uneasy about mixing

---

[5] http://www.psychoactive.org.il/108771/%D7%9E%D7%90%D7%9E%D7%A8
_%D7%9E%D7%90%D7%92 – %D7%93.

these fields, it did not suit my way of thinking. My view changed when I became familiar with feminist ideas about the interrelations between the personal and the political and about how the (masculine) separation of spheres of activity actually underpins the perpetuation of oppression and occupation. In conversations with Mirjam, my partner, and as I read the works of Judith Butler (1990) and Lynne Segal (1999), I realized that my earlier positions were reflective of the reigning oppressive powers. So when the same group of activists approached me again in the summer of 2006, during the second Lebanon war, I joined their activity. At this point in time, the group counted between twenty and thirty activists, some of whom had already participated in a workshop in Neveh Shalom/Wahat el Salaam/Oasis of Peace – a joint Palestinian and Jewish community – which was run as part of a training program for agents for change and in coordination with a group of West Bank mental health workers. For this group, the intensified activity around the second Lebanon war in 2006 was a landmark. A substantial number of professionals joined and the group chose its name, Psychoactive. Today, the Psychoactive list of electronic mailing list subscribers counts over 300 professionals and its many activities include conferences on the psychological implications of social and political issues; work with parents of autistic children in Ramallah; monitoring and intervening in cases of underage Palestinian detainees in Israeli military jails; publication of a monthly news sheet; participation in international events; participation in the organization of demonstrations and public meetings; reduced-cost therapy for activist victims in the Jewish-Palestinian domain and more. I do not describe any of the group's specific activities here – such descriptions can be easily found on the group's website – but I do focus on how it structurally included thirdness in its activities, a thirdness that emerges and dissolves each time depending on the issue at hand and on the group's dynamic.

Though it has no anarchist ideology, Psychoactive nevertheless is almost wholly lacking in any structure, lacking an established hierarchy, and practically lacking any rules – not even membership rules. The latter comes in the shape of filling out a form for joining the electronic mailing list and of active participation in projects and electronic discussions. To the best of my knowledge, membership in Psychoactive – in spite of its definition as a mental health workers organization – is under no official control; no request to be added to the listserve has ever been rejected. Some of the activists are not mental health workers. Currently, defined functions are those of the managers of the listserv (mainly a technical function), plenary coordinators, and editors of the electronic newsletter. The remaining functions are occupied by project leaders, who are the only persons with decision-making authority. Project leaders get consensually agreed authority to make decisions in the domain of their project, even when decisions are reached through the exchange of emails on the project mail list. This is the main form authority takes within Psychoactive and its goal is to advance projects, in terms that are both organizational (effectiveness) and motivational (the leader's willingness to lead).

The majority of those who are on the listserv are women and most are not active – neither through participating in the list's correspondence nor by participating in projects. Still, most members have attended one or more of the conferences organized by Psychoactive (the conferences are generally very well attended). This indicates, I think, that for most subscribers the main value of the organization lies in taking part in the singular discourse that Psychoactive developed. This discourse includes work-related announcements, discussions concerning working procedures, reflective and emotional responses to events and earlier correspondences, exchange of information and articles related to the group's activities and to human rights issues, and – perhaps most important to those who are not activists themselves – discussions about various issues at the interface between psychology and politics. There is a core of 50 to 100 women and men who are engaged at a fairly intense level of activity (writing to the listserve, leading projects and so on) and they often know each other personally. Of course, some members of Psychoactive also meet and communicate socially, outside of the group's framework. 'Projects' are usually initiated by a particular person who raises the idea on the listserve and gets responses and comments from the list. If there is support for the idea, then somebody takes the role of project leader, asks members to join the project and creates a smaller project list, consisting of those who expressed an interest in taking part. The smaller list then forms the project team and reports from time to time to the entire mailing list about its activities and progress. While these modes of working are not set down in any published regulations, they are widely accepted and practiced. Whenever the 'widely accepted and practiced' does not suffice due, for instance, to differences of opinion, then the activity tends to be discontinued.

Like in other postist groups, most of the communication in Psychoactive is constructive ('erotic' in my definition). Plans are proposed, information is circulated, participants encourage and support one another, activities are reported, praised or criticized and so on. A large part of the information that passes through the list is about the injustices of the occupation, harms done to Palestinians, the authorities' harshness, the damage the occupation also causes the Jewish population. While these matters are far from erotic in terms of their contents, they do mobilize shared feelings and address the Other and to that extent, they partake in the erotic discourse. However, like in other similar groups, the discourse that I call aggressive always makes demands on the group's resources and generates intense communication. Because I believe that the ability to act energetically over time is related to the ability to accommodate an aggressive discourse – by means of functions of the third – I now look a little closer at two episodes during which an aggressive discourse developed.

Perhaps the most turbulent period on the group's mailing list was the one following Israel's attack on Gaza in 2008. Psychoactive members were involved in the demonstrations that took place in different Israeli cities against the attack, as well as in organizing a wake to mourn the dead on both sides. Then, some people joined the mailing list who wrote in favour of Israel's right to defend the citizens of the South against the Qassam rockets which were being deployed from Gaza into the area. They expressed their opposition to the rhetoric that predominated on Psychoactive's electronic mail list, a rhetoric that directed itself against the attack, the suffering it inflicted on innocent Gazans and the moral indignity it had brought upon Israel. The ensuing debate was stormy and vociferous. Three sides could be observed: those who conceived of the attack as justified self-defence, more or less; those who saw it as outright murderousness, even in the already brutal terms that have marked the occupation for decades; and those who mediated between the former two positions in order to maintain the network as a pluralistic space for exchanging ideas. Following is part of an article that summarized this discussion (Buksbaum et al., 2009, p. 25):

All participants in these dialogues were living in a social reality that had no room for reflective encounters and compassionate talk. Our virtual conversations were constantly involving liminal experiences that fluctuated between emotional desolation and groping for identity. Conducting a dialogue in such charged and traumatic conditions tended to render it charged and traumatic as well, and much effort went into the restoration of safety in the virtual space. **Whenever such efforts were successful, we all felt relieved and even proud in our ability to offer an alternative to agonistic communication. When, however, the attempts failed and the discourse became**

riddled with dichotomies, clashes and oppositions, there was a sense of failure and despair. There were groups among the participants who felt they were required to straddle uncrossable lines in their identity, if they wanted to stay in the dialogue. A small number of them chose to leave the discussion. We hope that, like us, those who chose to stay – either as active participants or as readers – felt that they were supported in their wish to act towards change in a situation that was threatening and continues to threaten our region.

In this passage, the authors give powerful expression to the need, on the one hand, to confront the widely prevailing viewpoint of Jewish Israelis – which also came through in some of the contributions to the mailing list – (as in the opening line of the previous quote) and, on the other, the equally strong need for thirdness and for maintaining a closely attentive and sensitive discourse (as in the bold lines). As the authors note, even though some people left the mailing list as a result of these difficult exchanges, most felt that the balance between the confrontational nature of the debate and the list's containing function allowed them to express their feelings and ideas with relative confidence, without having to fear that the network might collapse or deteriorate into populism or talk-back type rant. Many spoke about how extremely important these debates on the Psychoactive mailing list were for them because they allowed them to speak up sincerely as part of a well-contained discourse.

For various reasons, these discussions were limited to exchanges on the mailing list and never occurred in the face-to-face meetings at plenaries. Another event which took place about a year earlier during the winter 2008, was dealt with, by contrast, mainly on a face-to-face basis; it too offers an example of how Psychoactive managed to generate thirdness from its inner dynamic. The episode concerns the recruitment of participants to the Mutual Acknowledgement Project. When I was asked to recruit Jewish Israeli participants for the project, I turned, among other people, to some of my fellow activists in Psychoactive. Because I was worried about creating pressure within Pscyhoactive, I asked those whom I approached not to mention the initiative in the context of Psychoactive. When the Aqaba workshop was near at hand, we told the Psychoactive list about the project generally (though, as said, quite a few had known from the start) and the upcoming workshop more particularly. Following the workshop, the participants from Psychoactive reported back to the list. A number of people in Psychoactive were badly offended by the fact that the recruiting of participants had been done under cover of silence and they voiced a strong complaint. They had close working relations with some of the workshop participants and they failed to understand how they could be so involved with each other in one activity and so compartmentalized in another. Like other participants, I understood how destructive the non-transparent recruitment had been and felt embarrassed at how unaware we could have been of its likely effect. The issue was discussed in the course of a number of plenaries, beginning with the complaints and the responses to it, and then in an effort to reflect on what had happened and what were the repercussions. Concurrently, more personal conversations between Psychoactive members were taking place, especially those who were most directly involved and implicated. All this took several months during which a small number of activists seriously reduced their activities whereas most of us felt troubled for quite sometime after. Still, the group managed to get a number of earlier-planned projects off the ground – in spite, that is, of the agitation and the breach of organizational trust – and the group as a whole managed to continue functioning.

I describe this episode as an example of the way in which group dynamic generates powerful energies exactly as a result of negative developments which threaten to be destructive. While it is not my intention to exalt aggression and its destructive effects, it still seems to me that if a well-enough functioning thirdness somehow gets to emerge, these negative energies set things into motion, generate activity and this then revitalizes the organization. When the offense first became public on the Psychoactive list, it seemed that it would be very hard to avoid serious damage to the ability to collaborate in a group of central activists. As for myself, I could not initially grasp what the fuss was all about because all I had done was to try and be efficient. There were some other activists who said the same thing. But in the course of the debate, both in the wider group and on an individual basis, I began to see the great importance of the nature of working relations and modes of action in the postist group: the quality of the relations between the activists is of no lesser importance than various dimensions of efficiency. It is not only by its outcome that the activity should be assessed, but, to a no lesser extent, by its sociability – i.e., the quality of the social relations underlying the activity. The postist group functions, as a *community* and as a group, which comes together on a value-laden basis but strives to realize these values in its working methods and in the quality of the in-group relations. This not only affects the group's ability to function over longer stretches of time but also the quality itself of the group's activities. Still, I do not believe it reasonable to expect that any emotionally invested activity can progress simply and smoothly, without upheavals. This is where the function of thirdness comes in. Phenomena like the one I describe here also occur in other activist groups and I believe that all activist groups have a need to process their own dynamics – with special attention to the functions of thirdness. Such work may improve the group's activity and reduce the degree of burnout in a social reality that is alienated and alienating. Psychoactive may play an important role in this respect by offering procedures for organizational thirdness.

10
Therapy and Politics

Compartmentalization and analycity

In this chapter, I return to matters of psychotherapy, to come full circle and institute the dual directedness between activism and psychotherapy. The previous episode of recruitment for the mutual acknowledgement project and the destructive character of exclusion and secretiveness throw a somewhat uneasy light on the very setting of analytic psychotherapy – a setting to which compartmentalization and confidentiality are key. I have no hard and fast opinions on this issue, and in my work as a therapist I try to cope with them in various ways – some of them quite radical from the point of view of regular analytic practices. In this chapter, I translate the questions that I faced when I encountered the offended responses of some of my fellow Psychoactive members into the psychoanalytic context. My point is that the foundation of all analytic psychotherapy, including its inter-subjective versions, is constituted by the asymmetry that sharply distinguishes and separates between therapist and patient. While the latter is intended to be as exposed as possible, to be sincere and transparent, the former must remain relatively anonymous, almost concealed, or concealed in principle. This is certainly the case for the initial stages of the therapy, but also to some extent during the resolution of the transference (Hadar, 2001). In terms of the ethics of being a subject, is not there something problematic in this situation, something we prefer to pass in relative silence, perhaps for the sake of *maximizing the gains* of therapy? There is of course an essential difference between the concealment that marked the process of recruitment for the mutual acknowledgement project and the concealment that is structural to the analytic process. In the first, those from whom things were kept hidden did not even know that this was the case, whereas in analytic psychotherapy, the patient is constantly aware – even if he may be troubled by it or even not in agreement with it. The first type of exclusion is far more hermetic and perhaps more aggressive yet, the refusal to offer information for which the patient explicitly asks, and which he – rightfully – experiences as relevant to the processes he undergoes in therapy constitutes a more active form of avoidance than concealment in the absence of such a request.

In this respect, *the gains of therapy* would relate to the patient's ability to experience and articulate subject positions with reduced pressure and threat (relative to everyday interactive situations). The exclusion of the therapist's subjectivity – whether in its dramatic Freudian form or in more osmotic versions, as in relational approaches – is exactly what allows the patient to develop qua subject, to talk uninhibitedly, without fear of competition and without oppression. To many patients, however, it feels as though there is something wrong, if not insufferable, about this division, which does not prevent us, therapists, from maintaining it with these patients as well, sometimes even more intensely so. The compartmentalized ethics of the analytic situation is further underlined by the dialectical relationship between subject and Other and the need for cyclic motion between release of and insistence on subject positions. This may well be one of the origins of the ethical failure of analytic reflectiveness which I discussed in Chapter 1. Later in the Chapter 5, in discussing the identification of the injury, I argue that this ethical failure can be located in a shortcut in positioning the subject and the Other. Because the patient does not have to try and know the Other or reach out to him, Otherness may be denied by both patient and therapist. Exclusion of the therapist's subjectivity clearly serves this type of short-circuiting – which is why resolution of the transference is so important. I regret to say that in spite of various attempts I made over the years to negotiate this problem, I don't have a clear procedural resolution of it. For the time being, we must be willing to live with this ethical discontent and do our best not to let it lead to abuses.

The therapeutic process involves one further form of exclusion on part of the therapist, this time of those who do not participate in therapy, in the sense that keeping its contents confidential is what makes therapy possible. This is not the same as medical confidentiality. The medical doctor can do her work irrespective of confidentiality; confidentiality, in this case, comes only to protect the patient as a result of his rights to both the facts and the story of his life. Analytic psychotherapy, however, crucially relies on confidentiality to mobilize its workings by allowing the patient to feel free to open up. Therapeutic talk always touches on the lives of third persons who are in some relation to patient or therapist, whether it be a professional relation, familial or a relation of emotional attachment. Though this third party might feel – and sometimes does feel – that the therapy excludes her from things that may be crucial to the way she conducts her life – this will not reduce confidentiality and may, in principle, even make it more indispensable. Analytic psychotherapy, moreover, will almost always create some conflict of loyalty between the patient's partner and the therapist. To varying degrees, patients will feel uncomfortable about exposing things that are very important to some third party while not informing the latter or asking for their approval. Without this shield of secrecy, there would be no analytic psychotherapy. This leads me to the conclusion that the patient's ownership of her life narrative is constitutive of her being a subject and this ownership is established through discretionary practices. Further down the line, exclusion affects a whole complex of relations of identification and differentiation which create, on the one hand, the subject's social place and, on the other, the experience of interiority or multi-dimensionality. As I explained in Chapter 1, subjecthood is experienced as a container whose ability to hold mental materials inside is predicated upon keeping some materials outside and in exclusion.

In my view, what is most important in the case I present here is to stress its ethical logic. If exclusion and concealment are morally reprobate in the broadest possible sense, then the analytic project disqualifies on moral grounds. If, however, the disqualification is not moral but ethical, i.e., related to subject formation in its concrete social relatedness, then exclusions are acceptable. There is no subject without them. The catch is that such exclusions can become pernicious because the ability to grow depends on the Other's recognition, on the formation of witnesses, others to whom the subject shows herself in all her vulnerability and from whom she receives recognition of her subjecthood. Following this path of being a subject, whatever form it takes, this dynamics of revelation and concealment involves a complicated juggling with exclusion and getting recognition. This exactly is what analytic psychotherapy aims to achieve: to generate an agreed upon system of exclusions in one domain (metaphorically represented by the walls of the therapy room) in order to make for greater exposure in the domain of another outline (openness within the room). This is not merely a matter of professional ethics but, more critically, of the ethics of the subject, the ethics that are at the centre of this book.

Political talk in analysis

At the very beginning of this book, I promised to discuss the question whether social and political issues might furnish a useful focus in analytic psychotherapy, but only at this point do I feel that there is sufficient background to return to it. Only at this point is there enough analytic and political material to approach the matter in an informed way, based on the insights this book has so far offered. That there could be political talk in therapy from the side of the patient – this will not come as much of a surprise. Because patients talk about everything, why would this not include politics as well? This is especially true about Israel, where people often experience politics as part of their everyday life. The one who really does not talk about politics or, at least, the one who publicly professes not to do so – with many exceptions (Samuels, 1994) – is the therapist, even though practitioners are increasingly more open to it (ibid). My experience with patients' political comments is rather diverse. They usually mention and often expand on dramatic events, especially those that have been traumatic or violent. Nearly all my patients, for instance, spoke relatively at length about the assassination of Yitzhak Rabin when it occurred. Some had a very emotional response and spoke about it in an extremely personal manner. I responded with empathy and a sense of having a common fate – not through interpretation in the analytic sense, but rather through 'reality interpretation' as Samuels (ibid) calls it, commenting on the nature as such of the related event. If the issue resurfaced in subsequent meetings, I reacted in my habitual interpretive mode, by considering the metaphorical pointers regarding the patient's life (Hadar, 2001). Without intending to do so, I evolved a pattern of no interpretation, on the one hand, and regular interpretation, on the other. There was nothing in the interpretive style to mark the specific subject matter, the fact that it related to a political subject. From my current perspective, this amounts to a denial of the specific nature of political contents and a lack of awareness regarding such specificity. Clearly, I had no idea about possible therapeutic implications that are related to political contents. This became especially obvious when a settler, who had decided to live in the occupied territories for ideological reasons, turned to me for therapy. I was not as politically active during that period as I am today. My patient could only know about my political attitudes indirectly, for instance because I used the notion of the 'green line'[1] as if it referred to

---

[1] The 'green line' refers to the pre-1967 borders of Israel.

a geographical fact. He had a way of provoking me by inserting offensive remarks about Palestinians and leftists, and sometimes he did so at length. Here also I did not give interpretations, not even to draw the patient's attention to the fact that he was being provocative, not even by way of interpreting the transference. It seemed to me that he was well aware that I would grow tense when he talked like this, and that he gained considerable satisfaction from it. Though professionally speaking, the therapy proceeded well. Eventually I took a justifiable opportunity to suggest that therapy may have exhausted itself and perhaps we could steer towards an end. He agreed.

Another episode that illustrates my reticence about political issues took place in 1991, during the Iraq war, when most of my patients left the Tel Aviv area in flight of Iraqi launched Scuds and did not come in for therapy. A few of them, however, did continue. These patients only rarely mentioned the war and spoke mainly about the things that usually preoccupied them such as their intimate relations or things concerning their professional development. This really impressed me, because I myself thought a great deal about the war and its consequences. My working hours during therapy acquired special meaning because they offered a break from these preoccupations. With hindsight, it seems to me now that these sessions came to carry such a special meaning for me exactly because they freed my mind of Saddam Hussein or the Scud missiles. A kind of an apolitical oasis.

My avoidant strategies altered considerably when around 2000, I decided that in the face of the increasing violence against Palestinians I should take a more active attitude in my opposition to the Occupation (Hadar, 2010b). Not only did I take a greater part in political organizations, I also started to teach about the Occupation as part of my academic commitments and to be more responsive to political remarks in therapy. Simultaneously, more people started coming in for therapy who had chosen me because of my political viewpoints – leftist activists, that is, and draft refusers (or conscientious objectors) for whom political talk formed an important element in the therapeutic discourse (I also know about people who put aside referral to me because of my political views). With time, I evolved a regular procedure for political talk. On hearing a clearly political comment from my patient, I would then start with my usual analytic investigation, by asking clarifying questions about the subject matter and about the patient's feelings and thoughts about this subject. If I know her well enough, I may ask the patient some challenging questions, ones that may dwell on gaps in her political storyline. I take this approach regardless of the patient's actual opinions, because it serves as an initial step of presenting more material about the issue, which is roughly analogous to ordinary analytic reconstruction (Hadar, 2001). Because political talk is polemical in essence, critically marked by positions and counter-positions, the mode of the analytic reconstruction, also, is to a large extent polemical. Therefore, it addresses possible contradictions and likely resistances. For me, the first encounter with political talk in therapy will bring out its specific nature – even if it is done in the rather minimal way of 'reconstruction'. My response to what the patient says will both resemble and be unlike the initial steps I have outlined earlier for regular therapy whose focus is the identification of the injury. There, the initial step is also reconstructive, and there too it might dwell on gaps and inconsistencies in the patient's description of the event. It does not, however, give special room to the problematization of the patient's reconstructive position, as I suggest in the case of political talk. I usually limit interpretations of a challenging nature during these initial steps by linking the degree of challenge to the degree of familiarity between me and the patient. Without sufficient familiarity, in the early stages of a therapy, the transferential intensities can be too unpredictable and potentially destructive.

Once the discursive field of politics gains a certain fullness of content, when it has become familiar enough – something which is always a matter of my subjective judgment – I start offering interpretations that make the connection between things that arise in the political discourse and the psychological biography of my patient. By way of an illustration, let me comment about what I could have done with the ideological settler whom I previously mentioned. What had caused him to turn to me was related to recurrent occasions on which he would act unpredictably, and in a way that always badly disappointed people who were close to him and about whom he cared. Sometimes this involved his excessive shirking of obligations. At times in therapy, he would give vent to detailed descriptions of his ideas for collective punishment of Palestinian locations in which there were people who had perpetrated violent actions against Israeli Jews. At that point, I could have suggested that he needed a lot of force in order to create discipline, that discipline, for him, was closely related to violence. I might have associated this to motifs from his childhood and to occasions when he had been disciplined, either by his parents or his teachers, in rather forceful ways. It could be an opportunity to discuss the subject of violence in his personal life, especially in the context of order and discipline. His sudden ways of dropping responsibility could be expressions of rebellion against the violence of enforced conformity, of having to meet others' expectations.

Where political talk stretches over sufficient time and the patient has had the opportunity to develop her ideas – as well as their interpersonal resonances – to a considerable extent, I may express my own views and – if this does not intimidate the patient – develop them. Though this is how I propose to proceed with self-disclosure in general (Hadar, 2001), there is something singular about the political case because here my views may clash with those of the patient, thus putting me into an antagonistic, potentially hostile position – and this, for me, needs special justification. I am unable to formulate a general principle to guide the therapist's political self-expression. So far I have only ventured to do this on rare occasions. But where I did express my opinion, I was persuaded that political confrontation contributed to the therapy in a specific, unique way, because of the patient's personality and the nature of the transference.

Gila first came to me for therapy at the end of a long career as an educational psychologist. It was a career that, on the one hand, had absorbed her, yet on the other, it had also frustrated her. She very much liked her job in terms of the work with the boys and girls, but she had not managed to create for herself the kind of place in the school that she had wanted, and so she felt isolated, unloved and not understood. She wanted the friendship of her colleagues and the appreciation of the management which were not clearly forthcoming. They were not totally absent but it was complicated – the principal also mocked her, something which always again, annoyingly, managed to hurt her. She should really have understood and internalized his limitations. Whenever he turned to her for her opinion he always spoke with irony. Also, the teachers tended to think she was a snob, taking a superior view of them – perhaps because she was a trained psychologist – people always think that psychologists judge them – or maybe because she had a doctorate, something they themselves did not usually have. She was aware that she did act in a superior way on occasion, but what could you do if people uttered such nonsense at times during staff meetings? They would talk with total confidence of things about which they did not have the remotest clue.

Gila was in a longstanding relationship but had no children. She had sometimes considered adoption but never got round to it. She knew all there was to know about adoption such as how it was done, and where, how much it cost, the legal aspects, and she had been in touch with adoption agencies – in Central America, Romania, Eastern Europe – but it never really reached the practical stage. Her partner was quite willing to be at her side in such a project. He was not enthusiastic but nor did he seriously oppose the idea. She would have known if he had really opposed. She was an expert in resistance, even if she was not a clinical psychologist. This was for the benefit of those who overvalue *clinical* psychology (relative to educational psychology). Her partner's lack of enthusiasm amplified her reservations. She really had wanted a child of her own, but it had not worked out. It had caused her much heartache when she was younger, during the first years of her life with her partner. If she had been more successful with the child, then she might have married too because the two seemed mutually dependent. But to get married just for the sake of getting married seemed pointless, a stupid concession to archaic religious ideas. Yes, she was Jewish, and proud to be so, not like me, Uri, for whom being Jewish was just a source of embarrassment. She took pleasure in lashing out at me, not just in this case. It was not as though she did not appreciate me – on the contrary, she did very much – but let us be honest, I could at times be rather thick, unable to quite follow her story. I would need reminders and she could not trust I would remember, or that my responses would be sharp. Therefore, she would sting me so that I would be more sharp, and it worked. In her younger years, she had been a political activist for Meretz (the leftmost party in Israel which is also Zionist). She had put a lot of energy into that, something which had caused much friction with her father, who was an old-guard, ideological Revisionist (traditional rightwing, Judeo-centric). Then it exhausted itself after some years, so she left political activism. She was rather forgiving about her father, particularly because she thought his views all in all reflected the limitations of Diaspora Judaism. Gila decided to be a good daughter, to let her father grow old in peace and stop arguing with him. She returned to university to continue her studies in psychology, completed the program in educational psychology and finished her doctorate. The fact that her parents were well off helped a great deal. Not that it compensated for their total inability to give her anything emotionally such as love or real appreciation. But she would not have been able to get her Ph.D. without their support. Scholarships and the money you could make as a teaching assistant would get you through two weeks in a month, in the best case. Subsequently, her job in the school was quite satisfying, along with her devotion to painting, which was her hobby. Her political-social interest had not vanished but she had never returned to any organized activity.

Gila's talk was interlaced with political comments which were directly related to her personal life. Such was the case, for instance, when she spoke of the relationship between marriage and children, as I previously mentioned. It happened rarely that I responded and when I did, only with a brief and non-committal remark. Things changed toward the Israeli army's disengagement from Gaza in August 2005. She became increasingly emotional as the date approached and spoke about it more and more extensively. Our conversations in the immediately preceding period had been marked by a certain numbness, maybe because energies in our sessions always involved an element of conflict and this had started becoming dangerous for Gila. She understood that I was not insensitive to criticism and that this was a way of mobilizing me, but at the same time she feared that it might also arouse my hostility toward her. I said that it seemed her fate, to be looking for the love of those over whom she held a degree of power, while their realization of her having that power could, sometimes, hurt them. At least in part, it seemed that her strength was in her ability to hurt. This reasoning lessened her prickliness to some extent but it also had the effect of taking the life out of our conversations. It sent her to sleep. The political talk in the run-up to the disengagement had a way of wonderfully reviving the conversation – always and irrepressibly so. Well, not entirely irrepressible because we never ended a meeting in the middle of political agitation (see the following paragraph). Yet, this was not entirely wonderful because, at the time, our talk could concern rather unpleasant themes like, for example, the personality of the then prime minister, Ariel Sharon. Gila had a big bellyful against him from a long way back, because the first Lebanon war had put him into eternal disgrace, as far as she was concerned. That it was he, of all people, who would lead Israel to an important withdrawal from occupied territories caused her obvious distress – a mixture of suspicion, resentment, and respect. He would clearly not go all the way and make peace with the Palestinians, but as a precedent, it was a far-reaching move, perhaps even of the proportions of the Oslo accords. I remember two of my own comments in this context. One was that if I had been a Kleinian, I would now have mentioned the difference between the good and the bad phallus, by analogy to the good and the bad breast. If the latter presents the infant with the problematic of its emotional attachments, then the former present it with the problems of its moral attachments. 'For you, Sharon forcefully represented this moral ambivalence'. Gila retorted angrily by saying that my formulation sounded to her more

Lacanian than Kleinian. This must have been a knee-jerk reaction, knowing about my Lacanian sentiments and having described him in the past as incomprehensible. In fact, I thought to myself how right she was. However that may be, she was annoyed that I came up with psychologistic reactions rather than with direct address of the issue at hand. About a month into Gila's frequent talk about the disengagement, with me responding by asking clarifying questions and offering interpretations, the pressure that I talk politics bore fruit. I considered the matter and came to the conclusion that political talk was irreplaceable in the sense that it allowed Gila to engage in confrontational talk without running the risk of being badly hurt by personal comments. This made it possible to be aggressive in a somewhat remote domain and thus be less vulnerable. I believed this was the secret of political talk, the source of its power. There was a certain logic to my taking a political position and to offering myself for confrontation, especially since she knew my opinions very well.

One of my first blatantly political remarks was that the comparison between the Oslo accords and the disengagement put the former in the right frame – as a failure to recognize the Palestinians as an equal partner in terms of status and rights. Repeated in other critical comments about the Oslo accord, which Gila clearly supported, triggered attacks against my close-minded and uncompromising attitudes. 'For you', she said, 'Nothing matters, it's all part of Jewish colonialism, you don't have to deal with inner conflict because it's all the same for you – whether it's Begin, Sharon, or Rabin. You are a leftwing fundamentalist'. At this time, Gila knew that my son was in military prison due to his refusal to serve in the army, and this too angered her, 'Isn't it ironical that exactly when the army is fighting Jewish settlers, your son is refusing to serve?' I responded by saying that the notion of changing the system from within[2] had not worked and that thousands of well-intentioned people were trying to do exactly that, while Israel's political positions were only sliding further down the slope. Israeli violence was only on the increase. Gila said, 'Perhaps. But meanwhile the notion of a territorial compromise between Israel and the Palestinians has become generally accepted. Would you have been able to imagine, five years ago, that Sharon would be the one to lead the most significant Israeli withdrawal from settlements?'. I replied, 'Maybe you are right, I would have liked to be optimistic. But I still

---

[2] "Changing the system from within" was often the rationale of military service for left-wing Zionists.

don't see how this disengagement will lead to anything significant. Being such a one-sided move, it can only enable us to go on treating the Palestinians in a colonialist manner, and it will be extremely hard to make progress'.

Even though it had been my own decision to go ahead with it, my political talk with Gila often felt uncomfortable to me. It was a kind of offense to my analytic superego, I should not have let myself. About ten minutes prior to the end of a meeting dominated by political talk, I would try and shift to a more classical form of conversation by offering a reflective interpretation. 'Such emotional intensities', I might have commented, 'Where do they come from?', and Gila might have responded, 'From being a person with values, from having faith in values, isn't that analytically conceivable?' I answered, 'What – like in a game between loyalty to parental authority and rebelliousness against it? Replacing one's parents with more deserving ones, parents-values, values-parents?' At this point she might have smiled, if she was in a good mood. 'Ah, parents! What would we do without them? How would we make interpretations?' Then I may have said, 'Yes, but when we talk of values we can confront one another without running the risk of becoming too personal. I understand that that has a relaxing effect, it neutralizes risk'. Gila replied, 'But it also emphasizes our separateness, separation, individuation, if you insist to talk in terms of parents and children, I can do so too'. Our political talk had a symmetrising effect which left its enduring mark on the therapy. Gila allowed herself to tell me things about my person more than most other patients. She was inclined to do so anyhow, but after the disengagement episode, this became more pronounced. My initial uneasiness about this strain of conversation dissolved over time. This therapy was one of my better ones.

11
Epilogue: The Ethical and the True

What, then, is the ethical which, by the present approach, does so intimately pertain to analytic psychotherapy? I hope now that we have reached the conclusion of this book, no one is surprised that the ethical in psychoanalysis consists of the formation, development and affirmation of subject positions and actions, grasped in their critical dependence on the other, the Otherness of the other and the subjectivity of the other. The ethical terrain is where subjects come and go and it is the aim of analytic psychotherapy to enlarge and enrich it in the patient's life. Because their subjectivity is reciprocally determined, the ethical domain stretches between self and other. This does not mean that one loses one's mind when one acts to suppress or obfuscate one's own or an other's subjectivity, but such action is always non-ethical, on the one hand, and psychically depleting, on the other. For me, therefore, any suppression of subjectivity embodies the non-therapeutic par excellence. Of course, this still leaves us with Jeremiah's protest at how wickedness prospers: 'Yet I would speak with you about your justice: Why does the way of the wicked prosper? Why do all the faithless live at ease?' (Jeremiah 12:1). The narrowing of mental life does not always lead to dysfunction. On the contrary, in certain roles good functioning requires just such narrowing, but my feeling is that the prospering wicked would not come in for analysis in the first place. Obviously, even if the narrowing of the psyche does not imply dysfunction, it is often possible to treat a functional disturbance by means of the psychic expansion of the kind attained by analysis. The ethical perspective that I have developed throughout this book, that of being a subject – let me call it the existential perspective, or better, by allusion to Lacan (1973/1998), 'the ex-sistential perspective' – is not the only ethical reading of psychoanalysis. There have been some major authors who approached the issues that my book addresses from the angle of truth, knowledge and consciousness. I call these the epistemological perspective or, again, by reference to Lacan, the 'epi-stemological perspective', which has the ironical added meaning, created by the prefix 'epi', of knowledge-that-is-ne arly-knowledge or truth-that-is-nearly-truth. Throughout this book, I have discussed epistemological ethics mainly in the context of diverse versions of self-psychology (mostly in Winnicott's version). It is, on the one hand, out of respect and admiration, and on the other, so as to achieve a degree of zoom-out, that in this epilogue I expand and relate more systematically to the ethics of truth and its implications for the ethics of psychoanalysis.

While the epistemological perspective is the result of the work of many, it is convenient to begin its story from Augustine, who in his *Confessions* (870/1993) created, more or less *ex nihilo,* the key concepts of subjectivity in the perception of time and thus the notion of auto-biography as the foundation of the experience of self. As a part of the link between symbolic representation (autobiography) and expe-rience of self, Augustine also demonstrated the value of sincerity in the construal of faith, where 'sincerity' is conceptualized as faithful-ness to truth in the individual's self-representation. Thus, Augustine established the extent to which faith relies on being true to oneself, an idea whose most classical reflection is in the concept and praxis of Catholic confession. The moral and psychological value of confes-sion resides in the individual's loyalty to the truth, to her inner truth. Its centrality in Christianity – as opposed to Judaism – is related to the fact that the former is a religion of interiority, of faith, whereas Judaism is a religion of exteriority, a religion of precepts, of dos and don'ts (though I am aware that Hasidism takes Judaism elsewhere). In this sense, my emphasis on being a subject – in contrast to a general-ized self and a 'true self' – reflects a rather Jewish version of psychoa-nalysis, one that is more inclined toward action than the Augustinian version of well being. I don't want to discuss the ethics of confession here because it has been done extensively by many before me (see for instance, Meninger's (1973) key work on the subject). Instead, I discuss more recent versions of the ethics of truth, especially the one devel-oped by Badiou (2001) in philosophy, and by Reiner (2009) in psycho-analysis. Interestingly, Badiou's and Reiner's versions use very different vocabularies and they are not aware of one another, but their ideas resemble each other considerably, to the extent of producing a similar ethics. As I understand them, Reiner's ideas present a psychological rendition of Badiou, but without showing awareness of this. Perhaps I should begin by laying out what their approaches share.

The first of these shared features is related to the formative role of the truth. For both authors, ethics is about the search for truth, commitment to truth and the willingness to express it wherever and whenever one encounters it, not giving in to pressures, either external (Badiou) or internal (Reiner). In the case of Badiou, truth depends on making contact with a certain state of affairs in a certain content domain: the personal, the political, the social, the mathematical, the musical and so on. Badiou calls the encounter with this specific state of affairs the 'event'. The event consists of the subject's (or 'someone's' as in Badiou's terms) encounter with a lack which she experiences as a problem or a challenge. Every event challenges the subject to perceive the truth to which it gives rise. This occurs around some problem, around something that demands a solution or a resolution, something that is lacking and presents itself as such in the event. The truth-demanding lack can be a mathematical or scientific problem, or a musical or artistic challenge. Ethically, the contents make no difference. For Badiou, the challenge of the event, its void, lack or absence are always internal to the event. The event and the lack mutually define each other as ethical. In this sense, the truth is always both internal and external, bringing together subject and object, rather like the situation in my notion of subject position.

For Reiner, truth is more internal, related as it is to the subject's natural inclination, her mental capacities, her inner sensitivities, similar to Winnicott's true self, which I already discussed in Chapter 1. Because there are always pressures to conceal the truth – which is the second feature Badiou's and Reiner's ethics have in common – its *revelation* requires special abilities, either special gifts (in Badiou) or abilities that may be acquired (in Reiner, by learning how to set free thought and the imagination, like in free association). Similarly, the *expression* of the truth and the determination to stand behind it and be faithful to it requires courage, namely, the ability to withstand pressures which are in some sense always social, even if they were internalized and transformed into deep, unconscious representations. Such internalized representations can act in the form of superego, for instance, or through the death-drive and aggression, which feature as a corrupting factor both in Reiner and in Badiou. For both authors, ethics is eventually related to a certain hyper-consciousness, a consciousness of a higher order than what is required in daily life, than what it takes to pay a bill or to find a certain address. In Badiou's thinking, this excess consciousness is related to formalization and articulation (of the environment of lack in the encounter with a certain state of affairs), whereas in Reiner's conception, excess consciousness is related to the analytic step of connecting to the unconscious, of allowing the processes of connection to inner experience. Let me compare these previous features to the approach I present in this book.

Fundamentally, the question of the truth is precisely not the question of ethics. I believe that in psychoanalysis the truth is extremely important (Hadar, 2001), but the dynamics of truth is not ethical. Rather, it is technical, a matter of skill, namely, the ability to enrich a particular semantic field so as to find in it new tracks. Such enrichment could operate just as well in a dynamics of evil, through the repeated attack on the subjectivity of the other. It is not just history that amply illustrates this, but in each of us, mastering a truth, whether internal or external, can lead to evil practices (shrewder subversions of the subjectivity of the other). This is the insight underlying what Lazar called 'reflectiveness as ethical failure'. In my neo-Kantian conception, the ethical and the epistemological are orthogonal, mutually independent, though they entertain interesting, non-trivial interactions. I already presented one way of considering this orthogonality in Chapter 1, where I reproduced the steps of the classical Cartesian logic. When a person says something, an immediate gap opens up between the contents of the statement and its existential conditions. In my perspective, because truth relates to content, whereas ethics relates to existential conditions, there is a logical gap between them. In that sense, the unveiling of the unconscious is not about the expression of truth – the unconscious does not encapsulate more truth than the conscious. Rather, articulating unconscious contents involves the defence of subject positions against internal assaults. What makes this ethical is the fact that articulating the unconscious is performative, ex-sistential. Of course, analysis constantly shifts between contents and existential conditions, thus realizing both its epistemic and its ethical potential. In this regard, its dual nature does not remove the orthogonality of these two dimensions. In certain conditions, the recognition and expression of truth may be dangerous and may require courage, whether the threat comes from the inside or from the outside. In these conditions, the ethical question becomes interwoven with the question of truth, but the crucial ethical issue remains the insistence on what is yours (truth, as it happens). Here, truth operations become ethical in a circumstantial manner. A person may with the same degree of success defend or be faithful to something that is not her truth, such as her property or her good reputation when these come under attack. These too can take courage and engage ethical moves, yet they do not involve the identification or expression of truth.

Another approach to the orthogonality between the ethical and the epistemological is from the quantitative angle. Truth, especially as it appears in analysis, is always infinite (Freud, 1937), because one can always go on questioning and interpreting. The productive power of contents is not in and of itself limited; it only becomes so due to the external circumstances in which articulation occurs. Analytic ethics, by contrast, is exactly the act of cutting off, bringing to a halt the infinite process of interpretation (Lacan, 1958a/2006). The ethical constitutes finitude within hermeneutic infinity. I formulate this in quantitative language in order to connect to Badiou, for whom the ethical always holds the infinite at its horizon, especially temporal infinity, i.e., the transcendence of individual life. I find it intriguing that both Badiou and I refer to Lacan in our conceptualization, but end up on opposite sides, which is not unheard of in the reading of other aspects of Lacan's theory as well.[1] For Lacan, the various analytic acts that come to cut into hermeneutic infinity, including the cutting of an analytic session, represent acts of the Real within the Symbolic (ibid). In Lacan's formulations, because the ethical clearly negotiates between the Symbolic and the Real (Lacan, 1959/1992), I understand the cut as the paradigmatic act of ethics (although Lacan does not say so explicitly). Hence the inherent link between the ethical and the finite. However, it is also the case that Lacan's cuts have truth revealing effects that are metaphorically similar to the effects of the closing of the camera's aperture. Cuts allow the subject to 'see' things more sharply. Either way, this may shed light on the finitude of truth, rather than on the infinity of the ethical.

If in Badiou the eternal is assumed so as to free the mind of pragmatic considerations (and opportunism), in Reiner the eternal comes in the guise of spiritual experience, of a rise beyond the self and a direct contact with being; it is a renunciation of the individual's clear outlines and of her distinctness from the rest of the world. Reiner (pp. 35–38) regards her approach as Bionian and refers to the mental domain which Bion called O. This domain entertains close relations with the process of *reverie*, whose therapeutic nature Bion stressed because it provides the individual with the raw mental material from which personal growth occurs. In Reiner as well as in Badiou, the eternal involves the

---

[1] This is especially so with regard to issues of gender, where some read his theory as sexist, whereas others view it as feminist, but this matter is outside my present scope.

transcendence of individual experience – the experience of individuality – but unlike in my own approach, this transcendence does not address itself to the other, neither seeks nor needs her. Paradoxically, this makes transcendence a wholly individual phenomenon, an act of self negation rather than socialization.

For me, like for Levinas, Frosh, and Lacan (to a certain extent), the *other* takes a formative role in the constitution of the subject and the ethics of being a subject. Truth, by distinction, does not arise in relation to the other, but in relation to the self (Reiner) or to the state of affairs (Badiou). Needless to say, Badiou and certainly Reiner recognize the crucial place of the other in relation to the subject: the former does so by alluding to the Lacanian impersonal Other (Badiou) and the latter to Bion's other, his O (Reiner), but neither of them takes the other as formative of the ethical. This is especially pronounced in Reiner, who believes in a fundamental gap between superego and conscience. For her, the superego is built on the basis of the internalization of bad objects, an internalization which gives rise to the false self, the self-denial of the subject's subjectivity, that is. Conscience, on the other hand, emerges on the basis of an articulation of the true self, by means, therefore, of a linking to the interiority of the subject. This approach makes a point of the need to neutralize the other in order to allow conscience to develop, because the presence of the other tends to be false. The test of otherness is the test that shows us the place of the other in the formation of the ethical, and it does not lie in the question of whether or not a given theory recognizes the subject's inability to live and function in isolation, as there exists no psychoanalytically aware theory in which subjectivity takes shape on its own. As Benjamin (2009a) emphasized, the real test of the place the other holds in a given theory lies in the place that theory ascribes to the recognition of *the other's subjectivity*. As long as we don't define the subjectivity of the other as formative of the psychological domain, the other can always be taken for a mere element in the subject's field of action, rather than as a partner in the formation of subjectivity as such. This also is the moment at which the other changes from being someone who constitutes the ethical domain to something that is part of the domain of truth. If the other is not active in the subject's consciousness, if it is unambiguously external to the subject, then its formation is a matter of identification and consciousness, a matter of truth. If, by contrast, the other takes an active part in the subject's consciousness – even in her being, by having a Real dimension, in Lacan's sense – then the other's inclusion in consciousness is a matter of action as much as of identification. It is a matter of giving place to the other, perhaps of commitment. In any case, this is a matter of ethics, not of truth. When we are speaking of truth, the subject's movement is one-directional, from the subject to the object of knowledge, whereas the movement in ethics is two-directional, from subject to object and back again to the subject. This return requires the occurrence of an encounter, of touch (Kosofsky-Sedgwick, 2003) or of face (Levinas, 2000).

In the present approach, the ethical constitutes a movement not only in the direction of the other, but also in the direction of the Real. This is of particular import when set against most religions, where the ethical is usually seen as related to the spiritual and, moreover, as transcendent of the concrete aspect of life. Here, the ethical is opposed to the pragmatic, the efficient and effective, and it is regarded as separate from the bodily and the quotidian. For me, by contrast, the ethical turns toward the real and the everyday. This way of seeing things has of course some influential philosophical and psychological antecedents. Foremost of these is Kant's (1788/2004) notion of ethics as a part of practical reason, and as opposed to pure reason which subserves the truth. Kant's ethics is practical because it suggests rules of action or conduct, not just of thinking. But Kant, like others and perhaps even more than them, links the ethical with the total (like Badiou's eternal) through the categorical imperative. As a result, the connection Kant forges between the ethical and the practical stays abstract (categorical). Lacan questions this in his construction of an analytic ethics. For Lacan (1959/1992), the ethical embodies a move-ment toward the real because it binds the symbolic to pleasure, the Other to desire. In contrast to a more intuitive meaning of the real, Lacan's Real emerges as a result of the gaps and lacks inherent in mental action, be it imaginary or symbolic. Desire turns toward the real because it cannot tolerate these gaps and lacks, so as to fill them up. As a result, it is precisely those gaps and lacks that drive desire, and it is they to which desire turns. The paradoxical nature of desire – its being driven by lack – is what constitutes it as something that is in excess of mere pleasure, as a dynamics that takes the subject beyond the pleasure principle. This is why *jouissance,* as Lacan calls it, and as distinct from pleasure, always is attended by frustration, is doomed to perpetuate the very thing that does not allow its gratification. Yet, it is through *jouissance* and desire – and still in the spirit of Lacan – that the ethical ties the symbolic to the body (see also Chapter 1). The route that is being outlined here (as the itinerary of analysis) is not a route of mentalisation, of a becoming-aware, or learning – but rather a course of tying up or even knotting up. Its point of departure is always already symbolic such as in a certain mode of talking, like in therapy. Yet, from the patient's statement, the ethical takes us not forward, to the abstract or the incorporeal, but rather backwards to the first person, to an emphasis on the speaking conditions. From there, analysis takes its subject towards the other, to the social, to solidarity and to the everyday of the body. I would say this is my lesson from Butler's (2004, 2005) inversion of normative discourse. It is at this site, where the body and solidarity meet, that the encounter between the good and the healthy also occurs. In Lacan's rendering of Kant, it is healthy to be good.

References

Abelin, Ernest L. (1980). Triangulation, the role of the father and the origins of core gender during the rapprochement subphase. *In* R. Lax, S. Bach and J. Burland (eds), *Rapprochement*. New York: Jason Aronson, pp. 151–69.

Althusser, Louis. (1984). *Essays on Ideology*. London: Verso Books.

Aron, Lewis. (2001). *A Meeting of Minds: Mutuality in Psychoanalysis Volume 4*. New York: Analytic Press.

Augustine, Saint. (870/1993). *Confessions*. Indianapolis: Hacket Publishing.

Austin, L. John. (1971). *How to Do Things with Words*. London: Oxford University Press.

Badiou, Alain. (2001) *Ethics: An Essay on the Understanding of Evil*, Translated by Peter Hallward. London: Verso Books.

Benjamin, Jessica. (1988). *The Bonds of Love: Psychoanalysis, feminism, & the problem of domination*. New York: Pantheon Books.

Benjamin, Jessica. (2004). Beyond doer and done to: An intersubjective view of thirdness. *Psychoanalytic Quarterly*, 73, 5–46.

Benjamin, Jessica (2008). *Injury and Acknowledgement*. Lecture given in honor of Sigmund Freud's birthday. Vienna, Austria.

Benjamin, Jessica. (2009a). *Acknowledgment, Surrender, Limits, Transgression and Hope*. Paper presented at the annual meeting of IARPP. Tel Aviv, Israel.

Benjamin, Jessica. (2009b). A relational psychoanalysis perspective on the necessity of acknowledging failure in order to restore the facilitating and containing features of the intersubjective relationship (the shared third). *International Journal of Psychoanalysis*, 90, 441–450.

Bhabha, Homi. (1994). *The Location of Culture*. London: Routledge.

Bourdieu, Pierre. (1991). *Language and Symbolic Power*. Cambridge, MA: Harvard University press.

Bowen, Murray. (1978). *Family Therapy in Clinical Practice*. Northvale, NJ: Jason Aronson.

Breuer, Joseph & Freud, Sigmund. (1895/1955). Studies on hysteria. *In The Standard Edition of the Complete Psychological Works of Sigmund Freud, Volume 2*. London: Hogarth Press.

Buksbaum, Tova, Maya Mukamel, Lirona Rosenthal and Uri Hadar. (2009). Psychoactive and operation 'Cast Lead': Therapeutic professionals' activism in the course of the Israeli army's attack on Gaza. *Community Mental Health and Wellbeing Bulletin*, 2, 12–30.

Butler, Judith. (1990). *Gender Trouble: Feminism and the Subversion of Identity*. New York: Routledge.

Butler, Judith. (2000). *Antigone's Claim: Kinship Between Life and Death*. New York: Columbia University Press.

Butler, Judith. (2004). *Precarious Life: The Powers of Mourning and Violence*. London: Verso.

Butler, Judith. (2005). *Giving an Account of Oneself.* New York: Fordham University Press.

Chomsky, Noam. (1956). *Syntactic Structures*. The Hague: Mouton.

Derrida, Jacques. (1998). *Resistances of Psychoanalysis*. Stanford: Stanford University Press.

Dimen, Muriel. (2011). *With Culture in Mind*. New York: Routledge.

Duckitt, John (2006). Ethnocultural group identification and attitudes to ethnic outgroups. *In* G. Zhang, K. Leung, & J. Adair. (eds), *Perspectives and Progress in Contemporary Cross-Cultural Psychology*. Beijing: Light Industry Press, pp. 151–161.

Eagle, Morris. (1984). *Recent Developments in Psychoanalysis*. Cambridge, MA: Harvard university Press.

Even-Tsur, Efrat. (2011). *Truth, Guilt and Responsibility in Witness Accounts of Soldiers Who Served in the Occupied Territories*. Unpublished MA thesis, Jerusalem: The Hebrew University.

Fanon, Franz. (1952/1967). *Black Skin, White Masks*. New York: Grove Press.

Fanon, Franz. (1961/1963). *The Wretched of the Earth*. New York: Grove Press.

Forrester, John. (1991). *The Seductions of Psychoanalysis: Freud, Lacan and Derrida*. Cambridge, UK: Cambridge University Press.

Foucault, Michel. (1966/1970). *The Order of Things: An Archaeology of the Human Sciences*. London: Pantheon Books.

Foucault, Michel. (1969/2002). *The Archaeology of Knowledge*. Translated by A. M. Sheridan Smith. London and New York: Routledge.

Freud, Sigmund, (1905). Three essays on the theory of sexuality. *In The Standard Edition of the Complete Psychological Works of Sigmund Freud, Volume 7*, pp. 125–172. London: Hogarth Press.

Freud, Sigmund. (1912). The dynamics of the transference. *In The Standard Edition of the Complete Psychological Works of Sigmund Freud, Volume 12*, pp. 97–108. London: Hogarth Press.

Freud, Sigmund. (1913). Totem and taboo. *In The Standard Edition of the Complete Psychological Works of Sigmund Freud, Volume 13*, pp. 1–161. London: Hogarth Press.

Freud, Sigmund. (1914). Remembering, repeating and working through. *In The Standard Edition of the Complete Psychological Works of Sigmund Freud, Volume 12*, pp 145–156. London: Hogarth Press.

Freud, Sigmund. (1919). The Uncanny. *In The Standard Edition of the Complete Psychological Works of Sigmund Freud, Volume 17*, pp. 219–256. London: Hogarth Press.

Freud, Sigmund (1920). Beyond the pleasure principle. *In The Standard Edition of the Complete Psychological Works of Sigmund Freud, Volume 18*, pp. 7–64. London: Hogarth Press.

Freud, Sigmund. (1921). Group psychology and the analysis of the ego. *In The Standard Edition of the Complete Psychological Works of Sigmund Freud, Volume 18*, pp. 65–144. London: Hogarth Press.

Freud, Sigmund. (1930). Civilization and its discontents. *In The Standard Edition of the Complete Psychological Works of Sigmund Freud, Volume 21*, pp. 64–148. London: Hogarth Press.

Freud, Sigmund. (1933). New Introductory Lectures on Psychoanalysis. *In The Standard Edition of the Complete Psychological Works of Sigmund Freud, Volume 22*, pp. 5–157. London: The Hogarth Press.

Freud, Sigmund. (1937). Analysis terminable and interminable. *In The Standard Edition of the Complete Psychological Works of Sigmund Freud, Volume 23*, pp. 216–254. London: Hogarth Press.

Freud, Sigmund. (1939). Moses and Monotheism. *In The Standard Edition of the Complete Psychological Works of Sigmund Freud, Volume 23*, pp. 3–137. London: Hogarth Press.

Frosh, Stephen. (2010). *Psychoanalysis Outside the Clinic*. London: Palgrave Macmillan.

Gadamer, Hans-Georg. (1976). *Philosophical Hermeneutics*. Translated by David Linge. Berkeley: University of California Press.

Grand, Sue. (2009). *The Hero in the Mirror: From Fear to Fortitude*. New York: Routledge.

Green, Andre. (2001). *Life Narcissism, Death Narcissism*, translated by Andrew Weller. London: Free Association Books.

Greenberg, Jay R. and Mitchell, Stephen A. (1983). *Object Relations in Psychoanalytic Theory*. Cambridge, MA: Harvard University Press.

Greenson, Ralph. (1965). The working alliance and the transference neurosis. *Psychoanalytic Quarterly, 34*, 155–181.

Hadar, Uri. (1998). Levels of discourse in surface analysis. *Clinical Studies, 4*, 27–48.

Hadar, Uri. (2001). *Analytic Discourse*. Tel Aviv: Dvir (Hebrew).

Hadar, Uri. (2009). Burning images. *Jewish Quarterly*, November issue, pp. 32–35.

Hadar, Uri. (2010a). A three-person perspective on the transference. *Psychoanalytic Psychology, 27*, 296–318.

Hadar, Uri. (2010b). *The Meeting of Ends*. The Psychoactive website at: www. psychoactive.org.il (Hebrew).

Hadar, Uri. (in press). The Benjamin Chreode. *Studies in Gender and Sexuality.*

Hagopian, Patrick. (2009). *The Vietnam War in American Memory*. Amherst, MA: University of Massachusetts Press.

Hegel, Georg W.F. (1807/1967) *Phenomenology of Mind*. London: Harper & Row.

Heidegger, Martin. (1927/1962). *Being and Time*. Oxford: Blackwell Publishing.

Jefferess, David. (2008). *Postcolonial Resistance: Culture, Liberation and Transformation*. Toronto: Toronto University Press.

Jung, Carl Gustav. (1971). *Psychological Types:* Volume 6 of the *Collected Works of C. G. Jung*. Princeton, NJ: Princeton University Press.

Kant, Immanuel. (1788/2004). *Critique of Practical Reason*, translated by Thomas K. Abbott, 1909. London and New York: Dover Publications.

Klein, Melanie. (1975). *The Writings of Melanie Klein, Vol. 3: Envy and Gratitude and Other Works 1946–1963*. London: Hogarth Press.

Kohut, Heinz. (1977). *The Restoration of the Self*. New York: International University Press.

Kosh, Talila. (2009). *The Ethics of Memory*. Tel Aviv: Hakibutz Hameuchad Press (Hebrew).

Kosofsky -Sedgwick, Eve. (2003). *Touching Feeling*. Durham, NC: Duke University Press.

Kristeva, Julia. (1982) *Powers of Horror: An Essay on Abjection*. New York: Columbia University Press.

Lacan, Jacques. (1949/2006). The mirror stage as formative of the I function as reveled in psychoanalytic experience. In *Ecrits,* The first complete English edition, translated by Bruce Fink. New York: W.W. Norton, pp. 75–81.

Lacan, Jacques. (1955/2006). The Freudian thing. In *Ecrits*. pp 334–363.

Lacan, Jacques. (1958a/2006). The direction of the treatment and the principle of its power. In *Ecrits*, The first complete English edition, translated by Bruce Fink. New York: W.W. Norton, pp. 489–542.

Lacan, Jacques. (1958b/2006). The signification of the phallus. In *Ecrits*, The first complete English edition, translated by Bruce Fink. New York: WW Norton, pp. 575–582.

Lacan, Jacques. (1959/1992). *The Seminars of Jacques Lacan, Book VII: The Ethics of Psychoanalysis*. Translated by Dennis Porter. New York: W.W. Norton.

Lacan, J. (1960). *The Seminar of Jacque Lacan VIII: Transference*. London: Karnac, 2002.

Lacan, J. (1962/2001) *Seminar of Jacques Lacan, Book X: Anxiety*, translated by Cormac Ghallager. Eastbourne: Antony Rowe.

Lacan, Jacques. (1963/2006) Kant with Sade. In *Ecrit*, The first complete English edition, translated by Bruce Fink. New York: WW Norton, pp. 645–668.

Lacan, Jacques. (1973/1998). *The Seminar of Jacques Lacan, Book 20: Encore*, translated by Bruce Fink. New York: WW Norton.

Laplanche, Jean. (1992). Interpretation between determinism and hermeneutics: a restatement of the problem. *International Journal of Psycho-Analysis*, 73, 429–45.

Laplanche, Jean. (1993). *Seduction, Translation and the Drives*. London: ICA publications.

Levinas, Emmanuel. (1985). *Ethics and Infinity*. Pittsburgh: Duquesne University Press.

Levinas, Emmanuel. (2000). *Alterity and Transcendence*. New York: Columbia University Press.

Mahler, Margaret S. (1972). On the first three phases of the separation-individuation process. *International Journal of Psychoanalysis*, 53, 333–338.

Memmi, Albert. (1974). *The Colonizer and the Colonized*. London: Souvenir Press.

Menninger, Karl. (1973). *Whatever Became of Sin?* New York: EP Dutton.

Milgram, Stanly. (1965). Some conditions of obedience and disobedience to authority. *Human-Relations*, 18(1), 57–76.

Miller, Eric, and Rice, Ken. (1967) *Systems of Organisation*. London: Tavistock.

Mitchell, Stephen A. and Black, Margaret J. (1995). *Freud and Beyond*. New York: Basic Books.

Nietzsche, Friedrich. (1974). *The Gay Science: With a Prelude in Rhymes and an Appendix of Songs*. New York: Vintage Books.

Ogden, Thomas. (1998). *Reverie and Interpretation: Sensing Something Human*. London: Kanac.

Ogden, Thomas H. (2001). *Conversations at the frontiers of dreaming*. Northvale, NJ: Jason Aronson.

Ogden, Thomas H. (2004). The analytic third: Implications for psychoanalytic theory and technique. *Psychoanalytic Quarterly*, 73, 167–195.

Pines, Malcolm (1985). Mirroring and Child Development. *Psychoanalytic Inquiry*, 5, pp. 211–31.

Reich, Wilhelm (1936/1951). *The Sexual Revolution: Toward a Self-Governing Character Structure*. London: Vision Books.

Reiner, Annie. (2009). The *Quest for Conscience and the Birth of the Mind*. London: Karnac.

Said, Edward W. (1978) *Orientalism*. New York: Random House.
Said, Edward W. (2003). *Freud and The Non-European*. London and New York: Verso.
Salomon, Roy (2011). *The Self in the Mind: The Self in Perception and the Brain*. Doctoral dissertation, Tel Aviv University.
Samuels, Andrew. (1994). *The Political Psyche*. London: Routledge.
Sartre, Jean-Paul. (1943/1958). *Being and Nothingness: An Essay on Phenomenological Ontology*. London: Methuen.
Sartre, Jean-Paul. (1944/1989). *No Exit and three Other Plays*. New York: Vintage International.
Schafer, Roy. (1976). *A New Language for Psychoanalysis*. New Haven, CT: Yale University Press.
Searle, John R (1969). *Speech Acts: An Essay in the Philosophy of Language*. Cambridge (UK): Cambridge University Press.
Segal, Lynne. (1999). *Why Feminism? Gender, Psychology, Politics*. New York: Columbia University Press.
Segal, Lynne. (2008). *Making Trouble: Life and Politics*. London: Serpent's Tail.
Spence, Donald P. (1982). *Narrative Truth and Historical Truth: Meaning and Interpretation in Psychoanalysis*. New York: W.W. Norton.
Spivak, Gayatri C. (1999). *A Critique of Postcolonial Reason: Toward a History of the Vanishing Present*. Cambridge, MA: Harvard University Press.
Weber, Samuel. (1991). *Return to Freud: Jacques Lacan's Dislocation of Psychoanalysis*. Cambridge: Cambridge University Press.
Winnicott, Donald W. (1965). *The Maturational Processes and the Facilitating Environment: Studies in the Theory of Emotional Development*. London: Hogarth Press & The Institute of Psycho-Analysis.
Yaffe, Alon & Hadar, Uri. (Unpublished). I am not the Subject of this Statement: A Pronominal Reading of the Lacanian Subject. Manuscript, Tel Aviv University.

Index

Printed and bound by CPI Group (UK) Ltd, Croydon, CR0 4YY

CPI Antony Rowe
Chippenham, UK
2016-12-27 18:34